Jesus: A Gospel of Love

Living Miracles Publications

Jesus: A Gospel of Love

ISBN: 978-1-942253-64-8

First eBook Edition 2023

Living Miracles Publications
12365 Sams Wash Rd
Box 8812 HCR 063
Duchesne, UT 84021
publishing@livingmiraclescenter.org
livingmiracles.org

This book was joyfully produced by the Living Miracles Community—a non-profit ministry run by inspired modern-day mystics devoted to awakening.

About the Author

David Hoffmeister

Christian mystic David Hoffmeister is a living example of peace and serenity. His compassionate nature and articulate, unwavering speech are a blessing to all. He is renowned globally for his teachings on spiritual awakening, which are presented in an accessible and practical way. His insight into the power of forgiveness, as well as his unique approach to mindful movie-watching to help let go of judgments, is unparalleled. His message is pure and leads directly to the divine.

For the past 35+ years, David has been spreading Jesus' message of love all over the world, visiting 44 countries across 6 continents. He regularly speaks at events and offers online workshops, like movie-based Awakening sessions.

David is famous for his practical take on Jesus' mystical teachings and always points straight to the Christ—the shared mind with our Creator.

His teachings have been translated into thirteen languages, and taken into the hearts and minds of millions through the intimate style of his books, audios, and videos.

The mystical experience ends the world of duality and conflict forever and is one of clarity, great joy, deep peace, and tranquility. The experience is not of this world, but radiates from within. It is not a concept; it comes into awareness when all concepts have been laid by. Forgiveness is the last concept.

Editor's Note

Each chapter in this book is structured into different subsections, starting with Bible quotes, followed by David Hoffmeister's teachings about those Bible verses.

David´s teachings are divided by a heart-shaped icon and Bible quotes are marked with ribbon-shaped lines.

At the end of each chapter, you will find a framed section containing parables or more in-depth teachings from David.

We hope that this structure will provide you with a meaningful and enriching reading experience, and we encourage you to engage with each section as you read through the book.

Contents

Introduction

Jesus: A Gospel of Love is an answer to the prayer of the heart for a present-moment, intimate and profound relationship with Jesus.

The teachings and life of Jesus Christ have inspired and influenced billions of people over the past two millennia. His message of love, compassion, and forgiveness continues to resonate with people of all backgrounds and beliefs.

The chapters in this book contain Bible verses and Christian mystic David Hoffmeister´s teachings, providing a direct answer to questions such as: "Jesus, what is my relationship to you? What is a miracle?" and, "How will the world end?"

This book aims to deepen readers' understanding of Jesus' message of love and to inspire them to live a life guided by the Christ.

Whether you are a believer, a seeker, or simply curious about Jesus and his teachings, this book offers a rich and inspiring exploration of some of the most profound questions. Through its pages, readers can discover the transformative power of love and the enduring message of trust and faith that Jesus Christ continues to offer.

This book is a gateway to opening to deep self-realization; that we are the Christ mind—we are love itself.

May this book comfort and bless us
on our journey Home to God.

1. Who Is Jesus Christ?

> "When Jesus came into the coasts of Caesarea Philippi, he asked his disciples, saying, Whom do men say that I the Son of man am? And they said, Some *say that thou art* John the Baptist: some, Elias; and others, Jeremias, or one of the prophets. He saith unto them, But whom say ye that I am? And Simon Peter answered and said, Thou art the Christ, the Son of the living God." (Matthew 16:13-16)

Jesus was a man who saw the face of Christ in everyone, thus recognizing the universal nature of God's love. Jesus Christ is a symbol of God's eternal love and a loving guide to remembering God's perfect oneness.

~♥~

Jesus said to his apostles, "Follow me." Isn't that great? A fisherman and a tax collector, and Jesus says, "Follow me." And they just looked into his eyes, and they did an amazing thing. The characters drop their businesses, their fishing, and their families. They drop everything and follow him. It must have been an amazing presence.

Imagine that in your own life. Someone comes along in the middle of one of your everyday days and just says two words to you. And the strange thing is, you look into his eyes and go, *I think he is right; I don't want to remain a figure in this dream. I want to wake up to eternity.* It's eternity calling.

~♥~

I want to take you back 2,000 years ago, to that point where Jesus was. He was growing up, and he was feeling inside his heart that he had a destiny. And we now know that his destiny is all our destinies. Knowing God and knowing our source is a shared destiny. And yet, he had to practice prayer and faith, and he had to practice patience, to wait on his time. When his time came, he would open up, and he would begin to extend the presence that he had become fully aware of.

~♥~

Jesus is the symbol of that deep devotion and presence to which we look for inspiration, guidance, and instruction.

~♥~

Many people wonder about the difference between the spiritual path of a monk who devotes twelve hours a day to meditation and that of someone like Mother Teresa, who is constantly on the move. Despite the apparent dissimilarity, it's the same presence inside. It's however the Spirit guides you to reach that "I Am" Presence. However, you're used, it's all to take you into that experience.

~♥~

I do these talks all over the world, and the talks in and of themselves don't really mean anything. It's the Presence from where the talks come from. Even the presence will be taken over by the ego and transformed into another set of words, another sermon, another talk, another discussion that will be recorded for posterity. It's just that I have found the most important way to come to the Spirit of Love, the Spirit of God, and the Presence of God is, very simply, to listen and to follow.

And even just listening won't do it for you. Even if you could hear Jesus speaking in your mind—if you could hear the Holy Spirit very clearly in a conversational tone—it still wouldn't help you if you didn't follow it. Even if you could hear it perfectly clearly, word for word, and without distortion, it wouldn't help you unless you followed it.

~♥~

Christ is a perfect divine idea, and Jesus is the name of one who demonstrates, represents, or symbolizes this divine idea. The name Jesus stands for a love that is not of this world, for love is eternal and the cosmos is temporary.

Jesus Christ is therefore a symbol, and the love the name represents is the Spirit that is one with God. Christ is our true identity. The Sonship is synonymous with Christ, and Jesus is the name of one who recognized the face of Christ in everyone and awoke from the dream of the world.

Jesus is a demonstration of the love that is the Sonship. Jesus points to God as being deserving of awe, and God is worshiped as the Spirit of God's love is shared or extended. The attitude with which one treats one's brothers and sisters is the attitude one has with the Creator, for these attitudes are one.

> "Enter in at the strait gate: for wide *is* the gate, and broad *is* the way, that leadeth to destruction, and many there be which go in thereat: Because strait *is* the gate, and narrow *is* the way, which leadeth unto life, and few there be that find it." (Matthew 7:13-14)

> "So the last shall be first, and the first last: for many be called, but few chosen." (Matthew 20:16)

> "Take my yoke upon you, and learn of me; for I am meek and lowly in heart: and ye shall find rest unto your souls." (Matthew 11:29)

Meekness is strength, and the meek perspective has literally conquered the world. The ego encourages fighting, battle, and "standing up for truth" against a brother. Actively aligning with Jesus means laying down the sword of judgment. Love never opposes. Opposing a brother shows weakness.

Fighting for or against something in form implies that you believe in the reality of the form while remaining unaware of the content behind the form. However, you will only find peace if you are aware of the Holy Spirit's content or purpose. Anger requires a scapegoat, and if you accept that attack is impossible, you will also accept that anger and projection are impossible. That is what Jesus meant when he said, "The meek shall inherit the earth."

The Holy Spirit does not work "in the world," but rather with the mind that *thinks* it is in the world. This is done so that the mind can first recognize that it invented the world. Once the mind has let go of the desire to project the error of separation "outward" into the rest of the cosmos and apart from itself, it accepts the Atonement and realizes there is nothing outside of the mind.

Atonement and healed perception are the same thing. You can see how this differs from saying, *Spirit, please come into the world and change my circumstances - find me a parking space, help me win the lottery, heal my body.* Atonement has transformed illusion into reality, and darkness into light. Maintaining the belief that the Holy Spirit can change an objective world outside of me is a mistake. When attack thoughts are released, there is an awareness of wholeness, which is the forgiven world as an all-inclusive mind.

~♥~

The ego is a belief in the concrete and specific, and it can only misinterpret the world's dream. In contrast, the Holy Spirit does not enter the world. Illusions do not contain truth. False beliefs are removed by the Holy Spirit as they are brought to or raised to Light. There is no *doing* or activity in forgiveness. Forgiveness shines calmly and passively, seeing the false as false.

Thus, the Holy Spirit works with the mind to completely release the ego's false belief system. Because the ego interprets one's self as a body in a world external to the body, it is the ego that attributes situations and events to Spirit, such as *Spirit found me a parking space* or *Spirit helped me lose 20 pounds.* These are "personal" interpretations, as if the Holy Spirit was working with separate bodies, objects, events, and situations rather than the sleeping mind, which believes in these particulars. The Holy Spirit does not perceive the world in the same way that the body's eyes do. The Holy Spirit's forgiven world perspective is not "personal", because it is all-encompassing and complete.

> "Then saith he unto his disciples, The harvest truly *is* plenteous, but the labourers *are* few. Pray ye therefore the Lord of the harvest, that he will send forth labourers into his harvest." (Matthew 9:37-38)

"And he began to speak unto them by parables. A *certain* man planted a vineyard, and set an hedge about *it*, and digged *a place for* the winefat, and built a tower, and let it out to husbandmen, and went into a far country. And at the season he sent to the husbandmen a servant, that he might receive from the husbandmen of the fruit of the vineyard. And they caught *him*, and beat *him*, and sent *him* away empty.

And again he sent unto them another servant; and at him they cast stones, and wounded *him* in the head, and sent *him* away shamefully handled. And again he sent another; and him they killed, and many others; beating some, and killing some. Having yet therefore one son, his well beloved, he sent him also last unto them, saying, They will reverence my son.

But those husbandmen said among themselves, This is the heir; come, let us kill him, and the inheritance shall be ours. And they took him, and killed *him*, and cast *him* out of the vineyard." (Mark 12:1-8)

"If the world hate you, ye know that it hated me before *it hated* you. If ye were of the world, the world would love his own: but because ye are not of the world, but I have chosen you out of the world, therefore the world hateth you. Remember the word that I said unto you, The servant is not

> greater than his lord. If they have persecuted me, they will also persecute you; if they have kept my saying, they will keep yours also. But all these things will they do unto you for my name's sake, because they know not him that sent me. If I had not come and spoken unto them, they had not had sin: but now they have no cloak for their sin. He that hateth me hateth my Father also. If I had not done among them the works which none other man did, they had not had sin: but now have they both seen and hated both me and my Father. But *this cometh to pass*, that the word might be fulfilled that is written in their law, They hated me without a cause." (John 15:18-25)

The world as seen through the eyes and heard through the ears is a screen of images. The world is just a hazy reflection of the deceived mind's attack thoughts. If one becomes aware of these attack thoughts and is willing to let them go, one is willing to clean up the film and let go of the judgments that block the light of awareness. Miracles require the willingness to let the light shine through without interference. When this occurs, the screen will *seem* to light up more and more. Because there is no world apart from mind, the world will reflect the light in one's mind.

~♥~

The mind opens up to the Holy Spirit's perspective, which reflects healed perception, as it lets go of the ego belief system of separation and distorted perception. This is a viewpoint that reflects Love and Oneness and provides a comprehensive interpretation of the universe. The cosmos is a moment of unified witness to abstract Love, now that the mind is in accord with the Holy Spirit's perspective. Thus, to realize that there is no world apart from mind is to be open to the recollection of abstract, Eternal Oneness, which has no opposite. Truth is simply that.

Salvation is truly in Christ, and the light has come. Christ is the lamb of God, and the lamb represents innocence. The lamb is pure white as a symbol of the purity of innocence. Innocence "resists not evil" because it has defeated the belief in death. And what was guilt but the conviction that death existed? Although Christ's innocence has truly removed "the sins of the world," God requires no sacrifice. Atonement is associated with innocence rather than sacrifice. It is written as follows: "For I desired mercy, and not sacrifice; and the knowledge of God more than burnt offerings." (Hosea 6:6)

"I have yet many things to say unto you, but ye cannot bear them now. Howbeit when he, the Spirit of truth, is come, he will guide you into all truth: for he shall not speak of himself; but whatsoever he shall hear, *that* shall he speak: and he will show you things to come. He shall glorify me: for he shall receive of mine, and shall show *it* unto you." (John 16:12-15)

Now is the appointed time. I use the term "mysticism" to mean union with God in Christ, and I speak using terms provided by the Holy Spirit in reference to the Bible, education, psychology, music, and movies, to name a few. I rejoice in allowing the Holy Spirit to speak, write, sing, and express the Presence of the Lord Jesus Christ. I know you understand this in your heart, for we share the heart of Christ.

God is completely unfamiliar with the concept of sacrifice. Sacrificing in any way is a violation of the commandment to be merciful as your Heavenly Father is merciful.

God's innocence is the true state of mind of His Son. Your mind knows God in this state because God is not symbolic; He is fact. Knowing His Son as He is, you realize that the Atonement, not sacrifice, is the only appropriate gift for God's altar, where nothing but perfection is permitted. Truth is the innocent's understanding. That is why their altars are truly radiant.

Christ is waiting for you to accept Him as your Self, and His wholeness as yours. For Christ is God's Son, who lives in His Creator and reflects His glory. Christ is an extension of God's love and beauty, as perfect as His Creator and at peace with Him. Blessed is the Son of God, whose radiance is from His Father and whose glory He desires to share as His Father shares it with him. There is no condemnation in the Son because there is none in the Father. Sharing the Father's perfect Love, the Son must share what is his, or he will not know the Father or the Son. Peace be unto you who rest in God.

> "These things I have spoken unto you, that in me ye might have peace. In the world ye shall have tribulation: but be of good cheer; I have overcome the world." (John 16:33)

"He that overcometh shall inherit all things; and I will be his God, and he shall be my son." (Revelation 21:7)

Only the ego seems to experience guilt. Be cheerful because you are not the ego. The ego associated "gifts" with things, money, and behaviors. The Spirit knows that gifts are the Thoughts of God. The ego's "gifts" never fully satisfy the yearning to give and to receive, yet miracles fill the "storehouse" of an open and willing mind ready to have miracles performed through it. Give the miracle as an offering of the present moment. Everyone is blessed in the holy instant of Christ's awareness. Feel how wonderful it is to be everything and extend everything without any limitations. Spirit expects nothing and provides everything simply by being. This is what it means to give as God gives. There is no scarcity or lack in God. When the ego's nothingness is revealed, guilt is revealed to be impossible. No trinket can provide the gift of forgiveness.

~♥~

The heart's sincere prayer is always answered in illumination, and beyond the words spoken is always the deep desire to know thy true Self. Ours is the willingness to forgive and be at peace, because lasting peace is our inheritance as the Christ. This is a symbol-filled world, and Jesus says that words are only symbols of symbols that are twice removed from reality. God answers the prayer of the heart. Any question or doubt is always about identity, and it is helpful to be reminded that words were made to maintain the belief in separation.

~♥~

Pockets of guilt are beliefs that have not been challenged and are still held to be true. The belief that time is linear rather than simultaneous is at the root of these beliefs. As the pockets of guilt are released, peace returns to awareness. You will know of your mind-training "success" by the peace you feel.

> "Jesus said unto them, Verily, verily, I say unto you, Before Abraham was, I am."

> "I am Alpha and Omega, the beginning and the end." (Revelations 21:6)

"Satan," "hell," and "sin" all describe the belief in separation from God—the so-called "fall" from Grace. God is Love, and Love has no opposite. In the Bible, this is stated as "Perfect Love casts out fear." In Genesis, the tree of the knowledge of good and evil represents the belief in duality, and biting into it represents attempting the impossible. Because God is pure Love and Oneness, duality is physically impossible. The world as perceived by the five senses is a dream in which the separation from God occurs, and the Bible says that Adam fell asleep. Nowhere in the Bible is it written that Adam (representing human beings) awoke, yet the Gospels clearly reveal that Jesus awoke to the truth of reality: "The Kingdom of Heaven is within" and "My Kingdom is not of this world" and "Before Abraham was, I am." Christ is mind awake, the I Am Presence, the Identity that God creates eternally in God's Mind.

Atonement is the correction to the apparent error of separation from God; universal atonement and forgiveness are available to all. The mind that chose to accept the Correction *returned for Christ elect* or remembered itself as the Christ, God's child. Jesus exemplified this decision for everyone by willingly accepting the Correction and remembering Christ's origin in God. This is the only decision that can be shared, because it is impossible to turn away from or be separated from God. This is why there is no "eternal hell," because the Holy Spirit has corrected mistaken identity, and awakening is simply a matter of accepting this Atonement.

God wills Spirit in Heaven forever, and so Spirit is. God communicates with you through the Holy Spirit. Because you perceive your brothers and sisters in form in your awareness, it will be meaningful to say to you that everyone will accept this Correction in due time because it is a decision that cannot be rejected. God's love is all-encompassing and has nothing to do with the ego concept of rejection. Love is total inclusion, and error has no meaning in the context of Love. Because God did not create time, awakening in Christ necessitates seeing the impossibility of linear time. There is no time in the holy instant, because the present moment is the gateway to eternity.

~♥~

Perception is reborn, or seen for the first time, when the Holy Spirit's purpose for the world replaces the ego's purpose of separation. And once Atonement is accepted, perception is no longer required. The divine Mind is completely abstract (formless), and creation is the light of understanding. God, being Eternal, does not take steps. Because creation *is*, it transcends the concepts of alpha and omega, beginning and end. Christ is God's creation, and therefore has no beginning or end. The Christ idea is eternal and has never deviated from its eternal Source. You've probably heard the expression "forgive and forget." As the world of illusion fades away, God and Christ are remembered.

~♥~

True perception, the happy dream, salvation, the real world, and so on all refer to the forgiven world after all judgments have been released. Perception is whole in this perspective because there is no division. This is the Holy Spirit's Point of View. The present is before time was or seemed to be. Therefore, the words "Before Abraham was, I am" and "I and the Father are One" reflect this perspective. Simply put, knowledge *is.* Pure being has no words or reflections. The cosmos and body are laid aside as a "final step" before remembering What is, pure being, which is knowledge.

When I was in graduate school, I used to take long walks in the woods and reflect on the purpose of my studies. And the ego would give me reasons based on fear of consequences, like needing a degree to get a good job or not wanting to be broke in a relationship. All of my reasons for being there were fearful, based on my fear of consequences. But deep down, I felt there was more to my life's purpose.

Becoming aware of this poor motivation for my life got me in touch with a deep desire to open up to the guidance of the Holy Spirit. I would ask, *Why am I here? Am I afraid of something? Is there something driving me to get all this education?*

Is there something pushing me from underneath? Am I afraid of something besides what the world would call a fully engaged life? The more I took the questions inward, the more Jesus was able to show me that it was freedom, peace, happiness, joy, love, and intimacy that I wanted. He showed me that I had many beliefs about what one has to do in this world to get those things. And it was those beliefs that were driving me. He said, "If you listen to me, I will show you how to experience the things you want through me. In other words, through listening to me and then following me, it will come from the inside of your mind. It won't come from any event or outcome in the world."

This turned me in the right direction. In the beginning, I was astounded to see that a huge percentage of my actions were motivated by the fear of consequences. It could have been tempting to judge myself at that point, but I was determined not to do that. I was happy to discover how plugged into the fear of consequences I was.

I was happy to begin to unplug with Jesus and the Holy Spirit's help. I found that to be very practical. It was something I could contemplate and ponder. I knew it was going to be a big job. I knew I wasn't going to take a pill and wake up the next day free of fear. I knew it would take contemplation and mind training.

2. Jesus, What Is My Relationship to You?

> "I am the vine, ye *are* the branches: He that abideth in me, and I in him, the same bringeth forth much fruit: for without me ye can do nothing." (John 15:5)

> "For whom he did foreknow, he also did predestinate *to be* conformed to the image of his Son, that he might be the firstborn among many brethren." (Romans 8:29)

> "Be ye therefore perfect, even as your Father which is in heaven is perfect." (Matthew 5:48)

We don't enter Heaven through fear. That was something misinterpreted by some very sincere Christians. The Bible quote, "Fear God, and keep His commandments" (Ecclesiastes 12:13) just means to hold God in awe. God is truly awesome. And we should be awed but not terrified of God. We don't need to tremble in the presence of the Creator of Love. That makes no sense whatsoever.

~♥~

The ego is nothing more than the belief that you can create yourself; and the solution, the Atonement, is nothing more than the realization that God created you perfect. A prayer to remember this is: *Let me accept myself as God created me rather than attempting to use time and space to invent, re-invent, and improve myself.*

~♥~

Fear arises from the belief that one can author oneself. Peace comes naturally to the one who recognizes God as the Author of oneself. You and the Father are one (in Spirit), and this is known in Heaven. The personality self was an insane attempt to deny this simple fact by making an "opposite" to Eternal Love. Yet Love is all there is and has no "opposite." This experience is the joy of awakening! Peace and forgiveness go together, for they both create the release of the illusion of a separate self. Forgiveness is the end of self-deception. Abide in peace, for God is the Author of reality—which is the self as Christ—and nothing can change Eternal Love.

"As a man thinketh in his heart, so *is* he."
(Proverbs 23:7)

The ego is the belief that it is possible to make a self or world apart from God or Spirit. The ego is the false attempt to make a *self* different from God. It is also the attempt to usurp God's place as the creator of reality. Atonement is the recognition that this attempt is impossible because Mind can't create beyond itself. Miscreation or projection is therefore impossible, and form and perception are therefore meaningless. The meaning of life is found in being as God created one's true Self (Spirit). Because of this, the perceptual world can only be forgiven or set free so that creation (Spirit) can be remembered. The memory of Heaven remains, though it seems to have been pushed from awareness and forgotten by believing in the ego. The Spirit creates and the ego makes, yet Atonement shows that creation is reality, and the ego's belief in separation from

God has *not* occurred. Such is healing. Such is enlightenment.

Jesus taught a lot of lessons through parables, which are like modern-day movies. And they let us have a very deep experience of exactly what we were praying for. We all want to feel like we belong. We all want to be happy and feel joy. We all want to learn how to relax in the present and live a life without effort, just being as God created us and not trying to make something of ourselves or accomplish something in the world. This is because God created us as Spirit and Spirit is perfect. Heaven is perfect. Why talk about anything but Heaven? Why not make Nirvana our default program and then go back to default and stay in default mode of Heaven?

> "Jesus saith unto him, I am the way, the truth, and the life: no man cometh unto the Father, but by me." (John 14:6)
>
> "I and *my* Father are one." (John 10:30)
>
> "Ye have heard how I said unto you, I go away, and come *again* unto you. If ye loved me, ye would rejoice, because I said, I go unto the Father: for my Father is greater than I." (John 14:28)

When it comes to accepting Atonement or salvation, the Bible can be a very helpful tool. The Word of God, or the Spirit of God is always available to the soul that is open, willing, and ready. The purpose of scripture is to provide a means for us to accept Atonement or complete forgiveness and thus remember our eternal union with God. The Holy Spirit interprets scripture for this purpose: awakening to the truth. In the Gospels, this was expressed as "I and my Father are one" and "You shall know the truth, and the truth shall make you free." (John 8:32) Heaven is the state of our eternal union, the truth of our being, and *now* is the closest approximation of Heaven. This is what it means to say, "The Kingdom of Heaven is at hand." (Matthew 10:7) Heaven is not a place or a location, but rather a state of mind (being at peace and happy). Heaven is eternal, as is God's Word (Spirit), which will never perish. The cosmos of planets and stars, earth, time, space, are temporal and will perish.

~♥~

There is a very famous passage in the Bible where Jesus is interacting with the woman at the well and he encounters her and she is nervous. She's a Samaritan, and Samaritans aren't supposed to associate with Jews, and she sees Jesus is a Jew, so she's a little nervous talking to him. Societally she shouldn't even be talking to this guy and then Jesus comes and he starts it off by saying, "Fetch your husband" or “Call your husband”.

But she doesn't have one husband, she's in a relationship with more than one man. So he's giving her a question and that brings up more fear and insecurity in her. *Bring me your husband*; she's involved in several relationships.

She flees in terror telling all of her friends, "There's a prophet there, He's reading my mind. He's reading my thoughts." But when she finally comes back and he delivers the famous line, "Drink of me, and you will never thirst again." Whoa! Now he's gone beyond reading the mind. It's the Christ speaking. Drink of Spirit. Drink of the Heavenly Father. Drink of your Source. Drink of the prime Creator. Drink of the Cause. And as the Christ, you will never thirst again.

That takes it way off the level of form where he seems to be there, and the woman at the well will try to draw him some water, and that will be his response to her. He just uses another basic situation, it's another situation in the world to teach, "I Am-ness", to teach eternity. That is Christ. That's our destiny. To reach the state of mind in which I will never thirst again.

> "Jesus said unto her, I am the resurrection, and the life: he that believeth in me, though he were dead, yet shall he live: And whosoever liveth and believeth in me shall never die." (John 11:25- 26)

We are training our mind to hear only one voice. That is why Jesus is such a great example and wayshower. Finally, it was stated that he heard one voice. He wasn't switching back and forth. It wasn't like some of the movies based on Jesus, such as *The Last Temptation of Christ.* It has him on the cross, looking at Mary Magdalene, and he is in pain. He is portrayed as being tempted on the cross. By the time he arrived at the cross, he had overcome temptation. Three years prior, he had been hearing one voice!

When he began his public mission, he began saying things like, "Before Abraham was, I Am." "I am the Way, the Truth, and the Life." That is not a man speaking. There is no one who declares, "I am the Way, the Truth, and the Life." That is the voice of the divine Spirit. So it really comes down to realizing that God's Will for me is perfect happiness. In terms of perception, the Holy Spirit is always the choice for happiness. It is the decision that will lead me to eternal happiness. That is the Way, the Truth, and the Life. This is the escape hatch.

> "Heaven and earth shall pass away, but my words shall not pass away." (Matthew 24:35)

When you have the experience of forgiveness, you have to experience that all specific beliefs are completely false. As a result, it puts your mind in a state of openness—complete open-mindedness, all-inclusiveness, and acceptance.

Peace of mind is an experience that transcends all theologies and concepts. Let's talk about it; I've never met a stranger. Who would be the stranger? If Love is open to all, then everyone is welcome. Then, there's that feeling of home. It's the presence of home. It's the point at which Heaven and earth cease to exist as separate states. It's the teaching that Heaven is here. Heaven is now. It is not a future state, nor is it something you hope and wish for.

Forgiveness is simply a name that we can equate with happiness. If our function while we perceive the world is forgiveness, then Jesus says, my happiness and my function are one. They are identical.

The belief that you can separate from God comes down to a question of authorship. The question is this: Am I the author of myself, or was I authored by God? If God is the author, I am Spirit because God is Spirit, and God authors in Spirit. If I am the author of myself, it is like saying to God, *Hold on there; I want to make myself up however I want to be. I want to experiment with being male or female, masculine or feminine; I want to experiment with being of this or that culture.* This is known as reincarnation. What is reincarnation but the belief that I can be the author of myself? I'm constantly remaking and reinventing myself in terms of form. You see, that is the core issue—who is my author?

As humans, we appear to have physical parents, but we have a divine parent who authors us in Spirit. We cannot be both. We can't be both physical and spiritual, because the physical is temporary and the spiritual is forever. That is the central question in my mind: Who is my author? Who is my creator? Who is my source?

When it gets confused on the horizontal level, like with mom and dad, there is going to be guilt.

Who among us has not had grievances with our parents? We think of teenagers sometimes saying to their parents, *Why was I born? Why did you even have me and bring me into such a crazy world?* The guilt gets projected in terms of the flesh, but the solution goes much deeper, way down into the mind. The core issue is an identity issue. Every time you have an upset of any kind, it is still, *Am I the author of myself, or was I authored by God?*

You might remember in the Bible where Jesus the wayshower said, "Why do you call me good?" This is Jesus Christ speaking: "Why do you call me good?" God is good. He was always pointing to the author; he never went back to a personal sense of self; he was always pointing back at the Creator and that is humble; that is appropriate.

Jesus is with us; he is like us in every way except one, and that is time. He has transcended time, but he is equal to us in every way. And when we transcend time, we say, "Ahh, you are me!" "I have been the Christ all along, but I was simply sleeping, and I forgot who I was and who authored me."

3. Speak on the Parable of the Prodigal Son

"And he said, A certain man had two sons:

And the younger of them said to *his* father, Father, give me the portion of goods that falleth *to me*. And he divided unto them *his* living.

And not many days after the younger son gathered all together, and took his journey into a far country, and there wasted his substance with riotous living. And when he had spent all, there arose a mighty famine in that land; and he began to be in want. And he went and joined himself to a citizen of that country; and he sent him into his fields to feed swine.

And he would fain have filled his belly with the husks that the swine did eat: and no man gave unto him. And when he came to himself, he said, How many hired servants of my father's have bread enough and to spare, and I perish with hunger!

I will arise and go to my father, and will say unto him, Father, I have sinned against heaven, and before thee, And am no more worthy to be called thy son: make me as one of thy hired servants.

And he arose, and came to his father. But when he was yet a great way off, his father saw him, and had compassion, and ran, and fell on his neck, and kissed him.

And the son said unto him, Father, I have sinned against heaven, and in thy sight, and am no more worthy to be called thy son.

But the father said to his servants, Bring forth the best robe, and put *it* on him; and put a ring on his hand, and shoes on his feet:

And bring hither the fatted calf, and kill *it*; and let us eat, and be merry: For this my son was dead, and is alive again; he was lost, and is found. And they began to be merry.

Now his elder son was in the field: and as he came and drew nigh to the house, he heard music and dancing. And he called one of the servants, and asked what these things meant. And he said unto him, Thy brother is come; and thy father hath killed the fatted calf, because he hath received him safe and sound. And he was angry, and would not go in: therefore came his father out, and entreated him. And he answering said to *his* father, Lo, these many years do I serve thee, neither transgressed I at any time thy commandment: and yet thou never gavest me a kid, that I might make merry with my friends: But as soon as this thy son was come, which hath devoured thy living with harlots, thou hast killed for him the fatted calf.

> And he said unto him, Son, thou art ever with me, and all that I have is thine.
>
> It was meet that we should make merry, and be glad: for this thy brother was dead, and is alive again; and was lost, and is found." (Luke 15:11-32)

Jesus is a revealer. He's revealing that God is all love. God loves you so much. He never gave up on you. Even when you fell asleep and thought you'd turned your back on God, he never left you. That's what the whole Prodigal Son parable that Jesus loves so much is about, and he teaches that over and over. Even if you've squandered your inheritance and covered over the light, you're still welcome to return to the light. No penalty. That's right. No consequences. That's a big love.

It's interesting that Jesus told the Prodigal Son parable over and over. It must have been important for Jesus to keep repeating that particular parable. That's probably one of the most famous parables in the Bible. So, what I feel is that there's an activation happening. There's a part of your mind that knows it's an authentic call coming from inside. There's also a part of the mind that says, *My world is empty without you, babe*.

We know when we're feeling those feelings of emptiness, like, *What's the point?* It's like that Beatles song, "Another Day." It's one of those days where we go through the motions of the day, thinking there has to be more to it. I don't know what it is. I have a hunch that there's much more than meets the eye—that there's a destiny. That my soul has a destiny, and that destiny will be fulfilled through joy. I will have more and more ascending steps of joy and more intense joy as I go towards this ultimate joy.

> "And His name shall be called Wonderful, Counsellor, The mighty God, The everlasting Father, The Prince of Peace." (Isaiah 9:6)

> "Another parable put he forth unto them, saying, The kingdom of heaven is like to a grain of mustard seed, which a man took, and sowed in his field: Which indeed is the least of all seeds: but when it is grown, it is the greatest among herbs, and becometh a tree, so that the birds of the air come and lodge in the branches thereof." (Matthew 13:31-32)

Only your willingness is required for the journey into your heart. The work is done by Christ or the inner Spirit. The light in your mind is ignited by your willingness and the power of the Holy Spirit.

The doorway inward easily opens with a little willingness. Witnesses to love appear at every turn. Symbols sparkle as we see with "new eyes," for our purpose is singular, and we see reflections of the thoughts we cherish all around us. The willingness to communicate attracts communication and completely dispels the belief in isolation and separateness. And as we communicate the love, we are aware that love is our being. We reap what we sow and receive what we give, and I rejoice that this divine principle is an eternal law of the universe. Place no limits on giving, and receiving will be perceived as limitless and endless.

Today, share a laugh and a smile with someone; and notice how good you feel on the inside. I've had so many joyful laughs and happy smiles in meeting my sisters and brothers. As I go about my loving and sharing, I am truly feeling the communion of the heart. Thank you for joining in the experience of our wholeness! Our oneness shines through the window of the heart and radiates throughout all of creation. Beloved child of God, you are holy. Let nothing prevent you from remembering thy own holiness.

> Jesus told the Parable of the Prodigal Son, in which one of the sons left after demanding his inheritance. Off he went and used his entire inheritance for riotous living until he had nothing and was hungry, until his only job was feeding the pigs and he was eating the husks. And after some time, he said, "Even my father's servants have more than me. Maybe I should go back." And he returned in shame; he returned in guilt. He went back with his head bowed low.
>
> But before he got close to home, his father came running down the road to greet and celebrate him. In the same way, our shame, guilt, and believed wrongdoings are met with open arms.

The father can only see the son's innocence, so he celebrates with a party by killing a fatted calf. Then the other son, the dutiful son, the son who tried to play it safe and do everything right, sees the condemned brother return. He says, "What is happening here? A party? I have stayed here dutifully by your side all along, and not once have you killed a calf for me. You welcome this wanderer—this betrayer, this weak one who blew it all—back and have a party." The dutiful one is angry. And the father says to him, "Dear son, all that I have is yours; it has always been yours. But your brother, my son, he was lost, and now he is found." There is nothing more important than being found and finding our true inheritance again, regardless of what seemed to happen when we were lost.

This second chance is the olive branch that is there for all of us. God is saying, *Just take the olive branch, just take the branch of peace.* This realization is what the second coming of Christ means. It's our self-realization. When the awareness of our true self dawns—the knowledge that all is forgiven and that we are one in God, where we have always been—we know that we are nothing but mind. This mind is whole and complete. It never dreamed of fear, loss, or separation. It is free and happy in God. It is guiltless—innocent!

All of Jesus' teachings were about loving one another. The Prodigal Son parable is a beautiful parable of forgiveness—of truly letting go of all past judgments and trusting in this loving Father, who is present to teach unconditional love. He is teaching us not to judge one another, not to judge another brother, but to just be there with open arms.

I've sometimes done sessions with people in which they just let all their darkness out. They tell me all their private thoughts. They tell me all their secrets, which they've never told another living soul on the planet, not even their mother and father. They've kept this secret for decades, and then when they tell me the secret, I just smile and hug them. And they say, *"Oh, my gosh!"* because they were carrying all this guilt around. And it doesn't matter what the secret is because I know it isn't true.

So simply seeing the false for what it is, not passing judgment on anyone or anything based on a secret, is what heals. Only the ego has secrets. The Holy Spirit has no secrets. God wants everything openly revealed. God is not a god of secrets or mysteries. That's the true meaning of confession. *"Can I tell you about this terrible secret I've been keeping and feeling guilty and ashamed about? Can I expose it to you and be loved? Will you still love me?"* Yes, I will! Because it's the Presence of God that loves us and knows that none of the secrets are true. So, it really works. It's very powerful.

4. Speak on the Creation and the Fall of Man

> "All things were made by him; and without him was not any thing made that was made." (John 1:3)

Your reality is Spirit, and God is the creator of Spirit. You could say God is the prime Creator. But a lot of the teachings about being a co-creator with God are still very much into manifesting, saying you can use the power of your mind to make the world any way that you want it. But what Jesus is saying is that the ego projected the world, and you're not going to find happiness in controlling what the ego made. Happiness can only be found by forgiving or releasing what the ego made.

~♥~

Thank you, God, for creating me like you. That's the best news I've ever heard. You created me like you, Spirit. So, that's important for us. I've done a lot of teaching over the last 35 years on cause and effect. So, I'm going to give the Cliffs Notes version, because this is important. In reality, God is the cause and Christ is the effect. The cause, God, created Christ, but the effect did not create the cause. I know it can sound like two things, but it's not really two things. It's one Spirit. But God is the prime Creator. Christ is created by God, and Christ has creations. And it's hard to grasp it in this world because there are no parallels. There are no examples. We don't have any examples of that in time. But that's the truth. I'm just giving you the straight truth.

The voice of God is the voice of Christ, because just as Creator and Creation are one, so is the voice that temporarily represents reality. The simple message of the Holy Spirit is this: God is Spirit. Christ is Spirit. God authors Christ eternally. Spirit is all there is, having no opposite. There is no author but God.

> "And God said, Let there be light: and there was light." (Genesis 1:3)

So we let go of the belief in the unhealed healer today by recognizing that we cannot give what we have not experienced. We must first experience what we intend to extend. Before the light of the world can be extended, it must be experienced. I must be certain of the mind that is within me in order to extend this gift. There is no other option.

The belief that error is possible pervades all forms of the unhealed healer. These are the manifestations of the belief that darkness, error, and evil exist. This is not the case.

Today, I accept the truth about myself in order to bless, heal, and comfort others. I have no other obligations today or in the future. I have no other goal or meaning in life. I cannot share irrational beliefs. I can only share God's Thoughts. Today, I am united with the Holy Spirit. I see past all substitutes for healing and open to the light that is in me and moves through me, so that I can recognize that I am the light. God declared, "Let there be light." Today, I recognize this light. This light is a healing source. I let the light shine today. I allow the healing to take place, knowing that the Holy

Spirit is the only therapist. In any situation where He is the guide, the Holy Spirit makes healing obvious. Today, I'll let Him do His job, knowing He'll tell me exactly what to do to assist anyone He sends my way. I agree that if I allow it, the Holy Spirit will speak through me and, Jesus says, I shall know my brothers "by their fruits" and they shall know themselves. Today, I let healing happen.

> "And God said, Let us make man in our image, after our likeness." (Genesis 1:26)

Creation is entirely at Heaven's level. In the sleeping state, you are unaware of your creations, but the Father extended Himself—created the Son in his likeness and image—and then the Son extended himself, and these are the things known as creations. It is entirely on the spiritual level. In other words, Spirit begat spirit, and so on. It's all one continuous line. You have no recollection of your creations while sleeping because your perception is distorted. It's one of those topics that you can only go so far in discussing. We know they are eternal and without change. They are perfect; they are infinite, just like the Father and Christ.

Because your behavior is automatically influenced by your thinking, the only place where you can make a significant difference is by changing the way you think. In your mind, there are only two thought systems: the ego's and the Holy Spirit's. The simplest way to distinguish between the two is to recognize that there is an effect for every cause. And there is only one Cause (capital C)! That is the Cause, and you are the Effect; you were created by your Creator. You were also made in His image and likeness, in the sense that He is eternal and you are eternal. He is unchanging, as are you. You are magnitude, and He is magnitude.

The only apparent distinction between the Father and the Son is that the Father (Cause) created the Son, whereas the Son (Effect) did not create the Father. There are some new age systems that claim that "I" am God, but this path is different. "The Father and I are one," Jesus said in the Bible. But he always talked about the Father and I and he would always return to the Father, saying, "Why callest thou me good?" There is only one good, and that is God. (Mark 10:18) He always pointed to the Father.

> "And the LORD God commanded the man, saying, Of every tree of the garden thou mayest freely eat:
>
> But of the tree of the knowledge of good and evil, thou shalt not eat of it: for in the day that thou eatest thereof thou shalt surely die." (Genesis 2:16-17)
>
> "And when the woman saw that the tree *was* good for food, and that it *was* pleasant to the eyes, and a tree to be desired to make *one* wise, she took of the fruit thereof, and did eat, and gave also unto her husband with her; and he did eat.
>
> And the eyes of them both were opened, and they knew that they *were* naked; and they sewed fig leaves together, and made themselves aprons.

> And they heard the voice of the LORD God walking in the garden in the cool of the day: and Adam and his wife hid themselves from the presence of the LORD God amongst the trees of the garden." (Genesis 3:6-8)

The fall of man is a perceptual distortion, a vast illusion in which the mind believed it accomplished the impossible: separation from its Creator.

Imagine this very powerful mind that was created in the image of the Father, turning his head and asking, *Could there be anything more than Heaven, more than everything?* This idea is a little puff of madness. It was a totally ludicrous idea, but, instead of laughing at it, the Son of God took it seriously and then fell asleep.

The mind was terrified of the light once it believed in the separation because the little puff told the mind, *Now you've really done it! You've rebelled against Heaven and turned your back on your Creator. Quick! We're going to flee and hide. We'll create a world of form, and because God is Spirit, He won't be able to come after us there; we'll be safe,* said the puff. In other words, this world was a projection of a tiny puff of a separation idea. It was built as a fortress to keep God out. God is both infinite and amorphous. Heaven is unchanging and eternal. However, this world is limited and fragmented. Everything in the universe is constantly changing; even the stars will burn out. It has a beginning and appears to be coming to an end.

Once the mind fell asleep, there were two thought systems: the fear-based thought system of the ego, the "puff," and the Thought from God's loving response, the Holy Spirit. Based on the premise that the impossible has occurred and that fear is real, the ego's thought system declares, *If you ever go back into your mind, into that white light, and back to God, God will get you and destroy you!* And the loving response simply repeats in the mind, "You could never do such a thing, God is not angry at you, your Father loves you, your Father will always love you."

~♥~

When the mind believed it had fallen from grace and was no longer connected to God, it was terrified. The ego voice, or fear voice, told the mind it was guilty and needed to flee. You could argue that the biblical Garden of Eden describes the world of time and space. The cosmos is just like a giant fig leaf with which the mind tried to cover itself. God is pure Love and unity. As a result, God cannot exist in duality. Duality is the hiding place.

The ego said to the mind that thought it had separated from God, *This is your new home now. Accept your body as your new home. We'll make up everything you appear to have in heaven. We will create a new type of love with our bodies. We will create a new kind of freedom through body movement. We will create a new kind of happiness based on sensual pleasures to replace your home in heaven.* Some belief systems even teach the body's immortality. But the body, like all worldly pleasures, is fleeting. They come and go, but they never completely satisfy.

The ego desired that God blessed its new world and make the fantasy of time and space a reality. The rage stems from the fact that God cannot do this! God is divine Love. God recognizes Christ as divine Love. This Love is infinite, perfect, abstract light, total joy, constant communication, gratitude. Because God would not be God if He granted the ego's wish, all anger is a temper tantrum, wishing for the fleeting to be true and real. Forgiveness dispels the illusion of the entire cosmos and recalls the Eternal reality that God created.

> "And they shall teach my people *the difference* between the holy and profane, and cause them to discern between the unclean and the clean." (Ezekiel 44:23)

> "Another parable put he forth unto them, saying, The kingdom of heaven is likened unto a man which sowed good seed in his field: But while men slept, his enemy came and sowed tares among the wheat, and went his way. But when the blade was sprung up, and brought forth fruit, then appeared the tares also. So the servants of the householder came and said unto him, Sir, didst not thou sow good seed in thy field? from whence then hath it tares? He said unto them, An enemy hath done this. The servants said unto him, Wilt thou then that we go and gather them up? But he said, Nay; lest while ye gather up the tares, ye root up also the wheat with them.

> Let both grow together until the harvest: and in the time of harvest I will say to the reapers, Gather ye together first the tares, and bind them in bundles to burn them: but gather the wheat into my barn." (Matthew 13:24-30)

> "And he said, So is the kingdom of God, as if a man should cast seed into the ground; And should sleep, and rise night and day, and the seed should spring and grow up, he knoweth not how. For the earth bringeth forth fruit of herself; first the blade, then the ear, after that the full corn in the ear. But when the fruit is brought forth, immediately he putteth in the sickle, because the harvest is come." (Mark 4:26-29)

> "And God saw every thing that he had made, and, behold, *it was* very good." (Genesis 1:31)

In Heaven, Christ remains in God's Mind and can never truly *leave*. In this world, the idea means that there are no problems apart from the mind, because ideas do not leave the mind that appeared to think them.

Everything that appears to be *manifested in the world* is actually a collection of thoughts and concepts. And ideas and concepts never leave the mind that created them. The ego's attempt to project thoughts to an apparent *outside cosmos* is delusional because everything is mind and there is therefore nothing *else* at all. This is also why all apparent illness is mental in nature and has nothing to do with physical symptoms.

Thus, salvation or enlightenment is merely an escape from false concepts that have no reality or existence. This disproves the illusory notion of "inner" and "outer," because mind is one in forgiveness and mind is *one* in reality.

~♥~

The Holy Spirit recognizes the error of separation but looks past it to the Atonement or Correction. The Holy Spirit is the present reminder of what is entirely beyond error, because the Holy Spirit contains the memory of God and Christ.

Before the deceived mind can awaken to eternal reality, it must accept the Holy Spirit's gentle dream of nonjudgment. In this forgiving dream, the universe appears as a seamless tapestry. Distinctions, categories, increments, levels, degrees, and parts are all gone, and only wholeness *remains*.

This perception of wholeness is itself an illusion and will not last, yet this illusion is the last illusion, for it is the gateway to the eternal.

Because God exists, the cosmos does not. Satan is not real because Christ is. Time does not exist because eternity does. "Perfect Love casts out fear" means that because Love is real, fear is not. As a result, Love and fear cannot coexist. When fear is experienced, Love appears to be blocked from consciousness. However, only Love exists, and Love is always present; thus, the experience of fear is merely an illusion to be dispelled.

When you turn on a light in a dark room, it does not fight the darkness; it is simply light. The light of Love shines in the same way, and there can be no darkness in light. Bring the error of darkness to the light of the Holy Spirit and see that only light *remains*. Beloved Child of God, there is only Love to behold.

The phrase "awakening mind" simply refers to the discovery or release of error. The Holy Spirit's purpose is to set free a deceived mind that believes in the *reality* of the time-space world. Forgiveness recognizes the false as such. Forgiveness is a miraculous thing.

> "Do ye look on things after the outward appearance?" (2 Corinthians 10:7)

> "For the things which are seen *are* temporal; but the things which are not seen *are* eternal." (2 Corinthians 4:18)

The time-space cosmos can seem very much like a dream, for it was the projection of the belief in separation. God, being perfect Love, creates forever perfect Love, and such is eternal creation. Christ is a perfect creation in the Mind of God and Christ creates forever perfectly in Love as God creates. In this sense, all that exists is Christ or from Christ.

Truth and error are not both true. Truth is true and only Truth is true. Because God/Christ/Creation is true, error is false or nonexistent.

God, Christ, and Creation appear to have been forgotten by the deceived or sleeping mind. It dreams of many parts separated by time and space, because it has forgotten the wholeness of the forgiven world offered by the Holy Spirit, as well as the eternal Heaven that is Mind awake in God.

~♥~

God's Will is also known as free will because it is eternally free, happy, peaceful, and joyful. This is the state of mind known as perfection—reality, or truth. In perfect Oneness and union, the Will is free, and this freedom is a feature of Spirit, or Eternal Creation, which is the abstract light of unconditional love sometimes reported in "near death experiences." This light represents total comprehension and Love, or Oneness. God only creates light and Oneness.

What does it require to remember God? Nothing in reality. You don't need to *do* anything to *be* what you are. If the illusion of time still seems real, what is your only need? You know the answer: the forgetting of this world of fragmentation, the forgiveness of illusions—the releasing of the past.

Don't put your faith in the ego and its laws of economics, medicine, nutrition, physics, friendship, and its doctrines, rituals and creeds that tell you that you must 'struggle' to survive.

Let go of the belief that you are confined to a body. Let go of the belief that you have a past or a future. Watch your cares and concerns disappear from awareness. Behold the blazing light of your true Identity in God, changeless and timeless.

The truth is now, the present moment, free of all illusory restrictions and limitations. In awakening to God you will first have a happy dream, cleansed of judgments and grievances. Joy and laughter will replace sadness and sorrow. The mind becomes completely "saved" from the belief in error, and what was error but a mistake to be corrected by the Holy Spirit, the Answer within. Now is the time of release, for happy dreams lead to awakening to Love and light, peace Eternal. Welcome home holy child of the living God!

> "Then said his wife unto him, Dost thou still retain thine integrity? Curse God, and die." (Job 2:9)

There is nothing left to seek for in this world when it can be exchanged for another one. No thought of gain or loss, winning or losing, success or failure ever had any meaning. Fantasy is not real and dreaming is not being *one*. You are ready to awaken to Oneness. And as you awaken the whole world awakens as well. For the world was never more than a misperception. As perception becomes whole, the single mind sees only wholeness. At last you are ready to see with inner vision, and you realize that physical sight was nothing but the illusion of being in the dark. The Light has come and it is time to rejoice! It is time! Teaching and learning true forgiveness is being aware that one is never upset by anything but erroneous thoughts, and that those erroneous thoughts can be released.

We were brought together by God to serve the plan of awakening, to treat each other with dignity, respect, kindness, and holiness, and to awaken to our divine Love. We approach our purpose for coming together with great reverence and devotion. It is the core of our life in God. Our relationship is our relationship with everything and everyone, for we live and love as God lives and loves, unconditionally, all-inclusively, and free of specialness. There is no jealousy or exclusion in Love. We join with all in experiencing the all-inclusiveness of the family of God, where no brother or sister is seen as separate or apart from the Whole of God. Our hearts are filled with Love and gratitude for our relationship in God.

We are glad that this joy is not dependent on where bodies seem to be or whether or not they seem to be together. We are created by a pure *idea*, and we are like our Source. We are Spirit as God is Spirit, and we are overflowing with thankfulness that this truth is dawning as the Mind we share. Our walk together is for the purpose of accepting our divine Source and laying aside all thought of the world as the source of anything.

> "There is nothing covered, that shall not be revealed; and hid, that shall not be known." (Matthew 10:26)

> "And ye shall know the truth, and the truth shall make you free." (John 8:32)

Jesus is telling us that there is a purpose in our minds called forgiveness, and that purpose will set you free, truly set you free—it will take you into your experience of who you are in the Kingdom of Heaven. And that is a mental purpose, not a physical purpose. The ego created all of these separate images and then assigned a purpose to each of them, as if purpose could be fragmented, and Jesus says, *No, purpose is unified. That's forgiveness.*

> Jesus said something amazing 2,000 years ago. "The Father and I are one," he said, which I think is amazing because he's saying God is the Creator or the prime cause, and Christ is the effect or the perfect extension of that prime Cause. "The Father and I are one," means that in Heaven, God and Christ are not two separate beings: they're just one spirit of Love. And this world is the belief that cause and effect are distinct; that the Son or Christ could somehow depart from the Father or Creator and have its own autonomous life—life in form—a temporary life.
>
> I was in university for ten years—undergrad and grad—and what I discovered is that no matter how different the disciplines you study in this world are, they all have one thing in common; and that is the belief that cause and effect are real in this world. So, every perception in this world is a denial that cause (God) and effect (Christ) are

together. Perception is a denial that Christ is an idea in the Mind of God and has not left its source.

The question is, who is my author? Was I authored by time and space? Do I start with my parents and conception, or do I start with a divine parent, a divine Source? That's what we're deciding between every second of every day. Who's your daddy? All we have to do is solve that one riddle. Who's your daddy? Then you're happy.

5. How Is Fear Abolished?

> "There is no fear in love; but perfect love casteth out fear: because fear hath torment. He that feareth is not made perfect in love." (1 John 4:18)

> "For by grace are ye saved through faith; and that not of yourselves: *it is* the gift of God." (Ephesians 2:8)

Forgiveness is a state where you can watch your thoughts and not give any power to the ego's thoughts. Then, eventually, those ego thoughts aren't there. The ego's thoughts can't even enter your pristine, holy mind. The light becomes so strong and so bright that the thoughts of temptation, the thoughts of ego, can't even enter!

~♥~

The Bible says perfect love casts out fear. That's another way of saying if we devote our lives to loving, then fear doesn't have a space. If we keep our garden weeded and clear and clean, then we have space for the fruits of the Spirit—and there are plenty of fruits.

~♥~

When you're watching the news, just remember that you're watching the ego's invention. How you react is your choice. Just remember that God has nothing to do with what you are perceiving because God doesn't know of separation. Love doesn't know of fear.

Perfect love casts out fear; that's exactly right. Once you come into alignment with the Source, that's perfect love, and fear is cast out for good. In fact, fear is not even there. "Cast out" is being kind to it—it just doesn't exist anymore. It's not like a big war is going on and you're saying, "I will cast you out!" No, love is laughing. This is no battle. Reality is love being itself.

When we look at Jesus's experience at the end of his life, when he was nailed to the cross, the ego would tell us that Jesus suffered. But Jesus had accepted the correction. He had no guilt, no pain, and no suffering on the cross. He was demonstrating, through the resurrection, that it was impossible to kill Christ.

~♥~

When anyone is tempted to give into feelings of hatred, this can be seen as a strong call for healing because the emotions of love and hate can never come together. Feelings of love and hate show that the mind is split, and it's very unnatural to try to hold onto both of those emotions.

When there is a prayer to heal this split mind, we can hear Jesus within us saying to bring love and fear together—and one will disappear because perfect love casts out fear. Hate must dissolve if you cease to protect it. So how do we protect hate? By seeing it in the world rather than in our own minds, by seeing it played out in the outside world rather than forgiving it inside where it's at.

~♥~

Miracles lead the way, for the way of the true mystic is to approach God through attraction, not through avoidance or opposition. As error is seen as false and without a real cause, its foundation disappears in the light of truth. Perfect love casts out fear, for belief has been withdrawn and replaced by the knowledge of life in God.

> "This then is the message which we have heard of him, and declare unto you, that God is light, and in him is no darkness at all." (1 John 1:5)

The Holy Spirit wants to strengthen your identification with the right mind by using you in miraculous ways. Your ability to transcend fear is what makes this possible.

On a horizontal plane, you cannot transcend fear. You have to transcend it vertically in your mind through your function. Therefore, whenever a question about fear or doubt is raised, the answer is always transcendence through love and being used by the Holy Spirit to bring about the release from fear.

Even though the personality self may believe it has a number of specific fears and challenges to overcome, the fear is actually the ego identification that is being held onto in the mind. The miracle takes care of that.

~♥~

When unpleasant or upsetting emotions arise you can actually adopt a "bring it on" mentality. Be glad that you have something to work with in terms of letting go because that is the point of awakening. We could use the phrase *letting go of fear*—letting go of doubt and really letting go of the hold of a false identity created to replace spirit or our spiritual reality.

~♥~

When Jesus says, "When I awoke you were with me." To open up to the confidence of Jesus' words, you must allow the spirit to come to your rescue and pull you through. Even though it doesn't seem like it in this world, we are eternal. Some people like to use the acronym F.E.A.R., which stands for False Evidence Appearing Real. Fear is merely a fabrication of reality, which is why the journey is really about letting go of everything that appears to be perceivable through the five senses. It is impossible to experience innocence and hold fast to a body-centric interpretation. Jesus responds, *Well, it's not that I'm asking you to see your brother without a body; what I'm asking is for you to see him sinless.* The body was created by the ego and was made out of hate. Is it your deepest desire to see him free from guilt? To witness your brothers and sisters as innocent? All it takes is a heartfelt wish; I hope my assumptions about my brother and sister were incorrect. I hope my assessment of the flesh was incorrect. I've been wrong about every body of evidence, and this body of evidence that has persisted for millennia is simply FEAR (False Evidence Appearing Real). It's as if the only kind of sword that exists is the sword of discernment used by the Holy Spirit to distinguish between what is real and what is false.

> "Verily I say unto you, Except ye be converted, and become as little children, ye shall not enter into the kingdom of heaven. Whosoever therefore shall humble himself as this little child, the same is greatest in the kingdom of heaven." (Matthew 18:3-4)

Imagine being as reliant on the Holy Spirit as a child is on his or her parents. Dependency has a bad reputation in this world; nobody wants to be dependent because it is seen as weak. But, in reality, becoming dependent on your internal guide, your intuition, is the ultimate source of strength—total invulnerability.

A friend of mine likes the analogy of Pinocchio wanting to be a real boy—an independent, autonomous real boy. So, after hearing that Pinocchio metaphor, her prayer was "Please get me back on the strings, Holy Spirit, move the puppet." That is exactly what we mean when we say "getting into purpose". You smile more, laugh more, hug more, and use kind words as if everything is fine. You simply allow the Spirit to flow through you and use your body to free your mind.

To begin you must get in touch with your own thoughts and beliefs. As long as you are distracted by the world and concerned with survival and body issues, you are postponing getting in touch with your underlying beliefs.

~♥~

Act on guidance and truly allow Jesus to guide the action component of the miracle. He will tell you where and with whom to bestow the miracles, and it must come from the Spirit.

~♥~

To remember the Christ Self and God's Love, one must be completely dependent on the Holy Spirit. As you follow the Voice for God within, your doubt thoughts will fade, and your apparent "needs" as you serve the *plan* will be met miraculously.

Now is the time to deepen our shared purpose, because this depth is required to take the steps that will surely follow. By addressing whatever is placed before you, you can nurture the awakening of the mind by being gentle and kind. Allow tomorrow to take care of itself. Future concerns and worries are never prudent or practical because they are always based on the past.

Accept the peace within to ease your way into divine providence, and watch as the Holy Spirit handles everything for you effortlessly and miraculously. You are a messenger of God's Love, and God's messengers are worth their keep while serving the Holy Spirit's Purpose.

> One time I was invited by this woman in Chicago to do a gathering. The gathering was at her husband's real estate office, but he did not attend. After everyone left the gathering, he came into the room and went through all his darkness and negativity with me for three hours. Later, the woman said that his stereotype or nickname was Archie Bunker (a 1970s TV character who was considered a racist).
>
> In the time we were together, the man told me which races should be exterminated and all that kind of stuff, and I just sat there in Presence, pure Presence. And then, near the very end of our time together, he just turned it all around

and said, "Well, I don't know. Maybe there is like a divine intelligence behind it all." And the Spirit just started moving through him. I was like, Oh my God! Even Archie Bunker channels the Spirit if it's just your desire. I had this strong desire to just stay there and see the innocence. I had such a strong desire that I had no intention whatsoever of going anywhere. I could just sit there beautifully in Presence.

I did a lot of listening that night, and at the end, the light did pop through. It was this feeling like, *Of course, the innocence has to break through. The darkness cannot hide the light.* The light is just perfect love casting out fear, and it's just a matter of divine reality and divine fact. To me, that's what this journey is about. We hang in with that determination to experience that love, and nothing can stop us.

6. Is Distorted Perception—Lack of Vision—the Main Problem?

> "Where there *is* no vision, the people perish: but he that keepeth the law, happy *is* he." (Proverbs 29:18)

> "When I was a child, I spake as a child, I understood as a child, I thought as a child: but when I became a man, I put away childish things. For now we see through a glass, darkly; but then face to face: now I know in part; but then shall I know even as also I am known." (1 Corinthians 13:11-12)

It doesn't matter so much the form of the decision, but if we bring it back to content, the two decisions that we're dealing with on a daily basis are the right mind and the wrong mind. A right-minded decision has no guilt; it is joyful, peaceful, loving, free, and happy. It's a decision you make with the Holy Spirit. And a wrong-minded decision is when you're looking through a darkened glass, as the Bible says in Corinthians.

It's not so much what the particular form is, it's that you are looking through a dark lens, and that's why the decision is so obscure. It is a common admission to not be able to tell the difference between the right mind and the wrong mind, because the resistance to that discernment and clarity is the ego's resistance to being undone.

The ego thinks it will be obliterated—destroyed—if you get clear on that distinction. And on this point, the ego is correct.

~♥~

The first thing that's necessary in coming to healing is this awareness that you have a perceptual problem. You can't possibly be reminded enough or too much by the Holy Spirit that it's a perceptual problem. Because this whole world and cosmos were made to make it seem like it is something other than a perceptual problem. It's almost like the ego is saying: You have done it, you have left the abstraction, you have left the Kingdom of Heaven, and now you have got images to deal with and you're stuck with that. Now you have got to make the best of it.

So having a healthy body, environment, neighborhood, or planet become ego goals to keep your mind from seeing it is a perceptual problem. It's like looking through a darkened glass, and you're not seeing anything clearly, you're literally hallucinating. It is seeing something that is not really there. A mirage in the desert would be the best analogy to describe the problem.

But until the mind comes to an admission that it's a perceptual problem, then it is on a wild goose chase, shifting around the images, trying to find a more peaceful environment, a better partner to be with, a better job, or it's dealing with bodily symptoms.

~♥~

This darkened glass becomes accepted as normal. It becomes accepted as just the way it is, even though it's so dark and distorted. And Jesus is telling us constantly that if you only knew what lies beyond this darkened glass, you would be in a state of wonder. You would be in a state of euphoria, exuberant joy, and supreme happiness if you could look beyond this limited lens of the ego.

The darkened glass is distorted. And it takes humility to admit you don't have a clear perception of the world and you need help. Nothing changed in my mind until I started asking for help; honestly, from my heart, asking for help. And then things started to shift, things started to become clearer.

~♥~

Many of us even had long years of education to become diagnosticians, to diagnose problems in the world. That's why the ego's so clever. You spend your whole career diagnosing, and then Jesus comes in and says, no, you're looking in the wrong place, you're looking in the wrong direction.

~♥~

There will never be a solution to all the problems in the world and all the levels. We can say we eradicated polio, but then we still have cancer, or there's still heart disease, or something. Wipe out some diseases; there are some new diseases. It just goes on and on, century after century. It's more like you're looking through a lens of fear and of illusions, and as long as you try and go to fix the forms that you think are the problem, the ego's just sitting back in your mind laughing and saying, *Good one. That will keep them locked in time and space for centuries, trying to solve that one.*

And yet, we have to get to a point where we go further back, even behind the ego, to be able to have gentle laughter at the very idea that there could be something other than love.

~♥~

"Let thine eye be single," (Matthew 6:22) Jesus said. He's not asking you to memorize anything. He's not asking you to recite anything. He's not asking for repetition. He's simply saying that you must first come to the recognition that you have a perceptual problem, similar to what they say in 12-step groups, "Hi, my name is so and so, and I'm an alcoholic."

We have to first come to the admission that it's a perceptual problem. But in order to do that, we have to realize that we don't really have financial problems. We don't have health issues. We don't have issues with the politicians. We don't have issues with the environment. We don't have issues with our families. It's a perceptual problem. It's seeing a fragmented world, perceiving a cracked, fragmented world, a cracked mirror. That's the problem, that's the distortion.

You don't see with vision; that's it. But that one simple admission is all that you have to make in order to slip easily into the real world. But without that admission, you are blocked from the real world. Without that admission, then the alternative is to be a human being, a construct dealing with a lot of different problems every day. Survival problems, psychological problems, problems that seem to come in many different degrees and directions, are part of a smoke screen to distract the mind from that one simple admission of, "I have a perceptual problem."

> "The LORD make his face shine upon thee, and be gracious unto thee: The LORD lift up his countenance upon thee, and give thee peace." (Numbers 6:25-26)

When you start to see beyond this world and see all of the things that are a part of the death wish, you are activated to say, *Okay, someone has to put an end to this and remember that it is a distorted perception.* It's not the people and actions; the death wish is in the mind; it's a filter. And as long as we keep perceiving through this filter, we are part of the death wish. And it is not God's will that we continue to be a part of this death wish—this darkened glass.

We have to feel our feelings fully, and we have to go past those distortions and dark feelings to the light. And it's important to realize that if we are not going through the darkness and we are not facing things and coming to that light, we are really wasting time. Delay is tragic in time and unknown in eternity, so you gradually lose tolerance for delay, which is what the activation is all about. *Why would I waste time doing nothing? I want the Holy Spirit to use time like a laser beam to cut through these deceptions and distortions.*

And you start to think, *Well, suddenly the moments look different, the hours look different, the weeks look different, the months look different, the years look different.* You begin to realize that what matters is not whether you speak or not, but what purpose your words serve. It is not so much whether you go for a walk as it is what purpose the walk serves. You begin to wonder, *What is it for?* With everything, there is a question. Instead of simply perpetuating time, you begin to say, *I want to use time in a way that frees the entire universe, that frees the entire Sonship.* Because time is the trick. As long as you are invested in time, you might say, *It's just going nowhere.* You're just spinning your wheels, going nowhere – fast or slow, doesn't matter; it is still going nowhere.

> "And he said, Go, and tell this people, Hear ye indeed, but understand not; and see ye indeed, but perceive not. Make the heart of this people fat, and make their ears heavy, and shut their eyes; lest they see with their eyes, and hear with their ears, and understand with their heart, and convert, and be healed." (Isaiah 6:9- 10)

> "For since the beginning of the world *men* have not heard, nor perceived by the ear, neither hath the eye seen, O God, beside thee, *what* he hath prepared for him that waiteth for him." (Isaiah 64:4)

> "Therefore speak I to them in parables: because they seeing see not; and hearing they hear not, neither do they understand." (Matthew 13:13)

> "For, behold, I create new heavens and a new earth: and the former shall not be remembered, nor come into mind." (Isaiah 65:17)

God is Spirit. Spirit is not a concept or a belief. Spirit can only be experienced because it is eternal and cannot be defined, explained, or described. God simply is. Christ simply is. Since there is nothing to forgive in Heaven, forgiveness itself is an illusion. The "highest" belief forgiveness—is not the experience of Spirit. However, the act of forgiving is the doorway or internal portal to remembering God. Therefore, the goal of all unlearning is to focus on forgiveness by removing the layers of false concepts and beliefs.

~♥~

Meekness is seen as weakness by the ego. In the eyes of the Spirit, meekness is strength and gentleness. When you are that gentle and loving, your perception will literally swallow up the world. Just before claiming your inheritance as a child of God, which is pure Love, you will literally see the world in a meek way. You can see that it is a beautiful interpretation of the proverb, "The meek shall inherit the earth." By literally replacing the false perception with the true perception, the meek will inherit the entire planet. It all comes back to the whole universe that is in my mind, instead of me being just a tiny person in the universe. You start to understand that, "I am the world," as Krishnamurti taught. "I am the world, the world is me." He was teaching unification of consciousness.

> "This is my commandment, That ye love one another, as I have loved you. Greater love hath no man than this, that a man lay down his life for his friends. Ye are my friends, if ye do whatsoever I command you. Henceforth I call you not servants; for the servant knoweth not what his lord doeth: but I have called you friends; for all things that I

> have heard of my Father I have made known unto you." (John 15:12-15)

> "Having eyes, see ye not? and having ears, hear ye not? and do ye not remember?" (Mark 8:18)

When you look at this world and you say, *Well, the ego made this world, then what's the point of this world?* And we could say that the only point this world has is forgiveness—that is, to see it with the Holy Spirit. That is the only point that this world has and the only point that is aligned with the retranslation of everything that the ego created in hate.

This world was made in hate and guilt as a distracting device, a separating device, and a means of reinforcing guilt, so the point of this world is to forgive it, and in that sense, to release it. It's not like you're trying to come up with something valuable about the world; it's about being willing to value peace of mind over images of the world in any instance. And that has been my entire practice to the point where whatever the body's eyes and ears seem to perceive and hear, whatever the feel, the touch, whatever the five senses report, after a while you start to realize that there's a small still voice in your mind that is the way, and these interpretations based on the five senses aren't going to get the job done. They will not get us back to the Kingdom of Heaven, so you stop valuing them, and yet life continues joyfully and miraculously, and nothing is lost.

~♥~

Don't worry, beautiful, beloved ones, all is not lost; the Holy Spirit and Jesus are foreshadowing. You may appear to be undergoing some lifestyle changes, and you may appear to be in a world that is different from the one that came before. But it is a reminder to us all that the cultures, the people, can all live in harmony if we all remember the purpose. And that purpose is to love one another, to love our source, our Creator, and to have an attitude of harmonious collaboration. Isn't that fun? I love the combination of those two words, *harmonious collaboration*. And what a wonderful world it is when we work together harmoniously.

I'm thankful that we could share these moments together. It lifts our hearts. When we are reminded of the full context, it lifts our attitude. And we are capable of facing whatever shadows or secrets the ego makes up, because we're created by Love.

Many times over the last 37 years, I've traveled all over the world during different seeming outbreaks of war. And a lot of times people will ask me, "David, do you think the world is getting worse or do you think the world is getting better?" And I say, it's a projection of the ego, and so, as a projection of the ego, it's an illusion. And there are no better or worse illusions.

My answer to: "Is the world getting worse?" No, it's not. "Is the world getting any better?" No, it's not. It's a mirror, so it's just a reflection of consciousness. When you heal, when you forgive, you see the world differently. When you don't want to forgive, when you want to be right about an opinion or know something about the world, it means you are looking through a darkened glass. And you would rather continue looking through the darkened glass than be at peace.

What is the darkened glass? It's the fragmented glass of distorted perception. It's got dark spots all over it. You can't see anything clearly when you look through the lens of the ego. You're seeing a projection of error. That's what the world is, it's a projection of error. God didn't create war. God doesn't create conflict. God doesn't create fighting. God doesn't create fear and upset. These are projections of the ego, and let's make no mistake, this cosmos and this world are projections of the ego.

7. How Does What I Perceive Relate to the Golden Rule?

> "Therefore all things whatsoever ye would that men should do to you, do ye even so to them: for this is the law of the prophets." (Matthew 7:12)

Amazingly simple and beautiful principle. If you just got that one thing out of the whole Bible, that would be spectacular. In other words, if I am kind to others, it is because I would like to be treated kindly.

Another way of saying this is, "As you sow, so shall you reap." I want to sow kindness, friendliness, love, and happiness so that I can reap all these things for myself.

~♥~

See nobody as guilty, and you will see nobody to blame. The innocence of the Spirit is apparent when one realizes that attack is impossible. A unified mind cannot attack or be attacked. And without the belief in attack, guilt has no basis.

The Holy Spirit gently leads us to a unified mind and a unified perception that is the forgiven world. When forgiveness has been accepted, the illusion of guilt has vanished from awareness.

It is possible to perceive any situation as extending love or calling for love. Let the Holy Spirit show you by aligning your mind with this guidance. Healing is unlearning the ego and thus releasing every scrap of ego belief, thought, emotion, and perception. If you are willing, the way will open, for nothing can obscure the innocence the Holy Spirit would have you behold.

~♥~

The Golden Rule depends on right perception. And how do we heal perception but by questioning our beliefs and looking at our thoughts? We perceive attack in the world because we still believe attack is possible, and really, what Jesus is showing us, ultimately, is that attack is impossible.

That is why Jesus could be defenseless; he could say from the cross, "Forgive them, for they know not what they do". He wasn't in any way saying that what they were doing was real, but he was saying that he had reached a point of peace and forgiveness and had transcended the belief in attack.

> "The soul of the wicked desireth evil: his neighbour findeth no favour in his eyes." (Proverbs 21:10)

> "And why beholdest thou the mote that is in thy brother's eye, but considerest not the beam that is in thine own eye? Or how wilt thou say to thy brother, Let me pull out the mote out of thine eye; and, behold, a beam *is* in thine own eye? Thou hypocrite, first cast out the beam out of thine own eye; and then shalt thou see clearly to cast out the mote out of thy brother's eye." (Matthew 7:3-5)

We all have experienced heartbreak, and I believe that our perceptions of the world are flawed because of our faulty interpretations, which are based on feelings of loss, guilt, and fear. Our issues stemmed from our own interpretation; therefore, we cannot place the blame on our parents, the nation, or the politicians. It was our own incorrect interpretation, and you guessed it—it was based on our own private thoughts! Yes, we still respect people's right to their own thoughts.

I recall a friend who would occasionally receive songs from the angels. She would begin to tell me about the song and sing it to me before bursting into laughter. On one occasion, she was trying to sing a song she had received from the angels, whose lyrics went, "I take my guilt in small doses; six billion bodies give a little to each," when she started to laugh. You see, that's from the angels; I give each of my six billion bodies a small amount of my guilt. The ego populates this world, so any grievance we have with a friend, coworker, partner, dog, cat, environment, country, or politician is simply an attempt by the ego to shift the guilt of our own private thoughts onto that person and say, *I would love you if you behaved differently*.

Get the speck out of your own eye before you get the beam out of your brother's eye, Jesus commands. Stop putting that there. You shouldn't try to correct people, tell them they're wrong, or tell them the world would be a better place if they just learned to act differently. The ego projects guilt onto the world to deceive you into believing that it is outside of you, but it is not, so the mind places it there.

> "But their minds were blinded: for until this day remaineth the same vail untaken away in the

> reading of the old testament; which vail is done away in Christ." (2 Corinthians 3:14)

> "And I will give unto thee the keys of the kingdom of heaven: and whatsoever thou shalt bind on earth shall be bound in heaven: and whatsoever thou shalt loose on earth shall be loosed in heaven." (Matthew 16:19)

The Christ is pure light, has no offense, and knows Heaven. The Christ knows Oneness. The Christ has become one with God. The sleeping and dreaming mind is offended by its belief in the ego or in something other than God. When you pray you are asking God to heal the offense within your mind, which is the ego. You're praying to let go of your death wish. You're asking God to help you let go of that which has nothing to do with God. Never has and never will. You're praying to let go of the separation.

~♥~

We are never offended by what other people say or do. We are afraid of love and deny our identity as love, which is where the offense comes in. Christ is always present, but whenever we commit an offense, we must pluck it from our minds; let the Holy Spirit pluck it, because it is always some self-concept that we believe in. We believe we are humans—a man or a woman, a teacher or something else, a student. To know Christ we must *pluck* the offense and come with wholly empty hands to God. Because Christ is the Spirit it can never be offended.

~♥~

We have never done anything good or bad. We never did anything. It's a complete disassociation from the doer, the timeline, and the story. We're back in the quantum field, where everything is completely connected but no people exist. In the quantum field, there are no people. There are no roles to play. It's a completely unified energy.

Everyone seems to go through a phase where they seem to raise the darkness to the light while still identifying with the darkness. There's still the feeling, "*I did it again; it's one of my major patterns;* or *I've been doing it for years*. The ego is still attempting to link the personal identity to a defense mechanism, *I've done this before.* And I use the example of when we were kids, and we folded the paper over and over again, and then we took our little scissors out and cut our little figure, which we then pulled out. The ego does this with false identities. A timetable is required. To maintain guilt, it requires a slew of images and identification with those images across linear time. When you begin to have these miraculous and expansive consciousness experiences, you begin to zoom into this atonement of pure innocence. You realize that you have never done anything at all. And that's the, "I need do nothing solution." That's when you can zoom in. It's the big revelation. It's the big reveal. It has surpassed all other happy surprises. Miracles are like happy surprises that happen along the way. The big happy surprise however, is that who I am is magnificent. My identity is spotless. I've always been who I am, what I will always be. Self-realization with a capital S is the ultimate goal.

I feel like everything that we do in forgiveness, which is just exposing and releasing illusions, is so that we can love. So that we can love God and love our neighbor as ourselves. Literally, as our self. Not like we are loving somebody else, but literally like we have this self-love that just wants to radiate, radiate, and as we give, we receive.

We are blessed. The more love that we let pour through our consciousness, and our awareness, the more aware we are of how powerful that love is. That is why Jesus was teaching that the problem of the ego is that it is a belief in reciprocity. "I'll scratch your back if you scratch my back." It is the opposite of the Golden Rule. The Bible was all about the Golden Rule and the ego simply flipped it around so we would be so concerned about what we can get from our brothers and sisters, that we would forget all about giving. The Gospels were all about "freely you have received, now freely give."

I have broken all the rules. I decided I would just travel, share, speak, shine, do healings, do this and that; and I would do it for free. And people said, "Well you are going to learn sooner or later. David, there is no free lunch. And you are going to learn that this world is about death and taxes" and the whole spiel about how foolish I was to think that I could go about giving. "You know you cannot just give, give, give. You are going to have to look out for your body and you are not going to survive in that kind of mode." And I thought, *Now wait a minute, Jesus is giving me a different direction.* He is saying, "Freely you have received." (Matthew 10:8) *You have received all this glorious happiness and wisdom and peace; now give it away, give it away everywhere, give it away without holding back.*

You might say it is my experiment. I just decided, I am going to record this stuff because it is so wonderful, and I am going to share it on the Internet, and I am going to put it all over the place for free so that anybody that has any inclination for it can have free access to it. To me that has been a real blessing because it is showing me that our whole system of reciprocity, our whole system of supply and demand, our whole system of scarcity and lack, is all based on an error. The only way we escape this error is by going the opposite way and going, "You know what, I am not going to buy into this anymore. I believe that an abundant love and an abundant universe is waiting inside of me and all I have to do is give it away to experience it for myself." That is what I believe; I am going to go against the whole system.

8. What Is a Miracle?

> "Thou shalt not avenge, nor bear any grudge against the children of thy people, but thou shalt love thy neighbour as thyself." (Leviticus 19:18)

A lot of times, people ask, "How can I be generous? How can I give glory to God?" And Jesus says, "Love thy neighbor as thyself." If you really love yourself and you radiate that love, that is giving honor to God, because God created you as love. So, just think how simple that makes it.

Instead of burnt offerings and some crazy rituals to please God, you just need to love yourself, and love your neighbor. That's how you love and honor God.

~♥~

Whatever you focus on, you reinforce, or you strengthen in your own consciousness. If you focus on the little hurts, if you focus on the little misperceptions or the little mistreatments, you retain them in awareness.

~♥~

Jesus said to love the Lord, thy God, with all your heart, soul, and mind, and to love your neighbor as yourself. He just emphasized those two, really. He did not emphasize the other eight. And what is the basis of the second commandment? Why would you love your neighbor as yourself unless your neighbor was yourself—unless you were not your brother's or sister's keeper, and they were simply reflecting your consciousness?

And you start to see that self-love, true self-love, is not a thing of bodies. It is your spiritual reality. When you love your neighbor as yourself, you are just loving. You are loving as your Source loves. Your Source makes no distinctions.

The Source does not love some and not love others. The rain comes, and the rain falls on everything. It falls on the trees, on the cactuses, on the rocks, on the people, it falls on everything. It does not discriminate, and neither does love.

~♥~

Jesus spoke about forgiving and being forgiven, but it appears that applying the Ten Commandments has been difficult and challenging for the last 2,000 years. Especially in living the first two of the Ten Commandments—to love God and to love our neighbor as ourselves, particularly in relationships.

It seems like the closer the kinship relationships—whether it is husbands and wives or boyfriends and girlfriends—the higher the homicide rate is among relatives than it is in the general public. So there seems to be something going on where there is some kind of specialness, some kind of error, or sin, or distortion going on.

In our "close relationships," as we call them, our expectations rise like the Loch Ness monster. How dare you? All the years I have done this for you! The vows you took! The promises you made! And on and on and on. The rage can come immediately to the forefront, like the Loch Ness monster.

Rage can come up more in close interpersonal relationships than when you are at McDonald's or when you are shopping at the grocery store. Most people have got a pretty good cover on that rage in the grocery store. You do not see people completely flipping out in rage in the grocery store, but if you go inside the homes, in the nests, the monster can come out.

~♥~

The practical steps in this awakening journey are learning to listen to the Holy Spirit and learning to trust the Holy Spirit. And then, as you build confidence, have increasing trust in the Holy Spirit; so that even when the Spirit's guidance seems to contradict what seems to be practical in this world, we start to realize this guidance, and the experiences that come from following this guidance, are the most practical experiences that we can have.

~♥~

If we have doubt thoughts along the way, it's that we are doubting our true identity, and the world just reflects that back to us. Friends, neighbors, or partners may reflect back to us the doubt that we have about our true self. And it's not their fault; they're just acting it out to help us.

We don't need to blame them. We don't need to feel that these people are holding us back in life because they're giving us a gift. The gift is showing us what we still believe in our unconscious mind. They're pointing to, "Choose again." Whenever we think we have an enemy, that's just a prayer for us to start to look inside in an even deeper way than we did before and choose again.

Jesus says if you think you have enemies, you have great need for prayer indeed. But he doesn't mean that there are actual enemies; he's saying that if you perceive that you have enemies, pluck these thoughts from your mind. Pluck them, do some weeding, and clear your garden of them. These attack thoughts are just doubt thoughts about our own identity that are being played out for us in this world so that we can pluck them.

> "A certain *man* went down from Jerusalem to Jericho, and fell among thieves, which stripped *him* of his raiment, and wounded him, and departed, leaving *him* half dead. And by chance there came down a certain priest that way: and when he saw him, he passed by on the other side. And likewise a Levite, when he was at the place, came and looked on *him*, and passed by on the other side.
>
> But a certain Samaritan, as he journeyed, came where he was: and when he saw him, he had compassion on *him*, And went to *him*, and bound up his wounds, pouring in oil and wine, and set him on his own beast, and brought him to an inn, and took care of him. And on the morrow when he departed, he took out two pence, and gave *them* to the host, and said unto him, Take care of him; and whatsoever thou spendest more, when I come again, I will repay thee. Which now of these three, thinkest thou, was neighbour unto him that fell among the thieves? And he said, He that showed

mercy on him. Then said Jesus unto him, Go, and do thou likewise." (Luke 10:30-37)

"Verily I say unto you, Inasmuch as ye have done *it* unto one of the least of these my brethren, ye have done *it* unto me." (Matthew 25:40)

The path of awakening through listening and following is this: *Be guided in every moment to carry out the plans that I receive by listening to wisdom that is not mine. Be open to hearing what needs to be done in the moment, and then do it. Listen, Learn, Do* is a method for overcoming fear and increasing faith in the Holy Spirit. Allowing miracles to be performed through your mind will make you more aware that now is the only time there is.

The willingness to witness and share miracles is the best preparation for any situation. When one is in the flow of the Holy Spirit, it becomes clear that everything is provided and nothing is lacking. You will be informed of any arrangements or preparations that need to be made through inner listening. The prompts come in a variety of forms, including words, thoughts, and feelings, and they always carry a sense of deep peace.

Perceived needs begin to dissolve as a miracle worker fulfills the function of sharing joy. This prepares the way for the experience of divine silence, a pure state of being.

"Give, and it shall be given unto you; good measure, pressed down, and shaken together, and running over, shall men give into your bosom. For with the same measure that ye mete withal it shall be measured to you again." (Luke 6:38)

Giving and receiving are the same; you don't have to wait to receive what you've given. Whereas in this world of time, you sometimes sow and have to wait to reap, this is not the case in Heaven. When God gives everything away, we can say that Christ is an expression of God's love. Christ possesses the same ability as God to give everything away. Give all of this love, and then you keep it in your awareness by giving it because you get back what you give. That's how you keep it in awareness. That's what love is; it just has to give because of what it is and receive because of what it is.

"Pilate therefore said unto him, Art thou a king then? Jesus answered, Thou sayest that I am a king. To this end was I born, and for this cause I came into the world, that I should bear witness unto the truth. Every one that is of the truth heareth my voice." (John 18:37)

"But when the Comforter is come, whom I will send unto you from the Father, *even* the Spirit of truth, which proceedeth from the Father, he shall testify of me: And ye also shall bear witness, because ye have been with me from the beginning." (John 15:26-27)

We are here to share the love, joy, happiness, and laughter in our hearts with each other, which is really with ourselves, as Jesus says. We are here to strengthen our awareness and draw closer to the Kingdom of Heaven, which is no small feat!

I used to believe that when I was in university and went to all these services, conferences, and so on, I was going to get something. I would go, take notes, listen to the speaker, and believe that I am here to receive something from the speaker. But I didn't realize I was there to give, to extend. And because giving and receiving are the same, we are blessed in that when we are kind, open-hearted, smiling, and laughing, we are not only extending to others but also extending to ourselves.

~♥~

Love and anger don't mix; they don't go together. So what we're opening to is that state of mind where you go through a purification in your own consciousness and then do whatever you want. As Saint Augustine famously said "Love and do whatever you want." Isn't that a lovely teaching? Love and do whatever you want. The purification of your mind has resulted in the state of living in the presence of love and then simply letting your actions flow from that love.

~♥~

The miracle is more of a means to an end, and Christ's vision, revelation, the Great Rays, or whatever you want to call it, are all synonyms for the same thing: light. It's not perceptible. So, it's almost as if, in a movie theater, you had this powerful light in a projector, and it was projecting through the film. The shadows that we see are like everyday life on the screen; it's that light, that's in the projector, that's the Christ vision, and so we're willing to move in that direction. Miracles cleanse our minds, they cleanse the film, they wash away the shadows, and some of us have actually been in those old movie theaters where the film burns or snaps sometimes. It would actually snap or burn, and then the whole screen would go to light, which is like piercing into what we could call Christ's vision. So, underneath it all, that is what inspires the miracles—Christ's vision—and miracles are quite interpersonal; they're still perceptual, so you know there will be so many miracles in your life.

> "They on the rock *are they*, which, when they hear, receive the word with joy; and these have no root, which for a while believe, and in time of temptation fall away." (Luke 8:13)

All service is capitalized S for Self. It's Christ Service, but it's also Self-service. It's extending Christ's love and light, and by doing so you're having the most natural experience you could ever have because you were created to extend love. And when you extend love, you experience the joy of the original creation.

~♥~

It's really beautiful and really simple, but the ego has just made up a bunch of other concepts to try to mix in, inject in, and throw us off track. And forgiveness is always a gift to yourself; you never truly forgive anyone else.

You're simply removing and releasing crazy ideas from your consciousness that don't belong there. And you're giving yourself and everyone else a gift. But you're not saying, *Well,*

God made me holy, so I have the power to forgive you for your sins—It's to forgive your brother for what he hasn't done, see the mistake in your mind, and let it go. That is how you take the enemy out; you pluck the enemy from your mind. Don't point the finger at your adversary as if they're in form. Pointing fingers at enemies in form demonstrates that you believe in grievances.

> "For I was an hungred, and ye gave me meat: I was thirsty, and ye gave me drink: I was a stranger, and ye took me in." (Matthew 25:35)

Let us not believe that our loving Creator is to blame for the fall from grace or that the loving Creator had anything to do with it at all. Because if God created you perfect, you must continue to be perfect. If God is all-knowing, all-loving, and all-powerful, then believe me when I say that this little puff of a thought called an ego is not creating conditions for God to meet. As a result, God cannot attack something he did not create. He must still honor the sleep, we will say, in the sense that he is unaware of it. So the Holy Spirit is analogous to our remembering the truth. It is the memory that remains in our minds that will never fade. It's so loving. It's like keeping that memory of the truth for us until we're ready to embrace and accept it.

And since that is a state of grace, even atonement is just grace. Grace is already present. It is available in any instant.

According to Jesus, this world ended a long time ago. As a result, the Correction is now available. It is the escape hatch, and nothing prevents the mind from accepting it. There is nothing preventing the mind from accessing it; it is fully operational. It is fully operational and readily available. So we can begin to let go of the victimization that something outside of me—some force greater than me—is keeping me from knowing who I am. No. That cannot possibly be correct. That's great news. The good news of the gospel, as they say, is truly wonderful news.

~♥~

The miracle is the choice to see the past as over and done with. The deceived mind, while sleeping or dreaming, believes it is living in the past. Yet life is eternal, and the closest thing to eternity is now. Miracles appear to pave the way for revelation, pure light, and the holy instant, in which the Great Rays are directly experienced.

> "And when he had called unto *him* his twelve disciples, he gave them power *against* unclean spirits, to cast them out, and to heal all manner of sickness and all manner of disease." (Matthew 10:1)

> "Heal the sick, cleanse the lepers, raise the dead, cast out devils: freely ye have received, freely give." (Matthew 10:8)

Everyone, all seven billion people, appears to have their own version of hell, but there is only projection—the attempt to get rid of something you don't want. To believe in the ego is to wish for death or hell. Making up your own perceptual nightmare with some good and some bad things, some pains, some happy memories, and some sad memories—it's a mix;

it's not reality. Reality is not a mix of the good and the bad. *What God created*, it says in the Bible, *he called good*. And we're saying it's all spiritual.

God was the one who created Heaven. God is Heaven. God is perfect love. Christ is perfect love and God's and Christ's creations are perfect love. But the earth (the time-space cosmos) is an attempt at the impossible, which is why Jesus says, *This world is an impossible situation*. Because only God's thoughts can be extended. The thoughts of this world are not God's thoughts; they cannot be extended.

So it's just one mind that appears to be asleep and dreaming the cosmos. And the mind has dreamed up and projected a world of bodies in which there appear to be private minds associated with each body, which have private thoughts, secrets, goals and ambitions for the future and past histories. All of that is part of the giant fiction—a giant fabrication that has no reality whatsoever.

~♥~

The hallucination will vanish when it is recognized for what it is: an impossible situation. There is no need for the impossible when you recognize that something is impossible. So we could say that when you try to share something that can't be shared, you have an authority problem, and this is where we get into time, space, and bodies.

Suppose you had a nighttime dream in which you dreamed up symptoms: maybe you were blind or deaf or you couldn't walk; maybe in the dream you had things done to you that appeared to be evil and dastardly. And then you woke up and thought, *Whooo, that was interesting, I had a dream in which I experienced these symptoms.* But when you awoke you just had a big happy smile on your face because you thought, *Thank God that wasn't real, thank God I just dreamed it.* So, if you start taking these physical symptoms seriously, it's because you forgot you were dreaming. That's the one mistake; you simply forgot you were dreaming and you're taking it as reality again, which is psychotic, schizophrenic, delusional, and hallucinatory. But when you believe those symptoms are real and serious, you've simply forgotten you're dreaming. Training your mind, allowing miracles to be performed through you to the point where the doer vanishes—and, eventually, all identification with the body and the person vanishes. And suddenly you're aware of dreaming; like a lucid dream, you're aware that you're dreaming the world. You're so happy when you come to the place of remembering.

A miracle is a way of looking at the world that gives you a little snapshot of the forgiven world, the miracle simply sees the false is false. Miracles do not create or really change at all; they merely look upon the devastation and remind the mind that what it sees is false. When you're in that still moment where you're still perceiving the world but you feel so at peace, the reason you feel at peace while you're still looking at the world is because of the miracle. You don't need to fix it, you don't need to improve it, you don't need to change it, you don't need to make it better, you simply have to see the false as false.

How you think of a brother is how you think of yourself. That's why in the Bible Jesus said, "Judge not, that ye be not judge." (Matthew 7:1) Because the one who's judging is also judging itself. If you criticize a brother, you criticize yourself. Projection is the ego's attempt to project fault onto something outside in the world, some other brother, as if there's some scapegoat, someone to blame. But Jesus is saying no, you're just doing this to yourself.

I want to teach you the vision of Christ so that you can see that you are the Christ. And this is why we practice. And this is why Jesus says that a teacher of God could heal the whole world without a sound. So much for being a great speech giver. So much for words. He's talking about divine silence. He's talking about the same thing that Eckhart Tolle is talking about, that Ramana Maharshi talked about, and everything I've been talking about for these 36 years: you can heal the world without a sound.

So don't try to guilt yourself if you don't say the right words. You don't have to be worried about saying the right words. You just have to want to see the innocence. That's all you need. Your mind is so powerful, that if you put that on your altar, and you say, "I want to see pure innocence," and that's the one focus now in your mind, then Jesus is saying that's it. That's what vision is. That's the gift, the gift of innocence. This lesson is not difficult to learn.

Well, that's a pep talk from Jesus! And the ego may scream, *Oh, that's impossible. He doesn't know what I've been through. If he had a childhood like I had, he would never say that. Or if he knew my neighbor.* But Jesus is like, "No, no, no. It doesn't matter about the childhood. It doesn't matter about the neighbor or about whatever seemed to happen. You have a gift, and you can give it and you can teach it."

9. Speak on the Beatitudes

"And he opened his mouth, and taught them, saying, Blessed are the poor in spirit: for theirs is the kingdom of heaven." (Matthew 5:3)

Jesus is not advocating poverty. I know sometimes throughout history, even in the convents and the monasteries, they sometimes have these vows of poverty, chastity, and obedience. Even the beatitudes mentioned how blessed the poor are. I think that is again an error only in the sense that what Jesus is saying is that poverty is ego thinking and true wealth and abundance are the result of right-mindedness. And from that definition, it is purely thinking and a state of mind. It has nothing to do with what seems to be the form or accumulated possessions and all that other stuff. It's purely based on a state of mind.

And when you open up to that right-mindedness, then your trust, faith, and confidence in the guidance grow. Then, of course, you are rich beyond any definition of wealth in this world because that's a wealth that can never be taken away from you. Store not your treasures upon earth where moths and thieves can steal them. Store your treasures up in Heaven. (Matthew 6:19-21) Put your entire investment in mind training and right-mindedness, Jesus is saying. Put all your faith in miracles, so much so that you become miracle minded.

~♥~

I would read about the saints and the mystics and poverty, chastity, and obedience, and I would ask, "What does poverty really mean?" And Jesus says poverty is ego-thinking. It has nothing to do with the forms. Don't try to define your abundance and your deprivation in terms of form. Just know that ego-thinking is poverty. When you make a vow of poverty, make a vow of disidentification with attachment, disidentification with possessions.

To be rich is to be in the beatitudes, to be in love, peace, happiness, and joy. There's nothing richer than that. Why should you be concerned with what appears to be poverty and abundance on the surface when the true abundance is the love, peace, and joy in your heart? You couldn't be any more abundant than having a peaceful mind. That's the Kingdom of Heaven. You can't get any richer than that.

It's just the ego that's made up this continuum from poverty and scarcity to richness and abundance. You will start to realize that you don't really want both, you just want peace. You're going for a state of mind, and whatever the form is, it's great! If there are lots of props and trinkets that are used in the experience, let the Holy Spirit use all the props of the world. You don't have to own them; they're all yours anyway. The Holy Spirit's going to use those symbols freely, without any connection or any sense of possessing them. The Holy Spirit is using all the symbols of the world for you to experience true abundance, and that's what it means to be truly rich.

~♥~

The great Russian writer Leo Tolstoy felt so bad that he had money and that there were so many peasants in Russia, that he gave away all his money and all his possessions to the peasants. But he still felt miserable. So, Jesus can't be just talking at the material level of selling all you have, giving to the poor, and *following him*. Because Tolstoy and others have tried it, and it wasn't a very pleasant experience. Give everything away, and then you feel poor yourself. Tolstoy joined the poor.

When Jesus said, "Blessed are the poor in Spirit," he must have been talking about a different kind of poverty. I always took poverty in the traditional monastery and convent vows of poverty, chastity, and obedience to just mean non-possession. Not that the form looked a certain way, but in your mind, you weren't possessing. People say things like, *Do you have the possessions, or do the possessions have you?*

I think there are a lot of people in the world now, even in materially advanced nations, that are starting to ask that question. Do I have the possessions, or do the possessions have me? Am I working and toiling to support my possessions, or are these things in my life serving the glory of God and my peace of mind? That's a very interesting question to ask yourself. *Are the symbols in my life—the symbols of bodies and cars and houses and whatever else—serving the Lord?* Are they serving my peace of mind, or somehow have I become a servant to them? Have I become a slave to a mortgage? Have I become a slave to loans? To payments?

> "Blessed are they that mourn: for they shall be comforted." (Matthew 5:4)

Every time there is a sense of pain or suffering, it means that there must be a decision made in the mind to go against

God's Will. But trying to live apart from the Creator, apart from the Source, is insane. So it's like a purge, a purification of desire through trust is what we're really talking about. And so deeply trusting that whenever anything other than perfect happiness arises, it is the time to be willing to open up and let go of whatever is being protected. There is some crazy alien belief down there in the mind that is still trying to hold on to the sense that there is something other than God's Will, and it's a very simple practice of purification. It's more like surrendering to God's Will rather than attempting to defend against it.

~♥~

Separation, death, guilt, and fear are all taught by the ego. Love, unity, oneness, and forgiveness are all taught by the Holy Spirit. They never meet. The Holy Spirit never meets the ego. And your mind will only meet the thought system to which it is attracted to. So, if you are attracted to love and the holy instant, you will learn the Holy Spirit's thought system. What does the Holy Spirit's thought system tell you? It declares, "There is nothing outside of you." That is what you must ultimately learn. But how is that possible? He's not referring to the person. There's nothing outside of you as a person, he's saying, "There is nothing outside of your mind." Because God created it, your mind is extremely powerful. You can also believe in something other than love. You can believe in separation but it doesn't make it true. When you believe it, it only appears true in your awareness. When you believe it, it appears that the world is fragmented, that you are struggling, competing, striving, making an effort, and pushing to make it. Make a name for yourself in the world. And Jesus simply says, "Let go. You don't have to be concerned about making it in the world. You must concentrate on forgiving the world, and the world will disappear and you will remember God."

> "Blessed are the meek: for they shall inherit the earth." (Matthew 5:5)

Jesus was teaching the beatitudes, he was teaching us the attitude that we could experience as a child of God; he was saying, "Blessed are the meek, for they shall see God," and he says, the reason the meek are blessed is because their strength will overcome the world, wait a minute. Jesus, what are you talking about? How are the meek strong enough to overcome this world? He's saying that if you're gentle, peaceful, loving, and have a very holy attitude, your perception of the entire world will change, and you will literally overcome the ego's distorted perception of the world with your holy perception, just like Jesus did. You have to have a different perspective if your body is on a cross with nails in your arms and legs and your response is "forgive them, for they know not what they do." That is a different perspective than the ego's perspective, and I'll tell you, it's a very high perspective. He was just saying, the world is insane, but I am not of the world. "Be of good cheer, for I have overcome the world." I have overcome it with the strength of my Christ vision, which is showing me God's love. The vision of Christ leads back to God, leads back to remembering God, and Jesus had already said, "My Kingdom is not of this world." He was teaching a spiritual kingdom.

~♥~

You can be truly loving and helpful when you are disidentified from concepts and roles. And what was so great about Jesus was that he was not identified with any of the concepts or roles. It didn't matter if they stuck him on a cross or not. He was completely unaffected by the dream, no matter how extreme it became. Because he allowed himself, he allowed his mind to be washed of the world's concepts and judgments. He was identified with the Christ idea! He was aligned in that flow, aligned to Source, and not identified with anything in the world.

Now, Jesus said in the Bible that we should be meek. And gentleness is meek. But how can you be truly gentle with yourself if you are still tied up in believing and identifying with ego concepts? Because it is only our mind's identification with concepts that brings in defensiveness.

If your mind is devoted to purpose, you're going to draw forth all kinds of witnesses of that devotion. Because that is how it works. We simply perceive what we believe. The world is an outward picture of an inward condition. It's simply a reflection of our consciousness back to us.

So really, whenever you want to know, what is the state of my mind, you could also say, *What is the state of the world that I perceive?* This gives me the most accurate indication of where my mind is in its mind training. As you allow yourself to be open to the Presence of God's Love, and as you become more and more focused on this purpose and calling, and the fear fades, you no longer perceive error.

But, because perception is selective, you're simply calling witnesses in the world to what you believe. And you have the power to change what you believe. You have the power to forgive rather than judge, to forgive instead of condemn, to forgive instead of holding grievances. It is extremely powerful and empowering to know that you can train your mind, with the help of the Holy Spirit, to a state of forgiveness in which, because perception is selective, you attract more and more witnesses to your consistency of alignment with forgiveness.

Until you become SO aligned with forgiveness that you see the world in a completely different way than you saw it before, isn't that exciting? That's the excitement! It's not the excitement of what's going on in the world. But it's more about the excitement of the mind's capacity to learn to truly forgive. And to see the world in a completely new light. You can see that you have the ability to alter your perception. That you are not stuck in a movie. You are the dreamer of the dream, and you can give the dream another purpose and therefore see the dream in a different way.

It's not through our deeds that we reach the state of enlightenment. It's through our purpose. And it is our willingness to be open, to follow and flow in that purpose steadfastly, that brings us to enlightenment. And it's not even about time; we don't have to think about how long this will take. That is just another belief that it will take that long to be who we truly are. We must begin to question this as well and declare, "I believe in miracles." I believe that miracles shorten time. Like, collapse the Alpha and the

Omega. They bring this illusory past and this illusory future together.

> "Blessed are they which do hunger and thirst after righteousness: for they shall be filled." (Matthew 5:6)

The belief in loss or sacrifice is at the core of the ego. On the other hand, Spirit is fully abundant, whole, and complete. This is what the ego is; it is the belief in loss and lack, as well as grief. It's always missing, telling us that we're missing out on something, or that we had something good in the past but no longer have it, and it's based on linear time, avoiding the present moment and avoiding eternity, and staying in this loop of not enough, never getting enough, and when I have something of value, it's taken away. That's what this whole cosmos is about.

So, being a miracle worker is the answer. We've tried to fill that sense of lack in so many ways, and the world appears to offer many, but when Jesus says, "Drink of me and you will never thirst again," he's really saying, join me in the miracle and we'll experience a fulfillment that has no lack, no missing. So that's one of those deep roots, and I know that for me, going down and getting to the core of that root was what the whole journey was about. Because as long as there is any sense of unfulfillment, any sense of, that inner sense of something missing, the mind just seems to seek in terms of form and never gets fulfilled, it simply does not do it in this world. So it's more of a negation of starting to realize, I need not seek for it in form, I need to find my function, I need to find my purpose because that's where I'm gonna find my fulfillment, and it's glorious!

> "Blessed are the merciful: for they shall obtain mercy." (Matthew 5:7)

One thing must ultimately be learned: guilt is always completely insane and without reason. Christ is the proof that the ego never was and never can be. There is no guilt in eternity. The past is no longer with us. It cannot touch us.

The journey to God is simply a reawakening to what you have always been and what you will forever be. Today, I accept the love that I am, and that extends from me eternally. I accept my identity in God as Spirit.

The Son of God was created out of love, and in love he abides. Goodness and mercy have always followed him because he has always extended the love of his Father. I shall dwell in God's Mind forever and ever.

> "Blessed are the pure in heart: for they shall see God." (Matthew 5:8)

Jesus says that forgiveness is a state of mind that is quiet, silent, and does nothing. It judges not. So it is a presence of mind that simply sees the false as false and does not react to it. It is a presence of mind that is aligned with the truth, and therefore, has no need to contest or try to change the world. It's just a demonstration of the presence of purity, and that's why Jesus said in the Beatitudes, "Blessed are the pure of heart for they shall see God."

~♥~

It's all about the love in your heart. If you only took one saying from Jesus and applied it to your life, that would be the end of it. "Blessed are the pure in heart: for they shall see God." You don't even need theology or philosophy; you don't need anything but love. The Beatles told us that, "All you need is love." They were right. That's right on.

~♥~

Nothing is more important than keeping your heart open to God's Love. Especially because God is Love, and if you want to know Love, knowing God is knowing yourself as pure Love. Because God is pure love and to know God, you have to really keep your heart open during these experiences of time and space.

The ego is constantly trying to say, *Here, know death, sickness, and guilt*. And your heart is telling you, *Oh, really? Is this the purpose of life? Sickness, struggle, pain, and death? Is that the purpose of life?* And Jesus responds, "No, actually, that isn't the meaning of life." Love and life are synonymous, but Jesus is telling us that life is eternal life. Life is life in God not in form.

> "Blessed are the peacemakers: for they shall be called the children of God." (Matthew 5:9)

I would say that inner peace is always the goal; it should always be at the forefront, and there is really nothing else we need to focus on except that inner peace; peace of mind is not a small gift, we are worthy. We were created in peace; we are worthy of that peace.

~♥~

God is everything; Spirit is everything; Love is everything; and the world of time and space is nothing. And yet, if we believe in nothing as our identity, we are unhappy, because we are children of God. We breathe, live, and move in Spirit and light. We are a child of light.

And when we forget our identity and believe in the forms, we begin to believe that we have to compromise every day. What am I going to compromise? What am I going to sacrifice? I would rather do this, but I have to do that. And, as you can see, the ego has set up a complex maze of time and space to keep us from being happy. It's designed to keep us guilty. And Jesus is saying "No, it's actually a device that the Holy Spirit can use to finally teach the mind that there is no sacrifice and that you are worthy of everything, and God's Will for you is to know Love, which is everything." Love is our identity.

> I was in the college of design and garden architecture for five years, and part of the training was learning art history and learning what is beautiful art and what is not.
>
> But the more I practiced mind-training and right-mindedness over the years, the more I started to feel that everything is beautiful. Because a still mind is where the beauty is.

That is the prettiness. That is the beauty. It is not about taking segments of it and saying that some are better than others. You have this sense of full gratitude and appreciation.

So, Jesus on the cross—what was that all about? Jesus says there was a lesson in the crucifixion, and it was to teach only love, for that is what you are. It can seem like that was an extreme example of teaching only love. But I think sometimes these extreme examples, like the crucifixion, have teaching value. It would seem to earth or ego perception that someone seemed to be beaten, torn, bruised, and carrying a heavy cross. But Jesus didn't perceive any attack at all; He didn't perceive any attack whatsoever.

So that is an extreme example. And for me, there is a joy; there is a steady joy like I am always watching a movie. It does not matter whether I am watching what the world calls a horror movie or a tsunami movie or, "Pocahontas" or whatever. There is a steady joy there.

And that is the beauty that I behold in the world, by not giving it value one way or the other. Everything in this world seems to be blurred by ego. It wants us to be complacent. You know how they say, "Familiarity breeds contempt." It wants us to find things that are cozy and familiar.

And I found that some of the countries I traveled to seemed to have the most extreme conditions of poverty, illness, children dying, and so on. And in those countries, I find that there is an underlying happiness and an underlying authenticity that I can feel being reflected back to me that is almost palpable.

When we are together, we can feel a very profound spirit there because we are not seduced by the comforts or conveniences of the ego. The things which can be like a lullaby, lulling you to sleep, where you make yourself comfortable with egoic means. It is almost like being lulled by ego tricks.

10. What Is the Devil?

"Then was Jesus led up of the Spirit into the wilderness to be tempted of the devil. And when he had fasted forty days and forty nights, he was afterward an hungred. And when the tempter came to him, he said, If thou be the Son of God, command that these stones be made bread. But he answered and said, It is written, Man shall not live by bread alone, but by every word that proceedeth out of the mouth of God.

Then the devil taketh him up into the holy city, and setteth him on a pinnacle of the temple, And saith unto him, If thou be the Son of God, cast thyself down: for it is written, He shall give his angels charge concerning thee: and in *their* hands they shall bear thee up, lest at any time thou dash thy foot against a stone. Jesus said unto him, It is written again, Thou shalt not tempt the Lord thy God. Again, the devil taketh him up into an exceeding high mountain, and sheweth him all the kingdoms of the world, and the glory of them; And saith unto him, All these things will I give thee, if thou wilt fall down and worship me. Then saith Jesus unto him, Get thee hence, Satan: for it is written, Thou shalt worship the Lord thy God, and him only shalt thou serve. Then the devil leaveth him, and, behold, angels came and ministered unto him." (Matthew 4:1-11)

> "And the great dragon was cast out, that old serpent, called the Devil, and Satan, which deceiveth the whole world: he was cast out into the earth, and his angels were cast out with him. And I heard a loud voice saying in heaven, Now is come salvation, and strength, and the kingdom of our God, and the power of his Christ: for the accuser of our brethren is cast down, which accused them before our God day and night." (Revelation 12:9-10)

The ego/error/devil was corrected by the Holy Spirit the instant the error seemed to arise. And now your only responsibility is to accept this Correction. What you believe, you will perceive, as long as perception seems to last. Believe the error, and you will seem to perceive abuse and addiction. Accept the Correction and you will seem to perceive a forgiven world shining in the light of the Holy Spirit. Accept the Correction and you have given up the attempt to reconcile "opposites." Accept the Correction and lasting peace is the only possible result.

~♥~

The devil is the ego–a belief in your own mind. Someone asked Gandhi about the devil once, and he said, "The only devils in this world are those running around in our own hearts, and that is where all our battles should be fought." It sure can seem in this projection that there are evil forces around us, but that thinking is false.

The ego is a belief system that is an attempt to deny awareness of love's presence. It sets up a cover or shield to cover over this experience of Love. For everyone who comes to this planet, the ego is there in awareness; no one comes to earth without believing in the ego. And we can say by definition that Heaven is the Love, and the ego is an attempt to run away from that Love, hide from that love, or cover over that Love.

The ego is a belief system that invents substitutes, so it's invented things like romantic love to take the place of Divine Love, and it has invented electric light bulbs to take the place of heavenly light, wisdom; and it's made up all kinds of substitutes to take the place of love.

~♥~

Jesus talks about unplugging the power of our minds from this erroneous faulty belief system that is attempting to deny love. In the end, when you have this experience of peace, it's an awareness that the ego is not. Love is all that there is, and that's the whole point of the spiritual journey: to have an experience that Love is everything. It's all in all. There is nothing but Love.

Jesus is calling us out of the world. He doesn't mean He is calling you away from the cities into the forest or something like that; Jesus just means He calls you to transcend the ego, to release it, to recognize and remember your spiritual nature, which is just pure Love and light.

There was a time when Jesus and the Apostles were going along, and Peter told Jesus not to go back to Jerusalem. And then Jesus uttered the famous response, "Get thee behind me, Satan." (Matthew 16:23) Peter's request was far from what could have been considered an outrageous request. Jesus was at the end of his public mission, and the Apostles knew there were those in Jerusalem who wanted him killed.

But Jesus was aware the script is written, and it is all prophesied what would happen. And it was just him tuning into Spirit and saying, "Get thee behind me, Satan." Not that he was saying it to Peter, but basically, Jesus is affirming the way things are going to go. There is a destiny that is being fulfilled. The prophecies are being fulfilled, and he is going back to Jerusalem. There is a big part of the whole Jesus story that would have been missing if he had not gone back to Jerusalem.

When you live in the context of a community with the guidelines of no people-pleasing and no private thoughts, there are going to be plenty of requests flying left and right to allow you to practice those guidelines. Can you do this or that? Can you turn the temperature up or down? A little more spice to the food, less spice. You get a group of human beings living together, and it is like marriage magnified. You start to realize that a lot of the people-pleasing is just this pattern the ego used to make this world, in a sense. It made a personality self, and then it made all these other personalities, and the personality self has all these preferences, yet it is so shaky.

You have the persona, or the mask, and the mask is shaky because it is not reality; that is one reason it is shaky. It does not have any good foundation. So, you have a shaky mask, and the ego works to strengthen it in part by getting praise from others, positive feedback, or other forms of acknowledgement. We would say these are all good things for stabilizing the personality. The mask is covering Christ. And whether you seem to have a good mask or a bad mask, a praised mask or a scorned mask, a mask is a mask; it is covering something. When we talk about no people-pleasing, it is really about starting to let your yays be yay and your nays be nay. It's about becoming more intuitive and following the Holy Spirit instead of your past learning or your past preference patterns.

11. What Is Temptation?

> "For in that he himself hath suffered being tempted, he is able to succour them that are tempted." (Hebrews 2:18)

Imagine that anytime you were tempted to perceive yourself as unfairly treated, you told yourself, I'm not in the mood to believe in unfair treatment. I'm taking a stand! I'm not a victim. I can't be mistreated.

It's not to deny the feelings, but if the feelings are coming up and that is what you feel, then obviously that is what you think and that is what you believe. But I'm saying to really take a stand in your mind because you are worthy of it. You are worthy of that peace. You are worthy of that love. You are worthy of that truth.

~♥~

As long as you hold on to a grievance, it seems like the past isn't the past. It seems like it's still active. It's still happening, and there's still an impetus to try to change something, fix somebody, control something, or defend something. That's where temptation comes in. Instead of just seeing it as it is—completely whole with no problems whatsoever—you think there's a problem in the field. In forgiveness, there is no problem.

This is the great temptation of this world: trying to come up with better outcomes and believing that you honestly know what the better outcomes are. It's only the ego that judges some outcomes as good and some as bad. For the Holy

Spirit, all things work together. The goal is to learn how to change your mind, or your perception of the world, to see as the Holy Spirit sees.

Don't be tempted to get into debates. Don't be tempted to get into arguments. Don't be tempted to take sides. Don't be tempted into opinions. Don't let who is right and who is wrong tempt you. Isn't that a sneaky temptation as you move through your daily life? Just the temptation to take a side.

Somebody says something to you, and there is a part of your mind that wants to jump on it. It wants to attack it, defend it, agree with it, or disagree with it. All of it is a temptation. Instead of being drawn into the temptation, ask yourself what it is that you truly want. From that focal point, you can ask to see with spiritual vision.

> "And lead us not into temptation, but deliver us from evil: For thine is the kingdom, and the power, and the glory, for ever. Amen." (Matthew 6:13)

> "Let no man say when he is tempted, I am tempted of God: for God cannot be tempted with evil, neither tempteth he any man: But every man is tempted, when he is drawn away of his own lust, and enticed. Then when lust hath conceived, it bringeth forth sin: and sin, when it is finished, bringeth forth death. Do not err, my beloved brethren. Every good gift and every perfect gift is from above, and cometh down from the Father of lights, with whom is no variableness, neither shadow of turning." (James 1:13-17)

> "And they came over unto the other side of the sea, into the country of the Gadarenes. And when he was come out of the ship, immediately there met him out of the tombs a man with an unclean spirit, Who had *his* dwelling among the tombs; and no man could bind him, no, not with chains: Because that he had been often bound with fetters and chains, and the chains had been plucked asunder by him, and the fetters broken in pieces: neither could any *man* tame him. And always, night and day, he was in the mountains, and in the tombs, crying, and cutting himself with stones.
>
> But when he saw Jesus afar off, he ran and worshipped him, And cried with a loud voice, and said, What have I to do with thee, Jesus, *thou* Son of the most high God? I adjure thee by God, that thou torment me not. For he said unto him, Come out of the man, *thou* unclean spirit. And he asked him, What *is* thy name? And he answered, saying, My name *is* Legion: for we are many." (Mark 5:1- 9)

The human condition on planet earth is about individuals. What we consider to be an individual is a person with private thoughts in a private mind apart from all the other individuals. So this is definitely a tapestry of pieces, many different pieces, seven billion separate pieces. There is a word that I like to use in place of *individual,* because most of the time people say that with pride, *I am an individual.* But what we really want in our heart is to be *indivisible*. Not able to be broken apart, indivisible, not able to be divided. Like the Light, like Christ—One Christ, One Light, One Mind.

~♥~

This is the great temptation of this world: trying to come up with better outcomes and believing that you truly know what they are because it is only the ego that judges some outcomes as good or bad. To the Holy Spirit all things work together for good and the goal is to learn how to change your mind or change your perception of the world. We're not attempting to make the world a better place in the way that the ego would judge a better place.

~♥~

Specialness is a filter in the mind, it is a desire to get something. It is completely opposed to the desire to give and extend. And when this desire to get is given faith, it seeks out things in the world to get that will seem to improve the self-concept. It's similar to going into a car dealership and trading in your used car for a new model; this is very much how it works with relationships and the self-concept.

~♥~

So, when you make that turn toward purpose, it has to light up your life and draw you in. Talk about the law of attraction! The attraction of your mind, your heart opening up for that love just seems to grow stronger and stronger. And what we would call temptation, the temptation to get, just fades away. It's not like you have to fight the temptations. It's more like you have to gently yield into this divine purpose, and the temptations just fade away. You are fulfilled. You are not looking for scraps to fill your empty cups. It is more like, *Ha ha, my cup runneth over.* That vibe, that kind of energy, just grows stronger in awareness.

The mind seems to have made up this image of a self, and it is dissatisfied with that self, so it wants to keep trading up. It wants all the perks and benefits of trading up, just like trading up for a new car. More bells and whistles. The prayer of the heart is really to give the self over to be transformed, to be used. It is the call to get into your miracle-working function and to get into your communication function to share and strengthen these ideas.

Until you open up deeper and deeper into your God-given purpose and function, there is no replacement for specialness. Specialness is this filter in the mind, this desire to get things to improve the self-concept. You have to have something else to pour your devotion and dedication into to take the place of specialness. This purpose will bring you the joy, the love, and the happiness that you do deserve because it is your natural birthright.

Through the ego, the mind tries to get happiness through inappropriate means, trying to get it in all kinds of ways that it really can't.

That is where the empty roads come in. There is all this investment to get something, and if there is no return, the ego says, *Okay, toss that one out.* Now go for the next conquest, or the next one.

You start to get wise to the ego's games, and you start to realize that you are just praying that prayer: "Lord, make me an instrument." You are praying to be used by God. You are praying to be truly helpful. You keep giving yourself over to that purpose, to that function, and the more you start to feel the fulfillment of that function. You feel happy, you feel free, and you feel content. And if you block that function by trying to get something else, then it is just another spin around the table of illusions. You try a different form, a different road, a different person, and it is that same emptiness that comes in again.

When you make that turn toward your God-given purpose, it lights up your life and draws you. Talk about the law of attraction. The attraction in your mind, your heart opening up for that love, just seems to grow stronger and stronger. And what we would call temptation—the temptation to get—just fades away. It is not like you have to fight against temptation. It is more like you have to gently yield to this purpose, this divine purpose, and the temptations just fade away. You are fulfilled. You are not looking for scraps to fill your empty cup. It is more like your cup runneth over. That vibe, that kind of energy, just grows stronger and stronger in awareness.

12. Speak on Perfect Equality

"For the kingdom of heaven is like unto a man *that is* a householder, which went out early in the morning to hire labourers into his vineyard. And when he had agreed with the labourers for a penny a day, he sent them into his vineyard.

And he went out about the third hour, and saw others standing idle in the marketplace, And said unto them; Go ye also into the vineyard, and whatsoever is right I will give you. And they went their way. Again he went out about the sixth and ninth hour, and did likewise. And about the eleventh hour he went out, and found others standing idle, and saith unto them, Why stand ye here all the day idle? They say unto him, Because no man hath hired us. He saith unto them, Go ye also into the vineyard; and whatsoever is right, *that* shall ye receive. So when even was come, the lord of the vineyard saith unto his steward, Call the labourers, and give *them* their hire, beginning from the last unto the first.

And when they came that were *hired* about the eleventh hour, they received every man a penny. But when the first came, they supposed that they should have received more; and they likewise received every man a penny. And when they had received *it*, they murmured against the goodman of the house, Saying, These last have wrought *but* one hour, and thou hast made them equal unto us, which have borne the burden and heat of the day.

But he answered one of them, and said, Friend, I do thee no wrong: didst not thou agree with me for a penny? Take *that* thine *is*, and go thy way: I will give unto this last, even as unto thee.

Is it not lawful for me to do what I will with mine own? Is thine eye evil, because I am good?" (Matthew 20:1-15)

As humans, we are equal. There is nobody who is ahead and nobody who is behind. Nobody is superior. No one is inferior. That equality is taking us to a unified experience of the living Christ. We knew it had to be through equality. There is no way that inequality has anything to do with God. How could God love one person more than another? How could God say, "I love the one who professes this belief, but I do not love the one who professes that belief?" That is ridiculous.

~♥~

I find that most people I meet hate this parable about the farmer. They say that maybe Jesus was a little "loco" on that day. Jesus was really teaching that there is no order of difficulty in miracles. The way he prefaced that parable is that he said, "The Kingdom of Heaven is like unto," and then he told the parable. People have been scratching their heads ever since, saying, "I do not know if I want to know anything more about the Kingdom of Heaven if it is that unfair." He is sharing an experience that levels out and unifies all of perception. In the perception of the healed world, everything is equal. The only fairness or justice is in a healed perception of the world.

The whole purpose of this world is to be used by the Holy Spirit to teach perfect equality, absolute perfect equality, regardless of the size of the bodies, regardless of how much these ones seem to learn, know, and don't know. All of that is going to be flushed up into conscious awareness for forgiveness.

When I was in South America many years ago, the mothers who had these little, small children said they were learning so much from them. What the mothers were learning from the small children was, *You're done.* What they meant was that this game of superior and inferior, this game of inequality, is over.

These old roles that are just projections and interpretations based on the ego have got to go. These struggles are really calls to let go of people-pleasing, to let go of control, and to go much deeper into this state of divine flow where there's an allowance to give your mind over to the Holy Spirit.

The ego's strategy towards all kinds of conflicts is basically to always say, "*If only something were different in the world.* It is always trying to change something on the screen to bring about peace. The mind is resistant to seeing that it just takes a change of perception in the moment. That is the one thing that the mind in the deceived state is so resistant to. In the end, that is what the Atonement is—to start to see there is nothing outside of me that can give me peace or take away my peace.

13. Speak on Charity

"Though I speak with the tongues of men and of angels, and have not charity, I am become *as* sounding brass, or a tinkling cymbal. And though I have *the gift of* prophecy, and understand all mysteries, and all knowledge; and though I have all faith, so that I could remove mountains, and have not charity, I am nothing. And though I bestow all my goods to feed *the poor*, and though I give my body to be burned, and have not charity, it profiteth me nothing. Charity suffereth long, *and* is kind; charity envieth not; charity vaunteth not itself, is not puffed up, Doth not behave itself unseemly, seeketh not her own, is not easily provoked, thinketh no evil;

Rejoiceth not in iniquity, but rejoiceth in the truth; Beareth all things, believeth all things, hopeth all things, endureth all things. Charity never faileth." (1 Corinthians 13:1-8)

True charity is very much like true empathy. When you come inside and get in touch with what's real and true within you, you can extend that truth to everything and everyone. It's in your mind. If you have the light in you, why not be a bringer of light? Instead of trying to play small and hide, why not be a bringer of light wherever you go? Why not be a bringer of happiness and joy? Let people feel the peace in your heart when you interact with them.

Part of being able to do this consistently is undoing the ego and the self-concept. Jesus says that whenever you feel the need to become defensive about anything, you have identified yourself with an illusion. You see? If you are identified with the body, of course, you're going to feel helpless at times; you'll feel weak. At times, you'll feel like you're not good enough if you're identified with the body. But the more you start to come back into your mind, the more you start to realize, *Oh, I have a powerful mind. My mind is part of God's mind. And that mind is very beautiful. It's just filled with light. It doesn't have any darkness in it, in its holy state.*

~♥~

Can we not honor our brothers and sisters as they take their seeming steps and do the best that they can? And can we not have charity for them? Can we not have a vision of seeing their innocence? Really, what they are is pure innocence behind these seeming choices in form as people. There is an innocence there. Can we not focus on that? Can we not overlook their failings, their misgivings, and even the perception of these things?

Remember the kindnesses he showed. Focus your mind on the generosity, focus your mind on the sweetness, focus your mind on the love, and let go of everything else because it is all for your mind. Whatever you focus on, you reinforce or strengthen in your own consciousness. If you focus on the little annoyances, the little misperceptions, the little mistreatments, or the little glares and glances that occasionally appear in your awareness, you retain that in awareness.

~♥~

Charity is seeing someone far beyond their accomplishments in form. Talk about giving them the benefit! You are seeing them closer to their true Selves than the way that they appear to be. That is called charity. Jesus says charity is always for you. The benefit is always for the giver of charity because, as you see them, you will see yourself. It is always a gift to yourself to see the good, to see the good in everyone.

~♥~

Jesus teaches true empathy, where he says you need to learn to always stay with what is real and true. Most of what we call empathy in this world is false empathy, and he's trying to teach us true empathy. He's trying to teach us how to be in a miraculous state of mind where we're so high that we look past the error entirely and we just answer the call for love every single time. The Holy Spirit knows only two orders of thought: that everything is love or a call for love.

~♥~

The form of prayer that might be called "praying for another" is a form of charity. Charity is seeing a brother or sister as much farther along than they appear to be in time, and so charity is a time-related reflection of Love. The Oneness of Love is a universal state of being that is eternal.

When we spend money with love, it is given freely, there are no questions asked. And love does not follow to see what the money was spent on. It is very much in the motivation of giving. I have a friend in China who lives on trust, and she lives a very simple life. She found out that a friend who was traveling with me had gum disease and her teeth were starting to fall out. So, this woman in China called me and said, "I want to help your friend go to the dentist." The woman from China wired money over to my friend's account so she could have the dental work done. And when the friend I was traveling with went to a dentist to have treatment on her mouth she was told that she would go for many treatments. It was going to cost quite a lot of money.

Sometime later, the friend in China called and said that my friend she'd wired money to had given away to a charity half of the money that was sent to her for her teeth. And she said, "I love her so much, but she just gave away more than half of the money that I gave her for her teeth." And she asked, "What is the lesson, what am I supposed to learn from this?" I said, “Whenever you give money, it has to be a gift. If you give money with expectations, it is fear giving the money because fear thinks it already knows how the money should be spent." So she asked, "What do I do? I want her to get her teeth fixed. But I do not know if I want to send more money because she may give that away too." I said, "Yes, that is the lesson. You have to pray, listen, and go with what feels good in your heart."

A little while later, the woman in China sent me an email saying, "I sent her more money. I love her so much. She has helped me so much. She is showing me how to live a life of trust." The trust is between you and the Spirit, and you feel good when you follow the Spirit. But you have to give up all the ego judgments and expectations because that is just fear.

14. What Does It Mean to Be Still?

> "Be still, and know that I *am* God: I will be exalted among the heathen, I will be exalted in the earth." (Psalms 46:10)

If you have debts, if you have loans, if you have responsibilities, do you think God set that up for you, or did God just create you as a perfect being? The ego puts you in this predicament of roles, duties, and obligations. God does not give you duties. God is pure Oneness, stillness, and love. God did not give you those laws, duties, and responsibilities.

You need to be unwound by the Holy Spirit, to loosen up, lighten up from what you believe you are on this earth. Bring all those concepts to the Holy Spirit. They will disappear, and you will come back to that beingness. The humanness will fade and the beingness will grow stronger and stronger, until you realize you have always been a being of light. The angels have been whispering to you ever since you were born into this world. The angels have been around you, reminding you that you are a being of light, a perfect creation of a perfect God.

This mesmerism of sleep is a known thing. I think that's a great context. That is where this guidance is taking you. It is taking you into the stillness, into the love and the light, where you do not have to do anything to prove your worth. Why? Because your worth was established by God, and nothing you think, do, make, or say can establish your worth. Your worth is established by God.

~♥~

Meditation starts out with practice. You do have to be vigilant for God and His Kingdom. You do have to work at training your mind to jump off the thought trains, as they say in Buddhism, or to sink beneath the leaves and let the leaves flow over you.

There comes a point when your life becomes a living meditation. You can be singing "Zip A Dee Doo Dah" and be in meditation. You can be walking or eating; your eyes can be open or closed. There can be someone screaming, and you realize that you can't be interrupted. (If all things work together for good, what would an interruption even be? It wouldn't exist.) I am talking about a state of mind that has no distractions. You realize that meditation doesn't have anything to do with posture or breathing. Those things can be helpful at the beginning, but Atonement is independent of the body and independent of time.

The Holy Spirit uses everything in form to reach the state of Atonement.

~♥~

Prayer is sometimes thought of as talking to God and listening for God's answer. Meditation is sometimes thought of as the practice of stilling the mind and sinking beneath the thoughts of the world. Even though prayer and meditation are often thought of as "activities" or "practices," they are actually continuous—meaning they are without beginning or end.

Prayer is desire, and it truly can be said, *Be watchful of what you pray for, for you will experience it.* It is possible to experience a stillness of mind that is involuntary and never controlled or forced. True meditation, like prayer, is being receptive, aligned, and extending in God's Love. They meet in the present moment as a living state of being. First, the mind becomes still and open to receive the Holy Spirit's guidance. The Holy Spirit's guidance dissolves the ego, and thus the ego's "chatter" seems to become less and less apparent in awareness. As the belief in time is undone, only radiant stillness "remains."

The aim or goal of prayer and meditation is always: be still and know.

~♥~

It takes great willingness to be attentive to the Holy Spirit. The mind that sleeps is in the habit of wandering. This is the chatter of the ego. Trains are a helpful metaphor; ego trains are constantly running through the mind. Attentiveness and meditation involve training your mind to hop off these trains.

Each time you notice you have gotten back on one, you hop off again. You train your mind to be aware of the silence that is beyond the trains. As you question the ego's belief system, you are getting at the underpinnings of the train. This way, you can dissolve the train before it leaves the station!

When you start giving yourself over to the Spirit, time will seem to collapse. You will have beautiful moments of stillness in which you lose all sense of time and space, but the two will never meet. You cannot maintain the experience of love and have a dedication to anything of time. Not to a career or a job, not to a child, not to a partner, not to the environment or saving mother earth, not to anything that seems to involve improvement even. Because who you were created as is pure Spirit.

You were created perfect, and everything in time is an attempt to improve on that perfection. That's why Buddha said to empty your mind of everything you think you know. That's why all authentic pathways to God involve stillness and emptying the mind of everything. You have to have the sense that you will not be obliterated by this emptying; you will actually be found. Through this emptying, you will find yourself.

Now, sometimes when I've traveled the world, people will ask that question: "What religion are you teaching?" And it finally got to the point where I asked Jesus for the best definition of religion. If I'm going to go and talk around the world, I'm going to encounter people and all these different religions—tell me what the best definition of religion is. And Jesus said, "Religion is inner peace." Oh, I like that. That's a great definition. That's the best definition I've ever heard. Religion is inner peace. And what's the best definition of spirituality? He said the same thing: inner peace.

Does spirituality have different dimensions?

Not really. And neither does religion, because inner peace is a state of mind. It's not a belief system. It's an actual presence. It's an actual state of mind. If you want to be religious in the truest sense, just find that presence of inner peace that you are, that everyone is, that transcends this world. And the same is true of spirituality. Find it.

Three of the simplest ways to access the Christ mind are: First, to trust your intuition or your higher power, pay attention to your emotions; they are barometers. Be genuine. Awakening takes a lot of mind training, and paying attention to your emotions is part of that.

Second, use simple language and do not pretend to be somewhere you are not. If you are hurting, that's OK. If you feel guilt, shame, and pain coming up, that's OK. Let your tears flow; let your anger come out. Let whatever is down there come to the surface; give yourself permission to move through it.

And finally, give yourself an opportunity to be in stillness. You can call it meditating, fishing, or sailing on the ocean. Whatever the form is, give yourself that peaceful, easy feeling, that time to decompress, unwind, and relax; that makes the intuition much, much clearer.

15. Does God Require Any Sacrifice?

> "For I desired mercy, and not sacrifice; and the knowledge of God more than burnt offerings." (Hosea 6:6)

> "Be ye therefore merciful, as your Father also is merciful." (Luke 6:36)

People have questions in this world, such as, "What happens after you die?" It's more of a question: If this seemingly physical realm is not reality, it's not safe and comfortable, and I can't put my faith in it, then where do I put my faith? Then God and the Spirit become the big question marks.

That's a part of this reversal. It's like amnesia—forgetting divinity, forgetting love, peace, harmony, and Oneness, and then becoming accustomed to images and false memories. Being lured into this illusory world, which seems to stabilize, and then fearing God or the Spirit as the big unknown. Don't take my world away from me. That's the ego's great claim. Don't take what little I have. Don't take it away from me.

It's going to take a retranslation because the ego is the belief in sacrifice. And once you become accustomed to the dream world, giving it up seems like a sacrifice.

~♥~

The Bible talks about the tribes of Israel and the Jews being God's chosen people. Well, God doesn't have any chosen people. Properly interpreted, it means that all are called, but few choose to listen. Few choose to listen because of the fear of sacrifice. What's this call going to cost me?

I think throughout the centuries, even when we talk about convents and monasteries, there was sincerity underneath taking all those vows and trying to live that life as a monk or a nun. But as long as there's a belief in sacrifice, it can still get very twisted.

The ego loves to quote scripture. There are a lot of things that have been taken out of context from the Bible and used in the name of fear, damnation, and hell. Jesus is saying those are just misinterpretations. Some of the thoughts that he has worked with are amazing to me! For example, "Vengeance is mine; I will repay, saith the Lord." (Romans 12:19)

Jesus reinterprets it as if the Holy Spirit is saying to you: "My child, give me that idea of vengeance; it does not belong in your holy mind." Vengeance is mine; give it to me. I can handle it. Wow, what a better interpretation of one that I had looked at as a very negative and condemning statement!

> "Let us hear the conclusion of the whole matter: Fear God, and keep his commandments: for this *is* the whole *duty* of man." (Ecclesiastes 12:13)

The Bible is very famous for saying, "Fear God and keep his commandments." I will simply reinterpret that right now with, *Be in awe of God the Creator and come to know this awe by forgiving the world, forgiving the ego, and forgiving the belief that one could ever be separate from a loving God, a loving Creator.*

> "For the LORD *is* good; his mercy *is* everlasting; and his truth *endureth* to all generations." (Psalms 100:5)

> "Keeping mercy for thousands, forgiving iniquity and transgression and sin, and that will by no means clear *the guilty*; visiting the iniquity of the fathers upon the children, and upon the children's children, unto the third and to the fourth *generation*." (Exodus 34:7)

> "But the wicked shall perish, and the enemies of the LORD *shall be* as the fat of lambs: they shall consume; into smoke shall they consume away." (Psalms 37:20)

> "For the wages of sin *is* death; but the gift of God *is* eternal life through Jesus Christ our Lord." (Romans 6:23)

> "O Israel, trust thou in the LORD: he *is* their help and their shield." (Psalms 115:9)

There is a line in the Bible where it says that the sins of the father are revisited in the third and fourth generations. With some of these things you think, *How could you reinterpret something like that*? However, Jesus does have a reinterpretation. It's about all of these opportunities for forgiveness that we're given. That is, after all, what generations are all about: opportunities to forgive.

So, it is not the father's sins that are revisited in the third and fourth generations; rather, the opportunity for forgiveness is presented over and over while you believe in linear time. In other words, Jesus is saying, *Choose again, my beloved one; do not cling to these vicious thoughts. You are making a mess for yourself; simply hand them over. Give me those thoughts*.

When you start to go through this awakening process and you start to have these miracles happen in your life, occasionally there may be some moments during the day where you feel like you are being asked too much by God. You feel you are being asked to give up something that you do not want to give up because you believe it is good, real, and valuable. This is a mental re-enactment of the crucifixion.

The ego is the belief in sacrifice. Jesus never taught sacrifice. He did not teach that you are going to have to sacrifice a lot to go back to Heaven. He said, "Follow me, think with me, live with me in the mind that I am, and you will know God and you will know yourself." Jesus was teaching self-realization; he was teaching self-actualization. He was not teaching sacrifice.

The ego is the belief in sacrifice. So, the deeper you go on this journey, the more there will be times when you will feel like God is asking too much of you or that you're being asked to give up something of value. That is the belief in sacrifice talking. It is ridiculous to think that you would have to give up something real to know who you are and who God is. And if you did have to give up something real, why would you want to know God?

If there were a sacrifice required for you to live in eternity, I would say there is something fishy about eternity. Eternity does not have conditions. Eternity is unconditional love. It is the ego that makes up all conditions. It is the ego that makes up all ideas of sacrifice.

So the Holy Spirit has a convincing job because as you go through the day, you are tempted to continue believing in the crucifixion. Now, I'm not talking consciously. I would say most people are not practicing a theology that says something must be sacrificed for love to be known, at least not consciously. We are talking about this unconscious belief in the ego that you have to let go of something real to know who you are. And that is where resistance comes up.

Whenever you find yourself getting into

resistance, this is what is underneath it. There is some kind of sense that something is being asked of you that you are not ready to let go of. Even though you may have already let go and let God, surrendered, and watched how glorious your life is, this unconscious ego belief in sacrifice is what is holding you back. And it is up to the Holy Spirit to convince you that there is no sacrifice to follow Him.

16. What Is the Meaning of the Crucifixion?

> "When the morning was come, all the chief priests and elders of the people took counsel against Jesus to put him to death." (Matthew 27:1)

> "For God so loved the world, that he gave his only begotten Son, that whosoever believeth in him should not perish, but have everlasting life. For God sent not his Son into the world to condemn the world; but that the world through him might be saved." (John 3:16-17)

Jesus says that the only message of the crucifixion was to teach only love. That is a radical interpretation when the ego perceives the crucifixion as one of God's beloved sons having to suffer and die, to be the lamb of God, literally, and take all the sins of the world on himself. An innocent son had to do it!

If you really trace that thinking back, you would get back to: what kind of God is it that would have his innocent beloved Son go through a suffering trial and turmoil in order to get to Atonement or salvation? From Jesus' perspective, he did not perceive the crucifixion as an attack.

Through the ego lens, it looks like an attack when somebody is kicking you and spitting upon you and screaming, "Kill him!" However, Jesus says that he did not share that perception; he saw it as a call for love. "Father, forgive them, for they know not what they do." (Luke 23:34) Jesus calls us to similarly change our way of seeing.

We can have such a trained mind that we go beyond the perception of ever being attacked and instead learn to see everything as either love or a call for love.

~♥~

Peace is not tied into appearances in any way. Jesus is a good example of accepting the Atonement and choosing to see the world differently. And yet, what seems to be happening on the screen seems to go on—including even an angry mob of thousands yelling "crucify him."

He did not share their perception. He did not perceive it as an attack because he was holding onto the torch of peace regardless of what was happening on the screen.

~♥~

Apostles who still believed in the ego wrote down the gospels. They were not able to understand many things that Jesus taught. Their egoistic ideas of sacrifice tainted their perception of the crucifixion. They perceived that God had an innocent son who suffered and died for the good of mankind.

But Jesus did not suffer, and the Christ cannot die! The resurrection was a small symbol pointing to a very great lesson: that you cannot kill the Christ. The crucifixion was an extreme teaching device, an extreme way of teaching love.

~♥~

When we forgave Jesus, the illusion, the example wasn't: "We can do this journey as a man." That was the story. The Christ mind is the actuality; it is here, and it is now. That's what it means to accept the Atonement. That's the correction—from the horizontal perspective of the story to the vertical perspective of the story.

If anybody has problems with the cross, just forget all the stuff about crucifixion, sacrifice, and the blood of the lamb. See it as the meeting point of the vertical and the horizontal—where the vertical remains, and the horizontal is gone.

~♥~

There is no one on earth speaking to you, telling you that you are the one. You have to know it for yourself. That is what accepting the Atonement for yourself means—accepting the correction.

Imagine if you get an inkling of this and you are having conversations, and somebody seems to be disagreeing with you. They can seem to be putting you down and speaking negatively. They could even be screaming and shouting at you. Or, in the case of Jesus Christ, they could seem to be putting spikes in your arms and legs and tacking you to a cross.

That would still not be able to take away the fact that you are the one, that you are the living Christ. That is what the crucifixion was meant to demonstrate: nothing can take away the awareness that you are the one. You have always been the one.

~♥~

You see how this mind-training is going to go. The Holy Spirit is going to love you, remind you, and give you the words to speak. You are going to have to learn and practice listening so deeply to that inner voice that, even if a brother or sister is speaking insanely, it is not going to have any effect on your remembering who you are.

~♥~

Jesus says you are tempted to believe that you are crucified all through the day. What does he mean? Every time you believe you are being unfairly treated by anyone, in any way, that is an attempt to reenact the crucifixion. You are attempting to reenact the crucifixion if you think you have been snubbed, if you feel offended, if you feel hurt, if you feel disrespected, if you feel mistreated, or if you feel abused. If you believe that abuse is possible, that mistreatment is possible, or that someone could be harmed against their will in this world, then these are symbols for what you still believe in.

> Now some of you have an issue with the cross. Because the ego has misused the symbol, and Jesus says the whole crucifixion was only a reminder to teach only love because that is what you are, that's all it meant. That was just part of a little skit that Jesus did to show that you can't really die.
>
> It was part of a little skit to show that you are innocent no matter what seems to happen in form. That was a little skit 2,000 years ago, where Jesus was showing that the body is of no consequence. Who we are is Spirit. Who we are shouldn't be affected by the perception of a dead

or live body, of a body taking a walk on a summer day, or of a body that's on the cross for several hours.

The cross has been used as a symbol of sacrifice, and that's why many have an issue with the cross. But the sacrifice isn't in history, and it isn't in the world. It's just a belief in the mind, which I am going to encourage all of us to give up today. Let's cough it up. We don't have to believe in sacrifice anymore.

Now it came to me one time to ask Jesus why the cross was such a negative symbol. And Jesus said, "Well, why do you keep looking at it that way then? Why don't you see it in a new way?" I said, "Ok, I'm all ears." He said, "The cross is just a symbol of the vertical plane and the horizontal plane intersecting."

The horizontal plane is time and space, and the whole cosmos of bodies, countries, different planets, and different galaxies. The vertical plane is where forgiveness is. The vertical plane is right-mindedness, seeing that nothing ever happened and that you are still as God created you. How glorious!

17. Speak on the Resurrection

"And, behold, there was a great earthquake: for the angel of the Lord descended from heaven, and came and rolled back the stone from the door, and sat upon it. His countenance was like lightning, and his raiment white as snow: And for fear of him the keepers did shake, and became as dead *men*. And the angel answered and said unto the women, Fear not ye: for I know that ye seek Jesus, which was crucified. He is not here: for he is risen, as he said. Come, see the place where the Lord lay.

And go quickly, and tell his disciples that he is risen from the dead; and, behold, he goeth before you into Galilee; there shall ye see him: lo, I have told you. And they departed quickly from the sepulcher with fear and great joy; and did run to bring his disciples word.

And as they went to tell his disciples, behold, Jesus met them, saying, All hail. And they came and held him by the feet, and worshipped him. Then said Jesus unto them, Be not afraid: go tell my brethren that they go into Galilee, and there shall they see me." (Matthew 28:2-10)

The resurrection of Jesus was a tremendous teaching example, taken in the context of his life and his teachings. He told his apostles and some of his followers exactly what would happen as he went through the crucifixion, defenseless, completely demonstrating everything that he taught in his life.

He knew that he was Spirit. He was at the level of the mind, and he knew that the death of the body was completely insignificant. Basically, the story of the crucifixion and resurrection is a great teaching example of the insignificance of the body and the power of the mind; a mind that is well-aligned with the Father knows life and is the manifestation of life.

~♥~

The resurrection is a decision, a final letting go of all strivings, purposes, and desires, leaving only the desire for the Father.

Jesus says that the resurrection is the acceptance of the Atonement for oneself. This is a decision that is made in the mind, and the body functions perfectly after that decision. In other words, once the decision is made, the body is simply a vehicle to be used by the Holy Spirit to let the light shine into the world, so to speak, and to let the Spirit be demonstrated to the world. In that sense, the Atonement is a decision, and it appears to be one Jesus made before the crucifixion. The drama of the crucifixion and the resurrection were all part of the teaching example that was to be left for the world to see.

~♥~

The resurrection occurred three years before the crucifixion if you use a time context, because those three years were used by Jesus in such a dramatic way—healing the sick and raising the dead—and what he was speaking of was not human. The words, "Before Abraham was, I am." (John 8:58) were not spoken by a man. It would not make any sense for a man to say those words. It was the Holy Spirit using the pulpit for three years as a demonstration.

So that is important to remember too if you start to think, *I am not going to get this until I die*. Jesus is saying, *No, do not wait on the resurrection. Do not wait to accept the Atonement until the body dies. It is not dependent on the body at all. It is a choice in the mind, and you can make it at any instant you want to make it.* It does not really depend on time. It is not a matter of waiting. It is a matter of willingness and readiness and making the decision.

Isn't that good news? It is not time-dependent, nor is it dependent on the body at all! For me, it is even more of an incentive. OK, then, let's get to it! Let's go!

~♥~

In form, Jesus was the same as all of us. He looked very human, but he was divine. He was completely divine. We know that because he even did a little skit at the end of his life called the crucifixion and resurrection to basically leave a calling card saying, *By the way, you can't kill the Son of God. I did a little skit for you there… but do this in remembrance of me. Remember my love. Remember my compassion. Remember my kindness. Remember my friendliness. Do this in remembrance of me.*

And now it's called the "sacraments" in some churches or the "Holy Communion." But he wasn't trying to set a ritual in motion for centuries. He was just saying, "Remember my love every time you sit down to eat." That's all Jesus meant. He wasn't trying to make it a special thing. He just knew human beings would be eating for many, many centuries and that mealtimes could be used to pause and remember that "I Am" Presence.

~♥~

From a spiritual perspective of awakening, you might say that, metaphorically, three years before the crucifixion and the rolling away of the stone was when Jesus seemed to have reached a point where he transcended all temptations and illusions. So basically, that is why he said so many profound things in his three years of public ministry: because it was the "I Am" Presence speaking.

Jesus wants us to be happy and joyful. He wants our brothers and sisters to see our happy faces and know how much God loves his Son. The message Jesus gave to the Apostles and the messengers before he disappeared and ascended back to the Father was, *Be happy. It's natural for you to be joyful. You are to be a witness to that happiness so that everyone knows that God is love.*

When we aren't happy, we're not really witnessing that God is Love. We're witnessing that we believe we don't know God or Love, and that is when we feel the sadness, sorrow, and guilt.

> Jesus used the cross, the crucifixion, as a teaching that there is no order of difficulty in miracles. Even in this most extreme example of a human being seemingly being put up on a cross with nails driven into his arms and legs, the

crucifixion was no different to him than taking a walk with the Apostles on a sunny day.

The miracle, you might say, neutralizes the world. The ego will say, "Well, that's boring." You mean you are going through this whole spiritual awakening just to neutralize the world? But the joy is in the sameness. The joy is in not getting caught up in that judgment. The joy is in having an identity that is no longer tempted to be attracted to some things and repulsed by others. It's just seeing the false as false.

In one sense, it does correlate with Buddha saying to empty the mind of all that you think and think that you know. It's the same kind of neutralization that all the sages from India have encouraged: to have a still, open, empty mind. The truth cannot fit into this world; the truth will never fit into images. We can never make the truth pantheistic. We can't say that the truth indwells a chair or in this body. The truth is so transcendent; it totally transcends all the images. All we're asked to do is be still and behold the world is false and experience the extreme joy that comes from that. That's as close to Heaven as we can come in perception. It's a state of pure non-judgment.

Not that we are even capable of judging. It is just

taking us back to this original stillness and innocence that existed prior to these categories and judgments. That's the thing that's the most delightful; that's what I have enjoyed the most: just being able to behold the world.

I will be out traveling, and someone will come and sit with me, and we could talk about anything; it doesn't matter. I'm not concerned about what they seem to believe in because I have transcended this idea that beliefs are important and that stories are important. I'm just able to behold the presence of Love without having to debate.

Imagine a state of mind where you can never get into an argument again. You've had your last argument, and you say, *I will never argue again.* And why would I never argue again? I don't have a point to make. This moment is the only one, and we are sharing it right now. If I'm going to make a political point, people will say, "What about this candidate or that candidate?" And I would say, "I don't know."

The present moment is the point, and we are already there. We can sink into the joy of this moment, realizing that there aren't any problems. All of our problems were hypothetical could-haves, would-haves, should-haves, and what-ifs. After a while, who wants to even use words when talking about what-if scenarios? What is the point? I would rather bask in joy and happiness than that.

18. Speak on the Last Judgment

"For the Father judgeth no man, but hath committed all judgment unto the Son: That all *men* should honour the Son, even as they honour the Father. He that honoureth not the Son honoureth not the Father which hath sent him. Verily, verily, I say unto you, He that heareth my word, and believeth on him that sent me, hath everlasting life, and shall not come into condemnation; but is passed from death unto life.

Verily, verily, I say unto you, The hour is coming, and now is, when the dead shall hear the voice of the Son of God: and they that hear shall live. For as the Father hath life in himself; so hath he given to the Son to have life in himself; And hath given him authority to execute judgment also, because he is the Son of man.

Marvel not at this: for the hour is coming, in the which all that are in the graves shall hear his voice, And shall come forth; they that have done good, unto the resurrection of life." (John 5:22-29)

"I heard a great voice of much people in heaven, saying, Alleluia; Salvation, and glory, and honour, and power, unto the Lord our God: For true and righteous are his judgments." (Revelation 19:1-2)

"The LORD shall judge the people: judge me, O LORD, according to my righteousness, and according to mine integrity *that is* in me." (Psalms 7:8)

Jesus was in a state of mind when he made the Last Judgment. In Christianity, the Last Judgment was a very frightening term. But Jesus says that the Last Judgment is really the Holy Spirit's judgment of our identity, which just sees the truth and let go of the illusion, which is really the only distinction, the only discernment, that counts.

~♥~

We are called to be the demonstration of love, and really, that means to not judge anything in form but to join with the Atonement principle. Said in another way, this means to join with the judgment of the Holy Spirit, which is really the guidance of the Holy Spirit unwinding the mind from the belief in all judgments and then opening up to the Last Judgment.

Growing up Christian, the Last Judgment always had a negative connotation. But it is not about God judging at all. It is really the Spirit's judgment of truth on illusion, which is that illusion is not real and does not exist. The judgment of truth on illusion is what we are going for, and that interpretation is very loving and joyful. It has no negative connotations. It has no destruction. It just means the truth is true, and only the truth is true, and that is good. It is a cause for celebration.

~♥~

The Second Coming of Christ is you accepting the Atonement for yourself. Your happiness, your joy, your laughter, and your love are the Second Coming. Wouldn't it be wonderful to know that the whole purpose of your life is to have a good belly laugh at the separation? To be able to laugh with all your heart at anything in this world—to not have a single appearance that could cause you distress, irritation, or annoyance.

~♥~

Every day I have to give myself a couple good laughs, and I have to look at something that just tickles my heart. I actually heard recently that someone—who was hoping to give me a better image in this world—said that I show too much leg by wearing shorts on my YouTube videos. Now that made me laugh: "Shows too much leg." I'm sure Jesus and the angels got a good laugh out of that one.

Somebody asked me one time, "Well, if you're so awake and happy and joyful and enlightened, how many enlightened students do you have?" Like they want to quantify enlightenment, like five, ten, or 15? What's your quota? "How many happy teachers have you produced if you're so happy?" And I just say, "Well, it's all one mind; it's not really quantifiable in terms of that." And it goes past all the centuries of disciples and devotees. It's just a state of mind. People don't get enlightened.

You may think about Buddha, Krishna, or Jesus, but if you take the person or personality and follow it back to the Latin root, persona is the mask. How can you have an enlightened mask? I mean, that makes no sense to me. You have to go beyond the traditional teachings that would say that there were human beings that reached the state of enlightenment. The mask never reaches the state of enlightenment.

~♥~

People have been talking for centuries about the Second Coming of Christ. When is Jesus going to come back? When you forgive the world and you wake up and you see that you are the Christ, that's the Second Coming. It's not that some man is going to come back with long hair and blue eyes and walk on water or on the clouds and say, "Come up here with me. I will rescue you from the world," like some people believe. And it's not going to be like the body is just raised into the sky in the rapture.

You've got to forgive the world, do your inner work, and accept yourself as the living Christ. That's the Second Coming of Christ.

~♥~

In this world, it seems that time goes forward and that we're moving towards a future end. But we are moving backward in time to a point that is prior to time. That is why Jesus said, "I am Alpha and Omega, the beginning and the end" (Revelation 22:13) because the Christ Presence is prior to time.

~♥~

The Holy Spirit has a judgment for the world? Yes, it's called the Last Judgment. It's not frightening. It's giving up judgment and accepting forgiveness, accepting the Holy Spirit's blessed judgment of the world. What? Some of us grew up Christian, and we were shaking in our knees thinking about the Last Judgment. But it's the Last Judgment that opens the way to the remembrance of God. And there's no guilt in that judgment at all.

The defining characteristic of the happy dream, of the right mind, is that there is no judgment. It is not that you have stopped judging; it is that you have this experience that you were never ever capable of judging in the first place. That is how the Spirit takes your mind higher and higher to the point where you just end up laughing. You just end up thinking, *My gosh, judgment was never a factor. It never entered into anything. It had nothing to do with God at all.*

But when human beings grow up and practice their religions, they end up with this idea that God is watching over them and keeping score. They get to a certain point in their lives, and what a score card they have going. What is for God? What is against God? What is in God's favor, and what is not? There is still the assumption here that God is judging.

But Oneness does not judge. Oneness just is. Being-ness just is. The whole idea of judgment comes from the ego. It has generated this whole world of sin, guilt, and fear. That is the unholy trinity: sin, guilt, and fear. The ego has made up the unholy trinity in place of the Father, Son, and Holy Ghost, and then it tries to do anything it can to perpetuate it.

So how do you go from a state of judgment to a

state of pristine non-judgment? The Holy Spirit can take on the function of judgment to help you get out of the maze. In a complicated maze, you need a helper who can help you with every apparent turn. The Holy Spirit is judgmental for the mind that believes in judgment and does not relate to abstraction anymore.

We would have had this problem solved long ago if we could just practice "All You Need is Love," from the Beatles. Then what do you need anything else for? It is all right there; "Let it Be." The Holy Spirit, Jesus, always does this; he tailors the guidance, like the prophets from Liverpool, the Beatles.

When I was growing up, I would even meet certain teachers who would tell me, "You cannot ever hear the guidance of the Holy Spirit." I would say, "Well, that contradicts what I have been going through. I have been going through an experience of following guidance for years." In fact, I could not even imagine waking up in the morning without guidance.

19. How Will the World End?

Jesus says the world will end in laughter because it was a place of sorrow. That sounds a little bit different than an arms race and defending yourself and storing food in case of a holocaust or an economic collapse. The world will end in belly laughter because truth or reality far transcends all these temporary images in the world. Whether they seem positive or negative, it doesn't matter. It wasn't fulfilling.

~♥~

When you start following that inner intuition and voice, get ready. Hold on to your hats because Kansas is going bye-bye. The whole construct is going bye-bye, and why? Because love, light, happiness, and joy are real. Why do we like certain fairy tales? We like happy endings. We don't like Grimm's fairy tales.

What's the happiest ending except to realize there was no beginning to this world? The world will end in laughter because it was a place of sorrow. Of course, the world will end in happiness and joy. Intuitively, we know that has to be the case because something inside us knows that, at the core of our being, fear cannot last. Fear is temporary, Love is eternal.

~♥~

There's a spike in searches that is occurring right now for the search term "end of the world." The end of the world is spiking today. Jesus says the world will end in laughter. It has to end in a different way than it began—than it seemed to begin.

If the world was made in hate, the world needs to end in laughter. It needs to end in healing. It needs to end in forgiveness. And in coming to that gentle laughter—not laughing *at* something or *down at* something—gratitude comes in: I was mistaken about the world. Thank you for showing me the light. Thank you for showing me the truth.

~♥~

In the end, it takes Jesus Christ to reveal the meaning of forgiveness, to reveal the meaning of the real world, the happy dream. What this is about is making your mind ready to receive the revelation. That revelation comes from Spirit to Spirit, which is our identity.

Revelation does not come from humans to Spirit or from Spirit to the ego. How is the ego going to receive the Spirit? The ego is the belief that there is no Spirit. The ego cannot make itself ready. Ultimately, that is why, even though we have terms like "time collapse" and "celestial speed up," you cannot really speed up what is already over and gone. You cannot really collapse what is already over and gone. Everything is aiming at an experience that the past is gone—and Jesus says it cannot touch you.

That is, of course, a step towards the fact that it never happened. The more you laugh at everything, the more you are getting the experience that Jesus wants you to have. The world will end in laughter. There is lightness, joy, and the sense that you cannot mess it up; you cannot do it wrong.

How will the world end? That has to be, for human beings, one of the most profound and intense questions that is ever asked. And the Bible attempts to answer it. All religions attempt to answer it. Even some philosophies try to answer it.

And Jesus is so nonchalant; he's so light and humorous. He answers the question with another: *Can what has no beginning really end?* You've got to love it. You know he's having some fun when he answers a question like that with another question.

Jesus is not really scared by this death belief at all, because he knows the world is not real. So, when he talks about mercy, love, forgiveness, and limitless gentleness, he's saying that there's a state of mind that will be the end of the world as it has seemed to be.

The world will end in joy because it is a place of sorrow. If you can feel the humor and the lightness, then that is a giant leap in awareness toward Heaven. Because laughter is how we enter Heaven. We do not enter it through Armageddon. We do not enter into Heaven through destruction. No, *nada, nada* to the destruction.

20. What Is the Meaning of Bearing Fruit?

"He spake also this parable; A certain *man* had a fig tree planted in his vineyard; and he came and sought fruit thereon, and found none. Then said he unto the dresser of his vineyard, Behold, these three years I come seeking fruit on this fig tree, and find none: cut it down; why cumbereth it the ground? And he answering said unto him, Lord, let it alone this year also, till I shall dig about it, and dung *it*: And if it bear fruit, *well*: and if not, *then* after that thou shalt cut it down." (Luke 13:6-9)

"And he spake many things unto them in parables, saying, Behold, a sower went forth to sow; And when he sowed, some *seeds* fell by the way side, and the fowls came and devoured them up: Some fell upon stony places, where they had not much earth: and forthwith they sprung up, because they had no deepness of earth: And when the sun was up, they were scorched; and because they had no root, they withered away. And some fell among thorns; and the thorns sprung up, and choked them: But other fell into good ground, and brought forth fruit, some an hundredfold, some sixtyfold, some thirtyfold. Who hath ears to hear, let him hear." (Matthew 13:3-9)

"Hear ye therefore the parable of the sower. When any one heareth the word of the kingdom, and understandeth *it* not, then cometh the wicked *one*, and catcheth away that which was sown in his heart. This is he which received seed by the way side.

But he that received the seed into stony places, the same is he that heareth the word, and anon with joy receiveth it; Yet hath he not root in himself, but dureth for a while: for when tribulation or persecution ariseth because of the word, by and by he is offended.

He also that received seed among the thorns is he that heareth the word; and the care of this world, and the deceitfulness of riches, choke the word, and he becometh unfruitful.

But he that received seed into the good ground is he that heareth the word, and understandeth *it*; which also beareth fruit, and bringeth forth, some an hundredfold, some sixty, some thirty." (Matthew 13:18-23)

"Every branch in me that beareth not fruit he taketh away: and every *branch* that beareth fruit, he purgeth it, that it may bring forth more fruit." (John 15:2)

An experience of true freedom can only come with forgiveness. Forgiveness is our function, our gift to the world. We have no life purpose other than this.

Our calling is to unwind from the false self that we made by forgiving our belief in it. When we fully look at our beliefs and release them, we are no longer bound by fear, guilt, and doubt. This is the ultimate unlearning and unwinding of the mind that will lead to a life of blissful freedom and joy.

~♥~

Laughter is the result of unlearning the ego's way of thinking and perceiving. It is a miracle to let go of grievances by allowing memories, beliefs, and judgments to surface in awareness and then letting them go.

This is forgiveness—when the temptation to perceive yourself as unfairly treated arises, surrender the thought, the perspective, and the desire to be "right" about the way it was set up or seemed to be, and let go into the miracle. As this becomes our habit, being a miracle worker is happily discovered as our function in all situations!

~♥~

In the Bible, it says, "As you sow, so shall you reap." (Galatians 6:7) This is another way of saying giving and receiving are the same, what goes around comes around, cause and effect are one, and there is no gap. This one universal law of the mind has seemed to bring harm and destruction to the mind, which seems to sleep and dream of a separate world of unreality. Yet this one universal law is the key to forgiveness.

If you realize that you always choose your state of mind and that what you choose, you choose for the whole universe, the belief in victimization has been undone. Misuse of a divine law seems to result in miscreation until the realization dawns that, in truth, it is impossible to misuse or miscreate. What God creates is Spirit, and Spirit creates only Spirit.

If you follow this divine logic, then you will experience enlightenment: the truth is true. Love is real.

> "And Jesus said unto him, No man, having put his hand to the plow, and looking back, is fit for the kingdom of God." (Luke 9:62)

> "Ye shall know them by their fruits. Do men gather grapes of thorns, or figs of thistles? Even so every good tree bringeth forth good fruit; but a corrupt tree bringeth forth evil fruit. A good tree cannot bring forth evil fruit, neither *can* a corrupt tree bring forth good fruit. Every tree that bringeth not forth good fruit is hewn down, and cast into the fire. Wherefore by their fruits ye shall know them." (Matthew 7:16-20)

> "Of his own will begat he us with the word of truth, that we should be a kind of first fruits of his creatures." (James 1:18)

> "Herein is my Father glorified, that ye bear much fruit; so shall ye be my disciples." (John 15:8)

> "Ye have not chosen me, but I have chosen you, and ordained you, that ye should go and bring forth fruit, and *that* your fruit should remain: that whatsoever ye shall ask of the Father in my name, he may give it you." (John 15:16)

Jesus set a lovely standard when he said, "You shall know them by their fruits." You shall know them by their living experience. You shall know them by their attitude and demonstration—as in the Beatitudes—their integrity, humbleness, and gentleness. You shall know them by the heart chords that resonate within you when you are watching or listening to them, or when you are in their presence. Keep this in mind as you go along, because nothing of this world is to tempt you or lead you astray. Watch carefully. Watch carefully to find symbols of consistency—symbols and witnesses that demonstrate a constant state of mind. Before you follow any of those witnesses—before you put your faith and trust in them—watch carefully for consistency.

"You shall know them by their fruits." What does that mean specifically? Watch them, listen to them, be aware of their attitude. It's really quite clear; you should recognize them by their fruits and follow the bringers of the fruits. You want to follow the demonstrations of love and the bringers and extenders of the fruits—the extenders of love, peace, joy, and happiness—the ones singing a happy song in praise of the Creator. It is very simple, direct, and straightforward. This is what the great awakening is for. It's all about joining, about coming together, about being happy together, about rejoicing together. I love the collaborative feel of it, where everybody's helping out, everybody's lending a hand, everybody has a contribution, everybody has a part to play. And Christ, the Holy Spirit, orchestrates the symbols within time and space, like a giant flash mob of the entire cosmos of images—a massive flash mob under Christ control orchestrated by the Holy Spirit to have an experience of unified awareness. That's all that anything is for. Forgiveness shows that the mind is unified. It has never been apart; it has never been fragmented; it has never been separate in any way. Forgiveness shows that Christ lives forever as an idea in the Mind of God. Hallelujah and all glory be to God, Amen.

~♥~

If you really want to get out of the quicksand, you must know the witnesses by their fruits, and trust. If you combine those, you can save yourself countless years of thrusting around in the quicksand and appearing to sink deeper instead of rising. People would go for decades without even thinking about facing, looking at, or letting go of unhelpful symbols and beliefs. But when you combine desire, willingness, and trust, you have a potent combination. It's not so much a matter of time as it is of willingness and readiness. Even if you are willing and nothing happens—you feel like your wheels are spinning—it simply means that somewhere deep down you are not ready. But that will come as well.

~♥~

Your joy, peace, and happiness are the means by which you teach that there is no sin. When you are happy, you are demonstrating that there is no sin. And when you are upset, you are saying sin is very real. We have to go beyond the words, theology, the body, and even the idea of separate minds. This is what forgiveness does. It overlooks the body and the mind of your brother, because there are no separate bodies and no separate minds in reality. And this takes you back to wholeness.

~♥~

This whole world is learned and based on upside down and backward thinking where cause and effect have been reversed. Even when you inquire into someone's background, *Well, I was born in 1958* ... and so on, it is obvious that cause and effect have been reversed to place my origin in the time and space universe. Consider questions such as, *Were you raised in a dysfunctional family?* and *What were the social conditions at the time you were born?* The social and cultural conditions seem to be a factor in who you are; the cause of who you are seems to be determined by the time/space cosmos.

That is what we have been taught. This world has been carefully built up based on that backward thinking, with enormous care in choosing its witnesses. Whether you are talking about a dysfunctional family, being mistreated in school, or having certain horrifying events that seemed to happen. When someone recounts their personal life history, it's still based on reversed cause and effect. It is believed that these events have caused a lasting effect on the mind. It is not seen that the mind has believed that it is guilty and that it called forth witnesses to reinforce the guilt. Instead, through the ego's lens, it is seen as if these events and conditions in the world are somehow causative.

> I had a friend of mine who was receiving all these songs from the angels, but then sometimes I would see her on the computer for long stretches of time, and I said, "What are you doing with your computer? What's going on with that?" She said, "I am playing hours and hours of solitaire." And I said, "Hmmm, well, you might want to ask

Jesus if that is the purpose of your computer." We went down to Argentina, and while we were there, that topic came up again. I just happened to quote this line from the Bible: "The branch that bears no fruit will be cut off." (John 15:2) When we returned to the Peace House, the land cable to her laptop was literally cut, and the laptop was gone. That is the only thing that was ever taken from the Peace House. So that is kind of an extreme example of the branch that bears no fruit being cut off.

We can learn to train our mind to consistently think with the Holy Spirit and to let go of the ego. We can control the direction of our thinking so that, in the end, we can choose to listen to only one voice and eliminate the ego altogether so that we never heed the voice of the ego.

Jesus is a great example of that. He told us, "Be of good cheer, for I have overcome the world." (John 16:33) He also says in the Bible that Satan is underfoot. (Romans 16:20) He is no longer listening to the ego and no longer needing to follow the dictates of the ego.

The ego is part of the management thing. When we have jobs in the world, we seem to have them for a practical reason: to survive. But the more you follow the Holy Spirit, the more you will be given lots of assignments, tasks, and things to do. And then, as you go deeper and deeper into that, you start to realize that the needs that you believe you have as a human being start to fade away.

I would say that initially, human needs are met in all kinds of ways. When I let go of my career, I was still perfectly provided for in many ways. More and more, I could just see that I'm in a state of mind where I'm just in acceptance. I don't have a desire for anyone to behave a certain way, to do something, or even follow something that I've said.

The Spirit is just radiating through me. But I don't have any desire to follow up. I'm happily on my way, shining my light like Johnny Appleseed and flinging my seeds all over the place in 44 countries. I'm a happy flinger! My joy is in flinging.

Jesus tells the parable that some of the seeds land in the fertile soil; some land among the rocks, and some land among the thistles, and no fruit comes up. I don't care. I'm in the joy of flinging. I don't even care where they land.

They could land on the concrete for all I care. Maybe they will germinate. With water and moisture, maybe they will germinate right there on the concrete. I don't care. I'm not interested. I'm into the joy of giving. The spirit is pouring through me, and I'm giving, giving, giving.

I put all this free stuff on the Internet. Over my years of traveling, event organizers will say, "Please can you not mention that all those books that you've got over there on the tables are free on the Internet as well because they're not going to buy any books?" I don't care. They can get them for free on the Internet.

Freely I've received, freely I give. I'm a happy flinger. I enjoy flinging. I don't care where the seeds go. It's all for me. It's for my mind. I'm a happy flinger. It's a way for me to stay happy. I'm sure Johnny Appleseed was the same way. He went around flinging his seeds. I don't think he was that concerned.

He was a born-again minister. He was into love. He was into flinging seeds. He wasn't concerned with, "Oh, look, that could have been an apple tree there. The seed landed on that rock, and there's no apple tree." He wasn't concerned with outcomes. He was into the flinging.

21. What Do These Sayings Mean?

> "And when Jesus had cried with a loud voice, he said, Father, into thy hands I commend my spirit." (Luke 23:46)

> "Beloved, now are we the sons of God, and it doth not yet appear what we shall be: but we know that, when he shall appear, we shall be like him; for we shall see him as he is." (1 John 3:2)

> "And whosoever shall compel thee to go a mile, go with him twain. Give to him that asketh thee, and from him that would borrow of thee turn not thou away. Ye have heard that it hath been said, Thou shalt love thy neighbour, and hate thine enemy. But I say unto you, Love your enemies, bless them that curse you, do good to them that hate you, and pray for them which despitefully use you, and persecute you; That ye may be the children of your Father which is in heaven: for he maketh his sun to rise on the evil and on the good, and sendeth rain on the just and on the unjust." (Matthew 5:41-45)

It is a pretty ingenious system that the ego sets up, because it sets up a game of guilt in which there's no escape in form. But in your mind, there is escape with the Holy Spirit, and Jesus is saying, "Please my brother, choose again, look with me." That's why he could say from the cross, "Forgive them for they know not what they do" (Luke 23:34) because he knew it wasn't about the bodies, even about the body of Jesus. He was detached, he seemed rather calm. That doesn't sound like someone who's identified with the body and bleeding on a cross. That sounds to me like Spirit that's speaking.

~♥~

"Into thy hands I commend my spirit", that is a beautiful phrase, Jesus was aligning with the Holy Spirit and God; even on the cross, there's an identification with the I Amness prior to time.

~♥~

We are learning from Jesus that the true meaning of forgiveness is to forgive your brother for what they did not do to you, and that means pluck the grievance from your own mind. If you have the interpretation that you've been wronged by anybody or anything at any time, at any place, pluck the idea that you could be abused out of your mind; pluck the idea that you could be mistreated out of your mind. Now we're getting into the true glory of Jesus Christ and his teachings. He was teaching, "Behold the great awakening and be glad because you are truly innocent!" What does that mean—I'm innocent? He means you never did anything wrong or right in form; you just misperceived the whole thing, you took the form and strung it out on a timeline, which, by the way, the ego invented. All those seeming mistakes that were made, all those wrongs and all those rights, are all part of a misperception of time and therefore a misperception of identity.

~♥~

Jesus is telling us that through the power of prayer, which is our power of purification, we can come to forgive the world and see everyone and everything in the same light, which is the light in our minds, which is the Holy Spirit, the reminder of God.

~♥~

Mastery through love requires the willingness to forgive—to release what fear has made. Surrender, yielding into the purpose and perspective of the Holy Spirit is what is required for awakening. There is nothing to be afraid of in this purpose/perspective. The ego is afraid of love, and you will be afraid of love as long as you identify with the ego. Simply refusing to protect or defend the ego's self-concept image reveals that the Spirit-Identity is invulnerable and requires no defense. *My safety lies in my defenselessness.* This is why it is always wise to *turn the other cheek*—be meek, forgive 70 times 7; resist not evil; love your enemies; and bless those who curse you.

> "Therefore whosoever heareth these sayings of mine, and doeth them, I will liken him unto a wise man, which built his house upon a rock:
>
> And the rain descended, and the floods came, and the winds blew, and beat upon that house; and it fell not: for it was founded upon a rock.
>
> And every one that heareth these sayings of mine, and doeth them not, shall be likened unto a foolish man, which built his house upon the sand:
>
> And the rain descended, and the floods came, and the winds blew, and beat upon that house; and it fell: and great was the fall of it." (Matthew 7:24-27)

> "And he said unto me, My grace is sufficient for thee: for my strength is made perfect in weakness." (2 Corinthians 12:9)

The ego's world is all about stuff, and everything in the ego's world is for sale. *What profiteth a man if he gains the whole world and loses his soul?* If we lose touch with the Spirit, we've lost touch with everything that's important. The ego says, *Forget about it; you can be content with time and space. You can buy a lot of things if you have a lot of money. You can own a lot of things. You can own the body and other people's bodies.* But Love does not possess. We are here to teach that we can follow guidance, that we can follow the Voice of the Holy Spirit and demonstrate that we are more than a body—more than something that must die, more than an ego, and more than separation—that we are really more than one self, and we don't have to be tricked by the ego.

> "Then answered Jesus and said unto them, Verily, verily, I say unto you, The Son can do nothing of himself, but what he seeth the Father do: for what things soever he doeth, these also doeth the Son likewise." (John 5:19)

> "For what is a man profited, if he shall gain the whole world, and lose his own soul? or what shall a man give in exchange for his soul?" (Matthew 16:26)

> "I can of mine own self do nothing: as I hear, I judge: and my judgment is just; because I seek

> not mine own will, but the will of the Father which hath sent me." (John 5:30)

> "Neither shall they say, Lo here! or, lo there! for, behold, the kingdom of God is within you." (Luke 17:21)

> "For where two or three are gathered together in my name, there am I in the midst of them." (Matthew 18:20)

> "Again I say unto you, That if two of you shall agree on earth as touching any thing that they shall ask, it shall be done for them of my Father which is in heaven." (Matthew 18:19)

The power of our joining is immense. Jesus said, "For where two or three are gathered together in my name, there am I in the midst of them." The ego has no response as we join together in this awakening—in this purpose. The power of our joining is a very strong synergy with enormous momentum and support—much greater than a massive tsunami—as well as the sense that we can't screw it up. The ego is constantly trying to convince us that we are destroying everything. It tells us this every moment of every day. But when we come together in *purpose*, there is the feeling that we cannot really mess it up.

> "And when he thus had spoken, he cried with a loud voice, Lazarus, come forth. And he that was dead came forth, bound hand and foot with

graveclothes: and his face was bound about with a napkin. Jesus saith unto them, Loose him, and let him go. Then many of the Jews which came to Mary, and had seen the things which Jesus did, believed on him." (John 11:43-45)

How did Jesus heal the sick and raise the dead? He didn't personally do it. He knew there was no sickness or death. He wouldn't even allow those thoughts to enter his mind because he knew they were ridiculous, and as a result, the people around him experienced that their symptoms were gone, whether it was demons, leprosy, blindness, or palsy. Anything you could imagine. Nowadays it's cancer, HIV—*no problem*—Such nonsense has no place in the glory of the Christ Mind. And that is what raising the dead and healing the sick are all about.

Miracles are for the mind that has ears to hear, or the willingness and readiness to behold them. Seeming changes in form reflect the shift in the mind of the miracle-minded, and though some of these changes seem to transcend *known physical laws*, in reality there are no "known physical laws." The only reality is the law of Love (Spirit). The divine law of Love, which has no limit or lack, was symbolized by feeding the multitudes and raising the dead. The beatitudes, or state of mind of knowing we are *blessed*, truly demonstrate that the miracle has occurred. Consistency is possible in this state of mind, which is a characteristic of awakening. *Consistent form* is a contradiction in terms, although behavior can seem to become more stable for the miracle minded. Miracles are not meant to be used as spectacles to induce belief. Miracles are a means of awakening for a mind that already *believes* yet is willing to go beyond belief and, *Be Still and Know That I Am.*

~♥~

It only took Jesus coming and demonstrating that sickness and death were impossible because, in his mind, he did not believe in them. He did not really go around healing the sick and raising the dead; it was more that in his mind he remembered who we all are as the Christ. And that presence of love and light was so strong that he drew witnesses for that love and light, so that death and sickness were impossible. That is why the sickness seemed to go away.

If you have two minds that do not agree, then that is where all of hell enters in. All doubt and fear enter in. And if you become so clear in your own mind of the impossibility of judgment, sickness, and death, then you set all the captives in the whole world—the whole universe—free. It takes the unified power of the mind—this is a key point. The ego has only one demand: to exist. And it needs the power of the mind to seem to exist. You can see that is why forgiveness involves exposing the ego and pulling your mind's energy and investment away from it.

> "And there shall be no more death, neither sorrow, nor crying, neither shall there be any more pain: for the former things are passed away." (Revelation 21:4)

There is no death. In the light of God's Love, this is realized. The ego has no foundation, and illusions are but error. Once faith has been withdrawn from the error, the error is no longer to be experienced as real. This is the meaning of awakening, the overcoming of death. When you allow the Spirit to raise the ego error to the light of truth (bring illusions to truth), the darkness of death is lifted. Death is not the death of the body. Death was the error that allowed the perception of separation from God to occur. To transcend the ego, then, is to transcend a belief in the impossibility of the impossible. Death is no longer appealing once it is recognized as an illusion. Who would choose illusions when the light of truth can be experienced as Love, and Love is no longer feared?

> "And we know that all things work together for good to them that love God, to them who are the called according to *his* purpose." (Romans 8:28)

In Heaven the mind is unified in Love, so to attempt to hold onto two thought systems, as if they both are real, is an intolerable situation. A cosmos was projected out to see the split in mind as if it was in the world. The sleeping mind sees good guys and bad guys, victims and victimizers, and an enormous variety of dualities—as if they exist in the world. The world is a giant distractive device to see the hurt and pain of the mind as if it is in the world. When the release of all remnants of fear happens, one sees the world through the eyes of the Holy Spirit as a whole tapestry in which everything works together for good.

The present moment is very literally the end of all war. When you have forgiven the error, you see a very different world. It is impossible to judge against anybody else, because you see that the mind is one.

~♥~

Everything that we are perceiving is working together for our good, for our highest good, even if we're not aware of it. Everything, without exception, is part of a well-planned awakening process. Everything, without exception, serves a purpose. That means that nothing happens at random. That implies that there is no such thing as luck—good luck or bad luck. Where are the *good* and *bad* if everything works together for good?

We have taken a deep dive. It's got to be the deepest dive ever when we start to realize that we are going for a state of mind—a perspective—that can look upon the world and experience all things working together for good. That will put a smile on your face, no doubt. That state of mind, that perspective, is of the Holy Spirit and Jesus, and it will put a smile on your face.

> "Let this mind be in you, which was also in Christ Jesus." (Philippians 2:5)

> "Finally, be ye all of one mind, having compassion one of another, love as brethren, be pitiful, be courteous." (1 Peter 3:8)

> "This do in remembrance of me." (Luke 22:19)

Jesus says that you can listen to one voice without interrupting your regular activities in any way. That is the most practical thing I have ever heard in my life! We become more consistently miracle-minded, allowing Jesus to truly guide us through miracles to revelation. That's how we get to revelation, not through formulas, rituals or any of the other things the world would have us do like eat the right things, say the right things, or repeat daily rituals. *No,* Jesus says, *Just come into alignment with my mind.* Allow your mind to become one with the Mind of Christ Jesus. You'll still look like a human being, just like Jesus did. To the body's eyes, he appeared to be quite human.

He appeared human, but he heard only one Voice, which allowed him to say things like, "I and the Father are one," (John 10:30) because it was true. That is why he could say, *Unless you become as little children, you will not be able to enter the Kingdom of Heaven.* Because he had entered the Kingdom of Heaven in that state of mind, he knew what it meant. He was as dependent on God as a small infant is on his parents. So when Jesus said, "I am the way, the truth, and the life: no man commeth unto the Father, but by me," (John 14:6) he meant it. He was referring to the Holy Spirit. That was the universal Spirit speaking and inviting all of humanity to return to the oneness of God's love throughout history. That was all there was to it.

> "And Jesus came and spake unto them, saying, All power is given unto me in heaven and in earth." (Matthew 28:18)

There is no personal power in this scheme, that we have to release the world to find the power of God. It is not personal power, nor power over others, but the light in our minds that is powerful. All power resides in the Kingdom of Heaven, not on Earth. It's a joke to think there's power on earth or powerful people.

> "Then spake Jesus again unto them, saying, I am the light of the world: he that followeth me shall not walk in darkness, but shall have the light of life." (John 8:12)

> "Ye are the light of the world. A city that is set on an hill cannot be hid. Neither do men light a candle, and put it under a bushel, but on a candlestick; and it giveth light unto all that are in the house. Let your light so shine before men, that they may see your good works, and glorify your Father which is in heaven." (Matthew 5:14-16)

> "For there is nothing hid, which shall not be manifested; neither was any thing kept secret, but that it should come abroad. If any man have ears to hear, let him hear." (Mark 4:22-23)

"Come unto me, all *ye* that labour and are heavy laden, and I will give you rest. Take my yoke upon you, and learn of me; for I am meek and lowly in heart: and ye shall find rest unto your souls. For my yoke is easy, and my burden *is* light." (Matthew 11:28-30)

We accept God's strength and God's Will for us as we put all weakness aside. Our strength is offered for all. Forget not the Kingdom of God for anything the world has to offer. You cannot behold the world and know God; only one is true. It's not up to you to decide which is true. God did not will the destruction of his creations, having created them for eternity. His Will has saved you, not from yourself, but from your illusion of yourself. He has saved you from yourself. Let us glorify Him whom the world denies, for over His Kingdom the world has no power. No one created by God can find joy in anything other than the eternal. Spirit is the gift. Spirit is our home. The son lives in the Father and cannot leave the Father. We pause to remember the story of the prodigal son, remembering what God's treasure is, remembering what our treasure is. This is Self Realization. This is Enlightenment. I am as God created me. "I am the light of the world." That is my only function. That is why I am here.

~♥~

The blanket of peace has spread across the face of earth. Tranquility is flowing to its corners. There is nothing left to do but celebrate, rejoice and bless. All the trinkets of the world that once caught the eye are valueless before the vastness of this present experience. All ambition and striving for future goals has vanished. All curiosity about the world and its ways has ended.

We rest in stillness so deep and unfathomable that time drifts by without its touch upon the Spirit. We listen. We hear. We rejoice.

> "And ye shall know the truth, and the truth shall make you free." (John 8:32)

Follow your heart on a journey of discovery. Listen to the Voice within and do what It says, even if it sometimes doesn't make sense according to what you believe are your *personal* best interests. Your passion to discover the truth will guide you on and draw others along with you. The journey is about forgiving the past and remembering the Love that is ever-present. Love waits only for welcoming and acceptance. When the heart is ready, the witnesses will appear. If you make ready the altar of your mind, God will come into awareness. God is always present.

> "But I say unto you, That ye resist not evil: but whosoever shall smite thee on thy right cheek, turn to him the other also." (Matthew 5:39)

Go into your right mind and be defenseless. Be accepting. Jesus taught that if someone smites you on one cheek, turn the other cheek. But Jesus was not talking so much about the behavior, like a literal thing; he was saying, *Come back to your right mind.* If you perceive an insult or attack—if you perceive something that is offensive—turn back to the love of the Spirit in your mind. Come back, turn to your right mind, and in that sense, you do not get into *defense.*

It's basically overturning the whole world, because the world is revenge: If someone does something wrong, they should be punished; if they do something wrong, they should face the consequences. No. Jesus says, *The meek shall overcome the world with their strength by turning the other cheek.* He's simply saying to calmly remember what you're here for: You're here for the miracle, you're here to be the light of the world. You're always here for only one reason, and that is to shine the light of Heaven, and to shine it for everyone and everything. Thus if we perceive an offense or an attack, he's simply saying, *That's a misperception—come back to me, return to your right mind.*

> "Whatsoever a man soweth, that shall he also reap." (Galatians 6:7)

As you sow, so shall you reap. This scripture refers to thoughts, and it is thoughts which motivate actions. "Blessed are the pure in heart: for they shall see God," (Matthew 5:8) refers to purity of thought. "Judge not, that you be not judged," (Matthew 7:1) means that the mind can elect a state of forgiveness, or non-judgment, and reminds us that any judgment the mind makes is made on itself. The incentive for freedom and peace of mind is therefore to be without judgment. This is the simple approach to awakening in Christ. *To teach is to demonstrate* (1 Corinthians 9:14) —*the Gospel being preached to every nation* (Mark 16:15) is meaningfully interpreted as demonstrating the unconditional Love of God to everyone by example—in thought, word, action, and attitude. This is also what it means to be the light of the world.

> "Take my yoke upon you, and learn of me." (Matthew 11:29)

> "And when all things shall be subdued unto him, then shall the Son also himself be subject unto him that put all things under him, that God may be all in all." (1 Corinthians 15:28)

> "And to know the love of Christ, which passeth knowledge, that ye might be filled with all the fullness of God." (Ephesians 3:19)

> "For the LORD shall comfort Zion: he will comfort all her waste places; and he will make her wilderness like Eden, and her desert like the garden of the LORD; joy and gladness shall be found therein, thanksgiving, and the voice of melody." (Isaiah 51:3)

> "I will lift up mine eyes unto the hills, from whence cometh my help." (Psalms 121:1)

> "Pilate saith unto him, What is truth?" (John 18:38)

> "Glory to God in the highest, and on earth peace, good will toward men." (Luke 2:14)

The message I'm conveying is that truth is within you, and that consistent peace of mind is a goal that you can and inevitably must attain, because it is the only reality. It is the peace that comes from tuning in to that small, still Voice within and letting go of another voice in the deceived mind, the ego (which is the voice of conflict, fear, and death.)

There are two voices in the deceived mind, and this is a means to help each of us learn to listen only to the Voice for God or the Voice for peace, and thus bring an end to self-deception. This Voice for God or peace may be referred to as one's intuition or inner guide. You can think of this Voice as an *inner knowing*, or a *higher power*. What we want to do is go deeper than words, which are just forms. We want to join in an intention to experience clarity and peace of mind. We want to come to the present moment, to the realization that right now, this very instant, one is perfect. It is not a matter of attempting to build and improve oneself.

The limited self, no matter how improved or inflated it appears to be, will never be the changeless, eternal Self that God created. One must avoid falling into the trap of believing that one's happiness, peace of mind, and salvation are somewhere in the future. The linear (past-future) time concept is part of the dualistic belief system that must be questioned. The experience of now is full of joy and contentment. God is not withholding anything from us or dangling a carrot of eternal peace in front of us, saying, *Here's Enlightenment, keep reaching... oops, you missed again.* Enlightenment is right here, right now, for the mind that is open, ready, and willing to recognize it.

In Matthew 10:7, "The Kingdom of Heaven is at hand" means it is *now*. Now is the gateway to the Eternal. For time and eternity cannot coexist. All is One with God, and I am grateful for the beloved eternity which is real and true. Now is the time of salvation!

> "There was a certain rich man, which was clothed in purple and fine linen, and fared sumptuously every day: And there was a certain beggar named Lazarus, which was laid at his gate, full of sores, And desiring to be fed with the crumbs which fell from the rich man's table: moreover the dogs came and licked his sores.
>
> And it came to pass, that the beggar died, and was carried by the angels into Abraham's bosom: the rich man also died, and was buried; And in hell he lift up his eyes, being in torments, and seeth Abraham afar off, and Lazarus in his bosom. And he cried and said, Father Abraham, have mercy on me, and send Lazarus, that he may dip the tip of his finger in water, and cool my tongue; for I am tormented in this flame.
>
> But Abraham said, Son, remember that thou in thy lifetime receivedst thy good things, and likewise Lazarus evil things: but now he is comforted, and thou art tormented. And beside all this, between us and you there is a great gulf fixed: so that they which would pass from hence to you cannot;

> neither can they pass to us, that *would come* from thence.
>
> Then he said, I pray thee therefore, father, that thou wouldest send him to my father's house: For I have five brethren; that he may testify unto them, lest they also come into this place of torment. Abraham saith unto him, They have Moses and the prophets; let them hear them. And he said, Nay, father Abraham: but if one went unto them from the dead, they will repent.
>
> And he said unto him, If they hear not Moses and the prophets, neither will they be persuaded, though one rose from the dead." (Luke 16:19-31)

All are called, but few choose to listen. The call is there. And, in terms of the world, few choose to listen, but everyone will listen in the end. That's the whole picture; everyone is called, but only a few choose to listen, at least according to the timeline. But in the end, everyone will listen, and everyone will answer the call; so the real joy is answering the call now.

That is what they refer to as being born-again: *What is born of the flesh is flesh, and what is born of the Spirit is Spirit.* When Saint Francis said, "I now am born again," it is powerful; it is to be new in the moment in order to truly experience Christ in the moment, which is everything. That is the joy we are all experiencing right now. It is this moment, and we are saying *yes* right now!

Jesus said to pray for your enemies. He didn't say to fight your enemies. He didn't say debate your enemies. He said to pray for your enemies. And he has clarified it by telling us that if you have enemies in your perception, you have great need of prayer, because the purpose of prayer is to pluck the offenses, the grievances, the judgments, and the opinions from your mind so you can see the Christ in everyone and everything.

God created you as a perfectly happy being, and the ego is the belief that you're something other than that. Jesus is teaching us that we have the right to remember love, we have the right to remember God, and we have the right to speak to and listen to the Holy Spirit, which is the remembrance of our Christ's identities and the bridge back to eternity.

~♥~

To inspire is to be in the Spirit. Whether you work in a soup kitchen, a hospital, or a homeless shelter, your attitude is what truly teaches. When I worked with dying patients in hospice care I was in complete joy. The doctors and nurses told me how helpful it was to have someone who was happy and peaceful in their midst because they were usually sad and depressed about the dying. I realized there was no death, so the Holy Spirit used me to speak to these people. I would be walking down the hall with a tray of food when someone would call me into their room. They would be alert and coherent, asking me questions about the meaning of life. Most of the time, they were simply hanging on for fear of disappointing someone. So, they were *people-pleasing* even in their final hours! "Don't worry about it," I told them, "Simply go to the light." The next day, I would be informed that this person had died. You begin to realize that life is not contained within this body. Life is a state of mind. It is strange to think that seven billion people are running around doing crazy jobs, stressed out, and trying not to die—when they are all afraid of living!

Nobody in this world is aware of how much they fear love. You come to see the fear of intimacy. You learn to drop not only the mask but also the fear of dropping the mask. The ego tells you to look at all your past relationships, how you put your heart on the line and got hurt. The ego says it is not safe to love. It teaches that love always leads to hurt feelings. Now we have to listen to the Holy Spirit and learn that it is helpful to forgive and love. You realize you cannot give something away that you do not already have. The more you love, the more you realize you have love and that you are love.

22. Speak on Time and the Meaning of Born Again

"Behold, now *is* the accepted time; behold, now *is* the day of salvation." (2 Corinthians 6:2)

"There was a man of the Pharisees, named Nicodemus, a ruler of the Jews: The same came to Jesus by night, and said unto him, Rabbi, we know that thou art a teacher come from God: for no man can do these miracles that thou doest, except God be with him.

Jesus answered and said unto him, Verily, verily, I say unto thee, Except a man be born again, he cannot see the kingdom of God.

Nicodemus saith unto him, How can a man be born when he is old? Can he enter the second time into his mother's womb, and be born?

Jesus answered, Verily, verily, I say unto thee, Except a man be born of water and of the Spirit, he cannot enter into the kingdom of God. That which is born of the flesh is flesh; and that which is born of the Spirit is spirit. Marvel not that I said unto thee, Ye must be born again.

The wind bloweth where it listeth, and thou hearest the sound thereof, but canst not tell whence it cometh, and whither it goeth: so is every one that is born of the Spirit." (John 3:1-8)

> "No man also seweth a piece of new cloth on an old garment: else the new piece that filled it up taketh away from the old, and the rent is made worse. And no man putteth new wine into old bottles: else the new wine doth burst the bottles, and the wine is spilled, and the bottles will be marred: but new wine must be put into new bottles." (Mark 2:22)

Spirit is eternal, and the world of flesh is temporary. When you bring darkness to the light, only the light remains. The light does not battle the darkness. Just like when you walk into a room at night and turn on the light switch, there is no battle. The darkness is gone.

~♥~

Many of the things in the story of Jesus that seem to be about time are very helpful learning tools for letting go of the belief in time. The Holy Spirit uses the symbols of time to teach that there is no time: "The Kingdom of Heaven is at hand." (Matthew 4:17) "Before Abraham was, I Am." (John 8:58) "Take no thought for the morrow." (Matthew 6:34)

Jesus is a great symbol of awakening. To be identified as Christ is to know yourself as Spirit. Yet a person does not awaken, and an enlightened person is but a symbol or learning aid as well. The mind that believes in history and in persons, places, and things is asleep. The Holy Spirit's perspective is the point of time, so to speak.

The Holy Spirit's perspective reveals that history—the timeline—is an illusion, and the vision of Christ—abstract light—is revealed completely beyond the veil of images.

~♥~

We know of St. Francis, the beautiful mystic saint who lived in the 1200s. He loved to quote Jesus. And Saint Francis said, quoting the Bible, "That which is born of flesh is flesh; that which is born of the Spirit is Spirit; I now am born again." (John 3:6)

He's talking about the present moment. He's talking about the same thing that Eckhart Tolle is talking about, that Mooji is talking about, and that Byron Katie is talking about. All the mystics and saints can't stop talking about the present moment because it is the gateway to eternity.

And so that's why when we trust, we are trusting in this moment. We are not trying to say that you need to trust the form. We're saying trust the guidance. Trust in your intuition in this moment. It will set your mind free.

~♥~

Sometimes Christians call it a "born again" moment. It is a moment where you surrender trying to deal the cards. You give up trying to control the relationships. You surrender trying to be the architect of your own life.

And something in your heart cries out, *I would rather be happy and free than to be the designer of my form and life in this world; I would rather be clueless about the world and cared for; I would rather be carefree and happy; I would rather be like a flower, offering my fragrance to everyone and everything instead of deciding who gets what and what it is going to bring for me.*

So we are going through a purification where we are just basically handing over our lives, however they have gone, so they can be shown to us anew.

There's a remembering and forgetting aspect to this. When you really come into the present, you really forget the past. There wasn't much work necessary to reach this point. A common thought is that, *I did the work, and everything that I've done has brought me to this point.* But the Holy Spirit says, "No, I've brought you to this point."

The past—the ego—will never bring you to the present. The Holy Spirit uses the symbols of the past to help us release the past. Even the illusion of the journey starts to fade into so much joy, that there's no sense in having a résumé of how you got back to Heaven.

It's like the given pool of love is just there. It just is! And it's waiting at all times. There are no stages of having to do the work. It's just been there all along.

The ego says the present is determined by your past; that is a common belief in this world. The ego says the past extends into the present, and then your future is just an extension of that too. You were guilty in the past, so you are guilty in the present, and you are going to be guilty in the future! The ego's use of time is depressing.

The Holy Spirit says the past is gone. The answer was given immediately when that first belief in time seemed to be believed in. When you believed in a world of separation, fragmentation, sickness, and death, God answered immediately, and it was over. All the pain, suffering, and sickness are over!

~♥~

The mind believed it was separate from God, and the plan of correction, of Atonement, was established simultaneously because God's plan is apart from time. The correction was given simultaneously.

However, for the mind that believes it is in time, it seems to take a lot of years; there seems to be a time lag. The Holy Spirit's use of time says you are completely healed, free, and atoned for in the present, and the past is gone; at any instant, at any single instant, if you completely let go of the ego belief system in your mind, you will remember God.

This is good news for a mind wondering how long it is going to take to give up all judgments, false ideas, and beliefs. The good news is that it has already happened, but you just do not believe it; you think that it is still unfolding.

One must be aware of the trap of thinking that one's happiness, peace of mind, and salvation are somewhere off in the future. The linear, past-future, concept of time is part of the dualistic belief system that must be questioned. There is great joy and contentment in the experience of *now*.

~♥~

God isn't holding out on us or dangling a carrot of eternal peace before us, saying, *Here's enlightenment; keep reaching; oops, you missed again!* Enlightenment is right here, right now, for the mind that is ready, open, and willing to recognize it. "The Kingdom of Heaven is at hand" means it is now. Now is the gateway to the eternal.

The idea that there is a separation from God created the time-space universe. The world and the belief that made it—the ego—are one illusion. Illusion, by definition, means something that is unreal or false. Illusion is make-believe, fantasy, or hallucination.

Time is an illusion. Space is an illusion. Change is an illusion. God knows not form. Truth knows not error or falsity. Reality knows not illusion. Eternity knows not time. Infinity knows not of the finite. Life knows not death. Limitlessness knows not of rules and conditions. Love knows no opposite. Joy knows not sorrow. Abstraction knows not specifics. God is One, and Oneness knows not of division, opposition, or multiplicity.

> "The lip of truth shall be established for ever: but a lying tongue is but for a moment." (Proverbs 12:19)

Your relationship with your brothers and sisters is your relationship to God. So, the more harmonious you are with everyone that you perceive, or even everyone you think of, that is your reflection of your relationship with God. To know God is to know supreme happiness. To know God is to know a sense of love, inclusiveness, and harmony. That's what it means to know God. It's not theology.

~♥~

The mind ran from the light in an instant of terror. The ego belief is that God is going to get you because you have really pulled off the separation from God. The mind was terrified and moved into the darkness, away from the light. For an instant there was a belief in the ego. That is all it is – the unholy instant. Here is the unholy instant where that tiny belief was believed in, and here comes the Holy Spirit simultaneously, as the answer to that, right there in the mind. God placed the answer to the insanity right where the insanity occurred. He did not put the answer out in the world because that is not where the *puff*—the insanity—is. The *puff* is in the mind. He put the answer in the same place as the problem.

~♥~

There is a perspective of the body and world that offers only blessings. This is the holy relationship. The body is seen as a symbol of communication and has no value in and of itself. The only helpful question in any situation in which the thought of bodies has entered is: *What is the body for?* Is it serving the purpose of awakening? Let the Spirit smile and laugh and hug through the body, and you will see the body in the light of forgiveness. In this light there is neither attraction nor repulsion, for what is wholly neutral can merely serve the One who brings healing. In this purpose is the experience of joy. Joy is ever fulfilling and offers the perspective that all things work together for good. Glory to God!

~♥~

Relationships seem to be a difficult undertaking in this world. They seem to be a mixture of love and hate, attraction and repulsion, joy and misery. Jesus refers to "special love" and "special hate" relationships as destructive, selfish, possessive, and exclusive. These are ego-based relationships that are songs of praise to their maker. The holy relationship, on the other hand, is a metaphor for a relationship that has been given over to the Holy Spirit for His purpose of forgiveness. The holy relationship is a healed relationship that reflects wholeness and completion.

Beyond all metaphors, one might say that the only real relationship is one of Spirit, of God and creation, of Father and Son. As the only real relationship is given by God, the holy relationship is learned of the Holy Spirit. As the scarcity principle is undone by the Holy Spirit, the sense of lack, inadequacy, weakness, and incompletion that is typical of the special relationship is replaced in the holy relationship by joining, extension, appreciation, and acceptance.

> "Without descent, having neither beginning of days, nor end of life; but made like unto the Son of God; abideth a priest continually." (Hebrews 7:3)

The teachings of Jesus were so profound because they came from God. When he said, "I and *my* Father are one," (John 10:30) he was essentially saying that we are the same Spirit, not the same flesh. "That which is born of the flesh is flesh; and that which is born of the Spirit is spirit." (John 3:6) That is the experience of being born again. It's more than just saying the name, "Jesus Christ," or, "I believe in Jesus Christ," and then carrying on with your earthly life. It's actually having that feeling of merging, where your will—as Christ—and God's Will are one. So, you go beyond "Not my will but Thy Will be done." (Luke 22:42) You actually enter a state of perfect happiness in which my will *is* Thy Will, and you share the same will as God. Isn't that more logical than believing that God has a different Will than you?

Every day you can ask yourself, *Do I want the problem, or do I want the solution?* Every moment of every day is an opportunity to truly become aware of who your Source is. It's like that YouTube video I have with the title, *Who's Your Daddy*? I saw that one day while browsing through my YouTube videos and that is a good title, *Who's Your Daddy?* Is your father the ego – a belief in separation, smallness, fear, guilt, and shame? Is that your father?

We are answering *Who's your daddy?* with the ego as long as we are identified with sin, lack, guilt, fear, pain, and these personality traits that we believe in. That is not our ancestors' legacy. We are valuable in every way. You are absolutely priceless.

> I was raised in the Judaeo-Christian tradition. I was raised in a Protestant denomination called the United Church of Christ. But I never really lit up in the Spirit until my late 20s. It was like a born-again experience, but not just professing the name of Jesus. I mean from my heart.
>
> I just really lit up with joy, passion, and happiness. And in that state of mind, our attitude does the teaching. It's not so much the words.

The words have to line up with our attitude. Because if we just go out and try to give lectures on the gospels, it's like everybody's saying, *Oh, please, how many more centuries do we have to listen to another lecture on the gospels?*

But if you are happy and joyful, then that does all your teaching. There may be words, or there just may be a lot of laughter and hugs. Words are so crude. I mean, they are helpful to us for a while, but then you get into this rapture-kind of experience of love, joy, and connection, and you really feel the sameness of everything.

We're all the same, so it doesn't really matter what we're talking about. We could be talking about anything, and there's such love that you join with the truth in them, and it goes way beyond the body and way beyond the words. It's the most spectacular experience that can ever be had.

And to me, that's what everybody is calling for: love and connection. Everyone is praying for that, whether they are even conscious of what they are praying for. I've had so many experiences with Jehovah's Witnesses and Mormon missionaries where I could feel the love and connect right with their hearts, and we just rejoiced together. There was no point in trying to split hairs over passages in the Bible or theology. The love just swept us away.

23. Speak on Judgment

> "Judge not, and ye shall not be judged: condemn not, and ye shall not be condemned: forgive, and ye shall be forgiven." (Luke 6:37)

Judge not. Those are probably the two most profound words in the Bible because it is the gateway back to eternity. But you may ask, "How do I not judge?" How do you stop a runaway freight train? If a freight train goes rogue down a steep mountain, how do you stop it? You don't. You just have to see beyond the runaway freight train. You just have to see that you never had the ability to judge.

You can never stop something that you never had the ability to do in the first place. That's the most frustrating thing for human beings. They are trying to stop judging, and they don't realize that they were never created with judgmental ability. God didn't say, "I bestow you, Christ, eternal loving and judgmental. I give you eternal life. I give you happiness, joy, peace, and the evaluation capability." That sounds crazy. Why would God give you all of the glory and then give you comparison and evaluation?

The mind can elect a state of forgiveness or non-judgment. This passage reminds the mind that any judgment it makes is made on itself. The incentive for freedom and peace of mind is therefore to be without judgment. This is the simple approach to awakening in Christ.

~♥~

Forgiveness is the great need of the mind that believes in the reality of the world of duality, multiplicity, separation, and conflict. The world of judgment is the veil of error that blocks the Love of God, Christ, and the Holy Spirit from awareness.

"Judge not, that ye be not judged." (Matthew 7:1) is the same as saying, "As ye sow, so shall ye reap." (Galatians 6:7) Sin, guilt, fear, and punishment are all make-believe, for God is a God of Love and is all-loving.

~♥~

The belief in sin, or lack, or separation seemed to set in motion an illusory cycle of guilt, fear, death, and punishment that can seem very real to a mind that is asleep and dreaming of exile. Yet be of good cheer, for Christ is innocent and has overcome the error that was the world. We live, move, and have our being in the heart of God, and God's Spirit is one with our spirit.

> "And the whole earth was of one language, and of one speech." (Genesis 11:1)
>
> "And the LORD said, Behold, the people *is* one, and they have all one language; and this they begin to do: and now nothing will be restrained from them, which they have imagined to do." (Genesis 11:6)

The Holy Spirit uses the body for only one purpose, and that is as a communication device to help the mind regain the awareness that true communication is through Spirit and that true communication is with the Creator. The Spirit must use what the separated mind believes in because the mind has fallen asleep and believes in separation and bodies. For example, as you go about your day speaking and maybe writing, the Holy Spirit will guide you through words to train your mind to return to true communion. The purpose of Spirit-inspired communication is to transcend interpersonal communication and enter into communion with God.

~♥~

Every mind that appears to believe in a world of separation and bodies believes communication is limited. Communion—mind communication, even telepathy—has been blocked and pushed out of awareness. The body has been literally imposed as a barrier to communication, which appears to be limited in this world if two bodies are not present. In other words, they cannot communicate with one another unless they use a telephone or some other form of material aid. This takes us back to the belief that the body and the world that we perceive is real. But the world was made to barricade and defend against communication.

The Holy Spirit is our channel of communication with the Father, and the world was made to block that. The Holy Spirit works with the lower mind to help it let go of its worldly beliefs. As the mind progresses, it appears that mental powers are gradually restored. Telepathy, clairvoyance, and intuition seem to be more prevalent, but this is merely the mind returning to its natural state. These are not supernatural powers that rare individuals can develop. These are very natural communication mechanisms available to everyone.

~♥~

What exactly is *prayerful communication?* It's being in sync with Spirit. It means that you will be open and receptive to being shown and given communication at all times. You're not going to react based on past patterns. You're not going to judge based on your past learning. You're not going to try to summarize or draw any conclusions based on past experiences. You're not going to hold an opinion based on your past beliefs. You actually have to practice prayerful communication: *What do you want me to do? What do you want me to say? Where would you like me to go?* This is an example of prayerful communication, where you're so in the prayer with God and the Holy Spirit that you're asking to be shown and given what the communication is in every moment; you're not assuming that you know. And, because most human beings have such a strong investment in the ego, most think of communication as just a reaction or response.

However, the prayerful practice of communication is to be sourced— tune into Jesus and the Holy Spirit, so that you don't want to extend anything other than what the Spirit gives you. In fact, you don't need to extend anything other than the Spirit because doing so teaches you that you are the Spirit. When you pray to the Spirit and listen and respond only to the Spirit's Voice, to one voice, you are aligned, and your identity becomes identified with the Spirit rather than the body or the person.

~♥~

As humbling as it may sound, words are really unnecessary because communication is just a word that applies to this world. We can discuss nonverbal or verbal communication, digital or written communication, picture communication, etc. That entire realm is within the scope of communication, as if there is actually communication going on in the horizontal level.

And you are starting to see that communication was just a temporary symbol to take you into communion. "Be still, and know that I am God." (Psalm 46:10) There are no words in communion. Words are not needed for communion. Pictures are not needed for communion. Imagination is not needed for communion. In fact, there is nothing that is needed in this world for communion. It is more about forgetting this world and surrendering by bringing these illusions to the truth and letting them go. You might say that disappearing into the heart of God is the whole mystic's journey.

> "And we have known and believed the love that God hath to us. God is love; and he that dwelleth in love dwelleth in God, and God in him." (1 John 4:16)

"The Lord is my shepherd; I shall not want," says the first line of the twenty-third Psalm. This line appears to contain everything because it describes the feeling of fulfillment in which everything is given at all times. Everything is in divine order. Everything is perfect. Nothing is lacking. There is no sense of ambition or striving and no thoughts on future goals. Contentment is a pervasive feeling of fulfillment in which the world does not need to be any different than it is. There is no situation that you believe should be different than it is right now.

~♥~

We don't begin our discussion with the idea, *God is Love*—or, *I am the Christ,* because most people do not have that experience. We start at the level of perception because people perceive themselves as being impacted by the outside world and struggling to keep their heads above water emotionally and financially. When the mind is identified with this small speck on the screen, it appears that the world has caused it. The mind that believes it is a body believes its origin is also on the screen, and it believes its earthly parents are its origin. When the mind is in this state it says things like, *I did not ask for this; I do not want a life like this; I do not like these things happening to me all the time; I want things to be different.* Everything is believed to be caused by something on the screen: the economics, the IRS, genetics, the husband, the wife, the heart condition, childhood trauma. *Some event out on the screen is the cause of my life being in shambles*. However, it is not the memories that cause trauma. It is the interpretation in this very instant; it's the mind recalling memories from the vaults of the past—and attempting to keep them by bringing them into the present moment—that is causing trauma to our minds.

~♥~

Some of the earlier saints would use the stepping-stone idea of, "Not my will, but thine, be done." (Luke 22:42) *Thy Will be done* is complete happiness. You can see that a prayer that says, "Not my will" is still identifying with the ego, but there comes a point when you say, *Thy Will is my will.* The Christ is the only one who can truly realize this, because the Father and Son—Creator and Creation—share one will, and that will is free. "Not my will, but thy will be done" is like a prayer, similar to when St. Francis recited his famous prayer, which basically ends with, *You must die to be born to eternal life.* It still has an egoic component to it. In reality, he was telling us to die to the ego in order to remember eternal life. Of course, Jesus is the example of *Thy Will is my will* and *I and the Father are one.* There was no sense of a separate will. It's as if Christ and God share the will for perfect happiness, which takes it to the fullness of what truly *is*. It is so different from the idea that human beings have free will. The ego made up that idea, and tries to pursue it with all its effort and energy in order to have its own autonomous, individual free will, which is nothing but a construct.

~♥~

God doesn't have a wish for human beings. He has a wish for the mind to see that it's not human; it's Spirit. That is the Will of God. It's for perfect happiness. It's not for a little happiness like I got an ice cream cone, a promotion, or a girlfriend who will last for so long, etc. That is not the type of happiness that God Wills for us. You may recall from the Bible that God is not a respecter of persons. I love that. "God is no respecter of persons." (Acts 10:34) The persona is an ego construct designed to cover over our Christ identity.

~♥~

God's Will for us is perfect happiness—to be home, to be the Christ, to be exactly as we were created. We talk about creative expression in this realm through music, dance, art, and theater, but that isn't even close to actual creation because creation is pure Spirit. God is Spirit, Christ is Spirit, and who we are is Christ. We have eternal creations that we have extended our love and light to, and they are waiting for us to wake up. It's as if they're waiting for us to come home and get to know them as they truly are. Our very creations are cheering us on to wake up from this dream. They are not cheering for us to try to manipulate the images or to make a better world. They are cheering for us to wake up from the dream of separation and enter into a happy dream, which is a dream of harmony, connection, and joy.

Whenever we hold a grievance, what we're just saying is that we believe that we were wronged. We believe that we were mistreated. We believe that something has gone wrong.

Oftentimes, when we're holding onto that feeling that something has been done against us, we don't really see that we're just wanting to be right about the ego belief system. We want to be right about the ego's world, and we want to collect evidence to perpetuate guilt.

Underneath all attempts to be right when you're trying to argue with somebody is just the attempt to perpetuate guilt. Why would we point the finger at somebody when we're just accusing ourselves of the same thing?

Years ago, Jesus told me, whenever you point the finger at somebody, just remember that there are three fingers pointing back at you. One for the Father, one for the son and one for the Holy Ghost.

The trinity is going; stop it! Quit condemning your brothers and sisters because you're just condemning yourself every time you fire that laser gun into the mirror.

The mind that thinks it can judge is really judging itself. It doesn't realize that it's setting up a prison, a vise, that will not allow it to know its true happiness.

24. Speak on Prayer

> "And whatsoever ye shall ask in my name, that will I do, that the Father may be glorified in the Son. If ye shall ask any thing in my name, I will do *it*." (John 14:13-14)

> "And all things, whatsoever ye shall ask in prayer, believing, ye shall receive." (Matthew 21:22)

> "If ye abide in me, and my words abide in you, ye shall ask what ye will, and it shall be done unto you." (John 15:7)

Prayers are answered in the sense that everything in the world reflects your mind, and your mind is where the prayer is. You could say that your faith is the power of the mind.

A helpful question is, *What have I put my faith in?* In this world, you believe you are sustained by everything but the love of God; pills, money, protective clothing, being liked, knowing the right people—a list of things that you have really put your faith in.

You have to start to realize that all those things have been part of a mesmerism to have your faith invested in something from which you will not benefit at all. So, the first thing I would say to anyone who wants to make the spiritual turn is: give your life over to God.

When you make the turn, all you're doing is saying, *How have I poorly invested? And how can I change my tune and my direction and turn to the Spirit?* To me, that's really what the turn is.

Practically speaking, that starts to mean that you are going to have to seemingly be given guidance to take steps to unwind from the world. If we still have the belief that we are sustained by all these things in the world, then we do need to go through a divestment period.

~♥~

Prayers are always answered, and there are no exceptions to how the mind operates. Prayer is also continuous. Inevitably, it becomes apparent that only a single desire or a single, unified prayer for peace will offer a peaceful perception of the world. When desire seems splintered, the mind has chosen to be unaware of the peace that is ever present.

Signs and symbols are an answer to the prayer. *Make it obvious. Give me a sign. Show me the way. Point me in the direction.*

~♥~

If you want to open to a greater love, the prayer of the heart needs to be one of valuing love and God.

Release all those thoughts in the mind from the past: all the could have, would have, and should have thoughts, the things that went wrong, the things that you wish had been different. And all those worries and concerns about where all this is heading, where will this take me, and what you will be left with if you keep up this journey

That is the prayer for the release of specialness. It's profound when you learn to let the Spirit tell you when to say no and when to say yes. It's always the answer. Yes, to God is to release judgments from my mind. You say yes to God by saying, *I do not know. I cannot judge accurately, so I will give it over to you. Show me how to see it differently.*

~♥~

The "Lord's Prayer" was taught as a model of prayer for generations beginning at the time of Jesus, though God knows the prayer of the heart before a word is ever spoken. Prayer is a medium of communication between the Creator and the creation in which answers and divine experiences come forth.

~♥~

To pray to Jesus is to pray to the Holy Spirit, for Jesus and the Holy Spirit are synonymous in function. They lead to Atonement or complete forgiveness, and the happy dream that brings an end to all dreaming. In the Lord's Prayer, Jesus is praying with everyone to the Creator.

Even the Bible statement, "I and the Father are one," (John 10:30), has two parts in that Christ is the creation and God the Creator. Creation and Creator are one spirit and share the same will for perfect happiness. There is no separation between God and God's creation. Forgiveness of illusion or error is its release, and this leads to awakening or remembering God's eternal Love.

~♥~

All one has to have is the willingness, and the Holy Spirit will undo the false self-concepts and replace them with forgiveness. Start with this prayer: "Abide with me, Holy

Spirit. Guide me in what to say and do and where to go." If you welcome and trust Him, you will experience immediate results.

> "Ask, and it shall be given you; seek, and ye shall find; knock, and it shall be opened unto you: For every one that asketh receiveth; and he that seeketh findeth; and to him that knocketh it shall be opened." (Matthew 7:7-8)

Prayer is a way for us to remember the Christ and God. In Heaven, prayer is a song of Eternal gratitude that is formless and changeless. In time, however, prayer seems to take the form in which it can be most beneficial. Since time and lack are the same beliefs, prayer—in the realm of time—takes the form of requests and answers for the sleeping mind, which is unaware of Heaven. Desire is what the heart wants or wishes for, and that is expressed through prayer. It makes no difference what words or symbols are used in prayer, because the image or perception witnessed by the mind is exactly what was asked for or desired.

As you sow, so shall you reap (Galatians 6:7) is a testament to the power of thought and prayer. *Let thine eye be single* (Matthew 6:22) means let your *desire* be single or let your prayer be *one.* A unified prayer is always one, it is never divided or splintered. *God, what is Your Will for me*? seeks absolute, eternal happiness rather than fleeting and transient illusions because God''s Will is for complete happiness. Any other use of prayer is a temporary misuse of it by the ego. Creation is synonymous with unified prayer, and creation, being everything, asks for nothing. The key to true prayer is to let go of what you think you need and empty your heart of false desires.

~♥~

True prayer asks only that the truth be true and accepts that Christ remains as God created him. This is true humility, because assuming that time and lack are real and then demanding that the script be better than it already is, is ego arrogance. According to the Holy Spirit, everything is already in divine order in the forgiven world. Regardless of what the mind appears to believe, the Holy Spirit always answers the sleeping mind in a meaningful and helpful way. This is an expression of the Holy Spirit's mercy, kindness, and compassion. What the ego invented is not destroyed by the Holy Spirit. The Holy Spirit simply reinterprets what was made, from the perspective of forgiveness and wholeness.

~♥~

The Absolute Oneness of Love has no opposite, and the belief in private thoughts and private minds—that is, in separate individuals—is the belief that Love can be broken apart and divided. Your heartfelt prayer is to feel and experience the Oneness of Love, and the witnesses who are summoned shine as a reflection of your prayer. The mind sees or perceives what it desires. As desire is purified, our perception heals and returns to wholeness. Praying for another who has not become aware of the error of duality, is a call to let go of the belief that anything other than God's Love can exist.

~♥~

You can relax because you do not need to know *how* to pray. Your prayers will be requests of needs as long as you believe in the ego, in lack, and in multiplicity. When you have thoroughly questioned the ego and allowed it to be undone by the Holy Spirit, you can truly pray: *Father, what is Your Will for me?* And this prayer is forever answered in the memory of Christ and God. The Holy Spirit knows the prayer of your heart, and your prayer is your desire. *As you sow, so shall you reap.* Prayer is continuous, and prayer is always answered, even if this does not always appear to be the case due to distorted perception. Split desire appears to produce a split mind that tries to serve two masters and thus perceives contradictory witnesses. Your deepest desire is to learn to completely forgive and to remember your Oneness with God. Because this is your prayer, everything that appears to be impeding or obstructing your forgiveness and union with God is being brought to light and exposed, so that it can be released.

~♥~

When you are bound tightly to the world of form, you cannot help but pray for it; this is the bottom of the ladder: *Help me; help my child; assist my Aunt Martha on her trip to India; help me contribute to the end of world hunger and poverty.* You can't help but pray like that if you believe in the reality of the world around you.

It is not incorrect to pray in this manner, but there are higher levels of prayer. *Help me see this differently* is a prayer because it returns everything to a perceptual issue. It says, *My perception is skewed; I require a fresh perspective. Instead of this, I need to see peace.*

Your desire is to pray. If your desire is single and complete, your prayer will always be answered. If your prayer is for

God and only God, the state you will receive is one of joy and peace. Yet, it could be tainted by your desire for other things such as wanting to hear from a loved one after an argument. Marianne Williamson, for example, puts it this way: "Do I want peace or do I want him to call?" It's a good example because getting a call sometimes seems more important than having peace of mind.

At the level of desire you can begin to see how important it is to connect with the ego's unconscious beliefs and purpose, and then to say, *Hey, I don't want those beliefs. I will not continue to follow the ego if I want peace. Who wants pain and misery rather than happiness?* That touches on the subject of prayer. It certainly moves away from specific prayers.

~♥~

The mind's desire is prayer. It's the internal altar. This altar appears to be defiled when the mind believes in the ego. The altar contains many idols rather than a single devotion to God. As a result, desire or prayer is splintered. As long as the mind believes in the ego, prayers will consist of requesting things and making petitions because the mind believes it is lacking. It is impossible to ask for prayers above the level of what the mind believes. The belief in lack and incompletion fades as trust in the Holy Spirit grows. It's like climbing a ladder. As your trust grows stronger, your need for things and control diminishes. *Father, what is Your Will for me?* is the highest prayer one can ever pray. This prayer is asked and answered immediately after the altar has been cleared of all idols. God's Will is for us to be completely happy.

"But seek ye first the kingdom of God, and his righteousness; and all these things shall be added unto you." (Matthew 6:33)

"And he spake this parable unto certain which trusted in themselves that they were righteous, and despised others: Two men went up into the temple to pray; the one a Pharisee, and the other a publican.

The Pharisee stood and prayed thus with himself, God, I thank thee, that I am not as other men *are*, extortioners, unjust, adulterers, or even as this publican. I fast twice in the week, I give tithes of all that I possess. And the publican, standing afar off, would not lift up so much as *his* eyes unto heaven, but smote upon his breast, saying, God be merciful to me a sinner.

I tell you, this man went down to his house justified *rather* than the other: for every one that exalteth himself shall be abased; and he that humbleth himself shall be exalted." (Luke 18:9-14)

"God *is* a Spirit: and they that worship him must worship *him* in spirit and in truth." (John 4:24)

"And when thou prayest, thou shalt not be as the hypocrites *are*: for they love to pray standing in the synagogues and in the corners of the streets, that they may be seen of men. Verily I say unto you, They have their reward. But thou, when thou prayest, enter into thy closet, and when thou hast shut thy door, pray to thy Father which is in secret; and thy Father which seeth in secret shall reward thee openly.

But when ye pray, use not vain repetitions, as the heathen *do*: for they think that they shall be heard for their much speaking. Be not ye therefore like unto them: for your Father knoweth what things ye have need of, before ye ask him." (Matthew 6:5-8)

"Behold, thou desirest truth in the inward parts: and in the hidden *part* thou shalt make me to know wisdom." (Psalms 51:6)

Prayer is sometimes thought of as conversing with God and waiting for His response. Meditation is sometimes thought to be the practice of quieting the mind and sinking beneath the world's thoughts. Even though prayer and meditation are frequently thought of as "activities" or "practices," they are actually continuous— that is, they have no beginning and no end. Prayer is a desire, and when you are watchful of what you pray for you will experience it. It is possible to have an involuntary stillness of mind that is never controlled or forced. True meditation, like prayer, is being open to, aligning with, and extending God's Love. They come together as a living state of being in the present moment. The mind must first become still and open to receive the Holy Spirit's guidance. The Holy Spirit's guidance dissolves the ego, and thus the egos chatter appears to fade away in awareness. As the belief in time disintegrates, only radiant stillness remains. *Be still and know* is always the aim or goal of prayer and meditation.

~♥~

What exactly did he mean when he said, "enter into thy closet?" If I told you to go to your closet and you live in an apartment, condo, or house, you wouldn't go out in your front or backyard to get to your closet. You also wouldn't go up on your roof. When Jesus says, "enter into thy closet," he means, *Go within*. That is significant. When he says, "Enter into thy closet," he really means, *Go to your inner chamber within your heart and mind.*

Next, he tells us, "Shut thy door." Close the door to your closet. What are you doing when you close the door? You're shutting off something and shutting out something. He is saying, *Go through your inner chamber, to your closet, and close the door.* Close out all of your perceptions about the world. Leave your preconceived notions of the world at the door because bringing those thoughts and images into your inner chamber will prevent prayer from working. That is not the goal of prayer. The prayer is to go within to the silence—to the light, which is why you must go to your closet and shut the door. Anyone who has ever meditated will tell you, *Let go of all the churning, riotous thoughts, sights, and sounds of this world.* Jesus is saying, *Leave the world behind. Do not bring it with you. But rather, close the door, and pray to your Father in private.*

What he really means is that you don't have to share your prayer life with the rest of the world. Because it is for your mental health. It's for your deepest core, the chamber of your heart. Back in the day, 2000 years ago, Jesus would make fun of the scribes, Pharisees, and Sadducees who went to the Wailing Wall. We still have the Wailing Wall over in Israel, and they would paint their faces, rock their bodies back and forth, and put on a big show.

No, there's no show with prayer. Jesus says, "Shut thy door, pray to thy Father which is in secret." He's saying, *We're talking about your heart's desire here.* It's deep down in your soul. He's leading you to what you really want. He is not requesting that you pray for your family. He is not requesting that you pray for your country. We're talking about right now, and we're getting deep, deep, deep. It goes deeper than that. It goes beyond world peace—that leads to the world outside. Jesus says, *Don't dare bring that world into your heart's inner chamber.* Because even a desire for world peace—with no fighting, no wars, however that looks to you—has no place in your inner chamber. You shut the door. You leave everything behind and approach the Lord thy God with holy empty hands. That's what he meant when he said, *Pray to your Father in secret.* He meant don't make a big deal out of it when you pray. Don't put on a show; this isn't for show. This is so intimate. It's just you and God. When you enter that chamber, it's just you and God. That's all there is to it. There is nothing else besides you and God. And the Word of God, with a capital W, is who I am as God created me.

When you go into that secret chamber, the deepest part of your heart, you know the only thing that can ever be known, through intimacy with God. That's right, you can never truly understand arithmetic, words, languages, or learning. You will never understand calculus or science. You can know God and who you are, and you can know it in the inner chamber of your heart and mind. But you must leave everything behind.

Years ago, I remember thinking to myself, *Is this practical?* Yes, it's the most practical thing, Jesus says it is more important than anything else—to leave this world and go to God. Nothing will ever be more important than your spiritual prayer life. Your income is unimportant; your family is unimportant, friendship, worldly success, and material possessions are unimportant. Jesus is saying, *It's that inner chamber where you go to know who you are and to know God.* That's all there is to it. Nothing else even comes close. There is no comparison.

> There is a line from the Bible that says, "If God is for us, who can be against us?" (Romans 8:31) And you can even say that if God is with you, you are never alone. If you're feeling alone and even praying alone, that's a perception.
>
> Whenever you perceive that anything is lacking in any situation, it is because you failed to give. You've never been lacking in any situation ever in your whole life. It was just this reluctance to give. There was just something you were holding back.
>
> We've all had that holdback. We've all heard

those lines: "Don't put all your eggs in one basket" and "Always save for a rainy day." We've been taught to withhold; that it is prudent to withhold, even in relationships. "Don't give it all away," "String them along a little bit," and "Make them work for it." Who taught us this stuff? Since God is a giver, why wouldn't we want to be givers—unconditional givers?

When we are praying, we can pray for opportunities to give. That is why I am so happy. I prayed for opportunities to extend, and then I started to get all these invitations to speak, and I became happier and happier.

I had all these chances to give it away. And then there is an eagerness to want to give it away, and that washes away the perception of lack.

Most of us were raised with the belief that God should give me this or offer me that. They were supplications. That was really what the prayers were. You don't tend to hear Buddhists making supplications. They say, "Open your mind, be still, be receptive, and open and listen."

The deeper you go, it is more that you are opening to a purification, a stillness of mind, where you want to have nothing on the altar except "God. I want you. Empty my mind, my altar." So, prayer is a means of emptying the altar.

We can't help but pray for what we believe we are lacking. That is just the way it works. Jesus is fine with that; it's just a lower run on the ladder. You'll go up the ladder, and eventually you'll get to the top of the ladder, and there will be one prayer left. In Jesus' terms, the last prayer is *Father, what is your will for me?*

Wow, that is a different kind of prayer than help me on my travels and make sure I have enough food to eat. *Father, what is your will for me?* is like saying, *Give me everything. Give me my complete inheritance.* I was a prodigal son or daughter, and I wandered off for a while in time and space.

But I am back. And I am asking for the whole inheritance.

We don't ask God for too much, but for far too little. It is like we are going to God with a little thimble, trembling, and saying, *Could you please fill my cup?* And Jesus is saying, "Get a bucket, get a pail, get a bathtub, get a pool. I can fill your cup until it runs over."

But if your asking is limited, then your prayers are limited. And that's a worthiness thing. A sense of loneliness or isolation comes from the belief in unworthiness, that you are not worthy of so much love. But as you ask for and accept the love that God is offering you, you'll feel it swirling more and more in your heart, and you'll just want to give it away abundantly.

I have a friend who told me she was praying for a sign on whether to drive an hour and a half to see me in Georgia. And then I remembered that about two hours earlier I had poked her on Facebook, and she said, "Yeah, you've never poked me before, so now I know I am supposed to come."

This is the Facebook prompt for how the Holy Spirit works. It was just a little symbol, and it was involuntary to poke her. The Spirit did it.

It just shows you there are just so many opportunities. Even the seemingly tiniest thing can make all the difference.

25. Speak on Union and Holy Relationship

"And the Word was made flesh, and dwelt among us, and we beheld his glory, the glory as of the only begotten of the Father, full of grace and truth." (John 1:14)

"Honour all *men*. Love the brotherhood." (1 Peter 2:17)

When the Bible says the Word was made flesh, it means it, with a capital "W," was made flesh, referring to Jesus. Strictly speaking, this is impossible; you can't turn light into images. Light is eternal, and light is not an image. The Word of God is God's will. It is Spirit, and strictly speaking, Spirit cannot be made flesh. As the Bible says, "That which is born of the flesh is flesh, and that which is born of the Spirit is Spirit." (John 3:6) You either perceive the flesh or you behold the Spirit. You can't have both. You can't have perception, which is unnecessary, and Spirit, which is eternal life; the two don't go together.

~♥~

Jesus was a man who symbolized the truth and demonstrated the truth. But remember, the form is not the truth. The truth is neither male nor female. The truth doesn't fit into the construct of time and space; it's literally beyond time and space. When you say, *I want to speak the truth, I want to tell the truth*, what you're really doing is asking your intuitive self, your higher self—the Holy Spirit, the universal presence—to put the words in your mouth that testify to Love. And it's more than just words, because if you speak eloquent words of beauty, harmony, love, and truth, but your actions aren't beautiful, loving, or harmonious, then you know that's just hypocrisy. We are here to have a transformation so that we embrace the presence of God's Love in our hearts and then we radiate that. We let the Spirit use the body for a period of time; and we let Spirit use the symbols for a period of time.

Jesus is calling us to the true Word of God. Our very being is the Word of God; our very being is the point of everything—the remembering of our true identity and God.

So, he's asking us to make the inner correction and accept the correction from the Holy Spirit. And that is the healing, right there; that's how we return to our experience of the Word of God. Scripture is like a trampoline; the only reason we have it is to bounce off the trampoline and go up. Love lifts us up where we belong, into the actual state of light. Desire the Lord, thy God, and you shall be rewarded by a direct experience.

~♥~

The ego teaches that relationship or union is about bodies together and minds apart; maintaining a sense of individuality while being coupled as a union. The Holy Spirit teaches a different view of union: minds joined as one, bodies may come or go. The ego tries to keep up a sense of privacy, where husbands and wives don't know each other's secrets. It is afraid of losing its individuality. Relationships are therefore best thought of as opportunities to unlearn the ego. The false sense of union will dissolve or fall apart. It is inevitable. It takes trust in all relationships to stay with the purpose of the Holy Spirit. The ego is appalled at the new purpose, so as you open to the Holy Spirit, sometimes it can seem like a very bumpy ride. You may be guided to stay in a relationship, to spend time being single, or perhaps to enter another relationship that will be another opportunity to unlearn the ego. Truly, the only union that is real is the mind of Christ mind, at one with God forever. This is union. This is what everyone longs for.

What we must come to realize is that there is only one decision that needs to be made—that of choosing the Holy Spirit instead of the ego. Although this still seems like a choice, it is a higher order of choice and the only one that's going to get us out of the illusion. Only the decisions we make with the Holy Spirit will unwind us from the maze of multiplicity and duality. We can call this choice Atonement correction, salvation, redemption, or whatever we want. It is the only real choice because it doesn't involve choosing between the images of the world. Instead, it is a choice to align our mind with the Holy Spirit, so that we may accept ourselves as God created us.

We must be willing to have our minds restored to holistic thinking. We can't find the truth in the parts because they don't contain the whole; the whole transcends the parts. Holistic thinking is thinking in alignment with God. Trying to think in terms of threads, parts, and specifics is trying to think against God.

It's so simple! All we have to do is make one decision. One decision! If we could even faintly grasp what peace, rest, and joy will result from the only decision that we need ever make, we would not wait a minute longer to make it.

> "For who knoweth what *is* good for man in *this* life, all the days of his vain life which he spendeth as a shadow? for who can tell a man what shall be after him under the sun?" (Ecclesiastes 6:12)

> "Then Peter opened *his* mouth, and said, "Of a truth I perceive that God is no respecter of persons." (Acts 10:34)

> "He that loveth father or mother more than me is not worthy of me: and he that loveth son or daughter more than me is not worthy of me." (Matthew 10:37)

As long as we have personal goals for a situation, they are goals to maintain privacy, private thoughts, private identity, and a personality self instead of the Christ. And they backfire because we're trying to will apart from God. When we pursue personal goals, have personal ambitions and personal outcomes that we want to come out of a situation that will benefit our personhood, our personality— That is a wish to maintain privacy.

"God is no respecter of persons" because the ego peopled the world, the ego has tried to trick the sleeping mind to think that it's a person and has all kinds of personal goals and personal ambitions. What about the holy instant? What about the present moment? What about waking up to eternity? Where does that all fit in? Jesus says that's primary; that's our reason for everything—*To go into the holy instant and remember our Christ nature in relationship to God.*

It's important to invite the Holy Spirit into all your relationships because Jesus is telling us that whatever you want to come of a relationship will hurt you. That's pretty strong, but he's basically saying that whatever the ego wants from a relationship will always hurt you. And whatever the Holy Spirit perceives, which is using the relationship to raise up these unconscious private thoughts and these unconscious private feelings of fear, shame, guilt, jealousy, that's the purpose of all our relationships. It's only for healing. We don't form a relationship to try to forge love on earth which is the typical reason why people get into relationships. We allow the Holy Spirit to show us the guilt in our minds that we may release it, open our hearts up to fully communicate, to be fully transparent with everyone and everything.

If you go to a business, a museum, or an apartment, every single person that we meet or think of is an opportunity to let the Holy Spirit show them to us in their truest state. *Show me the purpose, show me the spirit, show me that I'm always meeting myself.* Whoever I believe I'm interacting with, I'm literally meeting myself— not physically because God did not create the physical, but in my attitude, state of mind, and mood. *How am I reacting to myself? What do I believe about myself? What am I seeing reflected about myself in those I perceive in the dream?*

> "What therefore God hath joined together, let not man put asunder." (Matthew 19:6)

The Spirit has to induce the mind to give up this belief in the external world and the Spirit uses everything, including attraction.The Spirit uses attraction. And that is part of the bigger plan of flushing up the unconscious darkness into awareness so you can see it for what it is and *choose again.*

Every relationship is a total commitment to the Holy Spirit. That is an amazing idea. Imagine in your life opening to the idea that every relationship is a total commitment. You can see how this will take holiness, this higher purpose, and apply it to a much broader context—unconditional love. And the reminder that every relationship is a holy relationship is a really nice idea when you stop to think about it. Someone delivers your mail, someone you meet in an elevator or at your house, a waitress in a restaurant you visit, someone you see while walking down the street.... You gradually open up to the idea that every relationship is a total commitment. You can see how that appears to contradict everything we know about relationships. But as you get deeper into this purpose, you integrate everyone into this loving experience; it is inclusive. You see, you would not exclude anyone from that love.

~♥~

In terms of purpose, every relationship is a total commitment. You can see the ego shaking its head and saying, *Now what does that even mean? How is it possible for every relationship to be a total commitment?* It is directing us to return to the mind, to the purpose in the mind. There is purpose underneath all of these memories and images that unifies them all and brings us back to God.

Even if you don't use words like Holy Spirit, you can have a partnership and make love, peace of mind, joy, and happiness the top priority of that partnership. More than expectations; more than trying to get something from your partner; more than wanting to change your partner and make them different; more than all the ego projections, if you value love, peace, joy, and happiness and if you commit— if you *truly* commit to that—then that is the use (purpose) of relationships. Of course, you can apply it to everyone you meet; you will transfer that same commitment in order for it to become a full commitment.

That is how you return to agape love, how you come back to unconditional love, is to have the same commitment with everyone. You don't try to create a hierarchy of the really important ones in your life, separated from and ignoring the rest of the seven billion. Jesus says they are all you and all important, and you have to learn to extend the love to all of them, even the ones you think about, not just the ones you meet physically, but even the ones you think about, you have to send that same loving blessing because you need it. That is how you are going to find out that you are loved: by extending that love and committing to that extension of love. You see how this is the key to happiness, that your partner is never doing anything wrong to you; your partner is just reflecting what you believe and once you see something that you do not like, you need to come back to your commitment for happiness, for love, for joy, and let it go. Do not hold on to it, do not harbor it.

> If you look at relationships and you believe there's a hierarchy of relationships, that some are different from others, that some are more important than others, that some are more worthy of love, attention, and dedication than others, that is specialness; that is the guilt.
>
> Agape love—unconditional love—does not make distinctions between brothers and sisters; it sees everyone equally in that loving gaze.
>
> Everyone is equally loved; there is no higher, no lower, no more, no less. Love does not look at differences. Love doesn't know what it means to compare; it doesn't understand jealousy; Love doesn't understand envy. These are egoic meanings of love, and that's why Jesus says you're afraid of Love. You're afraid of the real deal because you believe in something called death that has covered your awareness of the true eternal Love. To come into this world is to believe in death. It's to believe that love can be fragmented, and that love can be special; love can be different. So, here's what Jesus had to say under the Holy Spirit's teaching: All relationships are seen as total commitments, yet they do not conflict with one another in any way.

You can only have perfect faith in each person's ability to make you happy if you have perfect faith in yourself, which you can't do as long as you still feel guilty. Jesus is going to show you that it is possible to be in love with everyone. You may not believe it. You may think that's ridiculous; you may think that's absurd. But Jesus is saying if you stay with him, and you follow the Holy Spirit... It's a fact that all relationships require total commitment. If you want to learn how God loves, you have to learn to love without exception. You can't make exceptions to love and know Love.

26. Speak on Lust, Fantasies, and the Desires of the Flesh

> "But every man is tempted, when he is drawn away of his own lust, and enticed." (James 1:14)

> "For all that *is* in the world, the lust of the flesh, and the lust of the eyes, and the pride of life, is not of the Father, but is of the world. And the world passeth away, and the lust thereof: but he that doeth the will of God abideth for ever." (1 John 2:16-17)

> "I delight to do thy will, O my God: yea, thy law *is* within my heart." (Psalms 40:8)

Struggles of the flesh, so to speak, are really struggles of judgment. There is no struggle in non-judgment or complete forgiveness. Forgiveness is the only goal worthy of your attention and effort now. It is our only purpose for this world, for forgiveness is the only purpose the Holy Spirit has for the world. The confusion and tug of war you experience are a result of listening to the ego (or Satan in biblical terms), for only the ego sponsors confusion and war. The ego always speaks first. Yet in the quiet moments, the Holy Spirit speaks of our innocence.

~♥~

Unconscious thoughts and beliefs have a direct effect on your way of life and habits. The confusion and struggles you feel about the flesh are really very deep-seated beliefs in your mind. Forgiveness (or the correction of error) has already happened, but you have to accept it in your mind. The task is to accept Atonement, or complete forgiveness, as Jesus demonstrated. It may seem like a mighty task, but if you are tempted to feel overwhelmed or intimidated by the task, ask yourself this question: "Would God have a plan for my salvation that could fail?" The ego is silenced forever in the glory of God's Presence.

~♥~

Forgiveness is already accomplished. Ask not to be forgiven, for that is already accomplished. Ask, rather, to learn how to forgive. The Holy Spirit leads you unfailingly toward learning this one lesson. In fact, the willingness to forgive is all that is asked of you. The Holy Spirit is the "how," and you will be guided every step of the way. The ego will seem to resist the final lesson of forgiveness, yet have no fear because the ego will go from awareness at last—and our holy mind rests in the Love of God. This is inevitable, for Eternal Peace is the Truth of our Being.

Is sexual expression good or bad, helpful, or harmful? What one does comes from what one thinks; that is why awakening is a purification of thought. Behavior modification is therefore never the goal, for behavior but follows the guide the mind chooses to listen to and follow.

Sexual desire is not better or worse than any other desire in the world, yet awakening is a state of contentment that is desireless. This is the peace that passeth all understanding in the world. All appetites are ego-getting mechanisms. Fantasy is the attempt to make false associations and obtain pleasure from them. As the miracle expands and becomes consistent in experience, these appetites fade, grow dim, and disappear. The ego was the belief in lack, and all apparent appetites reflected this belief.

Pleasure and pain are the same error. The miracle transcends the error by showing its falsity, its impossibility. It is impossible to seek for pleasure without finding pain, for both are the same error: the attempt to reinforce the "reality" of the body and world. Christ is Spirit, not a body, and to experience Divine Mind is to forget the body entirely. Awakening involves mind training. Step back and pay attention to the thoughts that come into awareness. Feel your desire for healing.

Preferences are judgments, and as the mind yields to the nonjudgmental perspective of the Holy Spirit, the awakening is obvious. Observe that as long as appetites seem to exist, there are the ego defenses of indulgence and repression. Neither is better or worse than the other, for they are the same illusion. The miracle offers a real alternative, and when one is consistently miracle-minded, defenses are no longer needed.

> "Then said Jesus, Father, forgive them; for they know not what they do." (Luke 23:34)
>
> "Lust not after her beauty in thine heart." (Proverbs 6:25)
>
> "*This* I say then, Walk in the Spirit, and ye shall not fulfil the lust of the flesh." (Galatians 5:16)

> "But I say unto you, That whosoever looketh on a woman to lust after her hath committed adultery with her already in his heart." (Matthew 5:28)

When the mind believes in the egoic belief system, it perceives its entire environment as lacking. That is the human condition, a cycle of lack followed by something to fill that lack. It gives some sort of satisfaction. Whether it appears to be physical or psychological satisfaction or both, it's the same kind of cycle. The mind has an unconscious belief in lack, and you could argue that the entire purpose of mind training, the entire purpose of exposing—of looking where the emotions are, the charges, the contractions, the constrictions, and everything else—is all part of healing. The Spirit meets the mind where it believes it is. As you journey towards wholeness, you focus on your mind training and expose those beliefs in lack—your entire perception of the world changes, as does your perception of the body. What appear to be external attractions, but aren't really external at all, you begin to realize are all being generated in consciousness.

> The ego is flushed up and exposed in relationships, and aligning with the ego brings illusory experiences of pleasure and pain. Distorted miracle impulses reach awareness as cravings, and in this regard, sexual cravings are the same as cravings for food, drink, temperature, stimulation, etc. Cravings are

always about what you don't have and what you want, and the miracle helps you get past this distorted view of the world. As the ego belief system is questioned, exposed, and released, the "lens of lack" is cleared of all obstacles to peace. When this happens, miracle impulses are experienced directly in awareness as Love and calls for Love.

Wholeness and completion are natural to the mind, and the miracle brings these qualities back into awareness. Complexity is always of the ego. The ego uses relationships to feel good, and since it is impulsive and unstable, it has no idea what it means to be committed to someone. Commitment to a monogamous interpersonal relationship is a step that the Holy Spirit can use (as with any commitment or discipline) to open the mind to the sole or ultimate commitment that one can make: accepting the Atonement or awakening God's Love.

I have referred to the ego's purpose for relationships as "Dixie cup relationships." The ego seems to throw its relationships away once it seems to get what it thinks it wants and moves on to the next relationship for another drink. Simultaneous sexual relationships, or "open" relationships as they have been called, seem to add to the complexity. A monogamous interpersonal relationship can offer a full plate of opportunities to expose and forgive the ego, and the undoing of the ego (forgiveness) is the only purpose for all relationships. The ultimate realization (self-realization) is the recognition that Creator and Creation share the same Spirit of Love. At best, all perceptual relationships reflect the Love of God, and this Agape Love inspires forgiveness and miracles.

The ego uses relationships for gratification—and the ego, being impulsive and unstable, has no conception of commitment. Commitment to a monogamous interpersonal relationship is a step that the Holy Spirit can use, as with any commitment or discipline, to open the mind to the sole or ultimate commitment that one can make: accepting the Atonement and awakening to God's Love.

The Holy Spirit guides surely. Simplicity is of God, and the illusion of complexity is the error to be forgiven.

You have every right to happiness; that is your inheritance, but you cannot look for it on the screen. It is within you; it is the Holy Spirit's purpose. And about pleasure and pain, let's face it; in this world, pain and pleasure seem to be very different. Experientially, they seem to be very different. So, what makes them single or unified? They are two things that share the same purpose; that is what makes them the same. How do pain and pleasure share a purpose? They both reinforce the body as being real. It is the same thing whether you are in ecstasy eating something you love or you have a throbbing headache. Is God in your awareness at one extreme or the other?

27. Speak on Celibacy and Chastity

> "All *men* cannot receive this saying, save *they* to whom it is given. For there are some eunuchs, which were so born from *their* mother's womb: and there are some eunuchs, which were made eunuchs of men: and there be eunuchs, which have made themselves eunuchs for the kingdom of heaven's sake. He that is able to receive *it*, let him receive *it*." (Matthew 19:11-12)

The Holy Spirit uses the body as a communication device to smile through, laugh through, hug through, be gentle through, and bring comfort through. Jesus says that the ego uses the body for pleasure, for pride, and for attack.

~♥~

Remember that the ego is the belief in separate self-interests that is being undone. The ego has a purpose that is being exposed and unveiled as a lie, and the Holy Spirit's purpose is being offered as an alternative to conflict. Nothing of value can be reduced to or explained at the level of form. It is all a matter of keeping the purpose in mind. "Sexual abstinence" based on repression is not helpful. "Sexual abstinence," which follows from chastity (purity of thought) or from the desire for purity of thought, and from turning the decision over to the Holy Spirit, is helpful. All body thoughts (e.g., hunger, thirst, preferences, cravings, etc.) raised to the level of the mind are wrong-minded.

I am not advocating an attempt at controlling behavior. I'm trying to get you to be more open to changing your mind by accepting that it is changeless and whole. All physical impulses are distorted miracle impulses. The miracle calls you Home. Through the ego's dense lens of lack, miracle impulses reach awareness as bodily cravings, which seem to be satisfied by imagined fantasies or false associations of bodily behaviors (e.g., eating food, drinking liquid, sexual activity, etc.). The little willingness being asked for is really the willingness to have a change of purpose and thus a change of mind.

Sex in a loving relationship dedicated to the Holy Spirit and guided by the Holy Spirit is, in this sense, an act of affection and can continue to be so until the mind has become so unified in purpose that there are no cravings or desires for form of any kind. When this desirelessness happens, there is truly the miracle of Atonement, and Christ is fulfilled in the Divine Love of knowing God in Spirit. The miracle of Atonement transcends or dissolves the attraction to guilt in the sleeping mind. Sex solely for the purpose of pleasure and sensual gratification is an ego motivation, attempting to reinforce the "reality" of the body, and this always involves the illusion of guilt. As one deepens in awakening, the desire for anything of this world evaporates or fades away—and joy radiates from within! All seeming needs or lacks are gone in Divine Love. Let the Spirit within guide you in everything, moment by moment.

> The ego doesn't like obedience, but that gets to the authority problem. If you believe you are an autonomous being who has a separate will apart

from God, that you've been able to make up a world unlike God's Spirit and you've been able to take on this sense of an autonomous character in the dream, then you would need obedience to get back into alignment with that inner voice to get the puppet back on the strings. To be a servant like St. Francis talked about, "Make me an instrument," so that I may truly know myself as God created me.

All of a sudden, the Spirit gave me a lot of high interpretations of a lot of things. It wasn't like they were all wrong or they were completely missing the mark. I just needed to really know the high direction. Because I couldn't really dedicate myself to something just out of a blind faith just because it was in a book or just because so and so said it was, so I was supposed to believe them. I needed to really, really feel an alignment and a connection with what I was going to devote my life to. Then, when I did, that made the devotion just seem to grow stronger and stronger. And I never looked back. I never would give into comparison of *could have, would have, should have*. People would say, "Oh, but you've given up so much." I said, "Nonsense, I feel like I've given up nothing." Sacrifice is not a part of authentic awakening to God; we are not really asked to give up something of value. We are just simply asked to be shown the valuelessness of these ego pursuits. They just lead us nowhere. They are like dead ends.

One day, I went to the dictionary, and I looked up chastity, and I read the beginning words of chastity in the dictionary: Purity of thought! Ah, that's what that vow is about. Purification. Of course it would have to be if you're coming home to know God and your mind in its pristine, clean stillness. Of course, it would involve purification.

28. How Would You Have Me Look upon the Body?

> "What? know ye not that your body is the temple of the Holy Ghost *which is* in you, which ye have of God, and ye are not your own?" (1 Corinthians 6:19)

> "For he that soweth to his flesh shall of the flesh reap corruption; but he that soweth to the Spirit shall of the Spirit reap life everlasting." (Galatians 6:8)

> "That which is born of the flesh is flesh; and that which is born of the Spirit is spirit." (John 3:6)

Life is more than the body. As you approach true forgiveness, the body will become increasingly unimportant in your perception, and you will have experiences of the vastness of the mind. As it becomes apparent that you are mind—wholly mind, purely mind—the concept of the body will fade, grow dim, and disappear from awareness. What remains is abstract light, and the light of God is our eternal home.

The ego belief system has projected a world in which you seem to exist as a body and seem to be dependent upon a job, environment, and other people for survival. The true vastness of the divine mind has been pushed out of awareness and forgotten. To turn this seeming situation around and bring an end to the amnesia about Heaven, it is necessary to forgive—to release the false beliefs and thoughts that seem to produce a fearful world that God did not create.

In truth, there is only one mind, because Spirit exists as perfect oneness. Yet in this world, every "body" seems to have a private and separate "mind" of its own. The belief in private minds and private thoughts IS the ego. Each seeming interpersonal relationship, therefore, presents an opportunity to accept the union, or oneness, or wholeness, of the divine mind that God creates eternally.

~♥~

The dream of bodies cannot be realized, and bodies do not join. The body was made as a concrete symbol of separation, yet given to the Holy Spirit, it serves solely as a means or symbol of communication. In Enlightenment, the recognition of the pure oneness of mind, the body has no purpose because it has no existence. At no single instant does the body exist at all. The body is always remembered or anticipated, but never present. This means that the body is an illusory, time-based concept. Illusions are one, and so forgiveness lets them all go together.

There is a perspective of the body and the world that offers only blessings. This is what Jesus calls a holy relationship. The body is seen as a symbol of communication and has no value in and of itself. What is the body for? "Does it serve the Light?" is the only helpful question in any situation in which the thought of bodies has entered. Let the Spirit smile, laugh, and hug through the body, and you will see the body in the light of forgiveness. In this light, there is neither attraction or repulsion, for what is wholly neutral can merely serve the one who brings healing. In this purpose is the experience of joy. Joy is ever-fulfilling and offers the perspective that all things work together for good. Glory to God!

~♥~

Life is neither of the body nor in a body. Life is an eternal state of Mind. There is no death, for nothing real can die. Forgiveness shows the falsity of illusion, allowing for the remembrance of God and Christ. Christ is not born and does not die, remaining eternal as God created Christ in Spirit. If you seem to be discouraged by judging "progress" remember the teaching of Christ: "Judge not, that ye be not judged." (Matthew 7:1) Time is self-judgment, and the Holy Spirit's only use of time is to teach that there is no time.

These words witness to this simple fact. Because Christ is *fact,* time and Christ cannot coexist. It only takes one instant for Atonement, yet this instant is without an opposite and thus is completely certain. Miracles will seem to build your trust, yet Atonement is a moment of complete trust that yields to *absolute* certainty. You cannot fail to accept what is inevitable, and God's plan for salvation *is* inevitable. Innocence is our birthright, and nothing can change what God created perfect and eternal.

> The key to eternal life is forgiveness. It's through forgiving your brother, and that means simply meeting your brother without a past. That is no small order; that is giant! We are praying for deliverance, we are praying for resurrection, we are praying for divine innocence—to see the

perfect innocence of who we are and who everyone is. So that is a huge prayer. We are going for the escape from fear and guilt.

Every time you look at a person or a body, you have a choice of interpretation. There is another way to look at the body and the world that is of the Holy Spirit, and it's a miracle; it is truly a miracle. This is a moment where you perceive the world without judgment. Beyond all the judgments of the world is a pristine interpretation that leaves you with a smile on your face because you behold the world as the Holy Spirit sees it, you behold the happy dream, you behold the forgiven world. You see the whole world sparkling. And the main characteristic of this interpretation is that you still have a self-concept, but the self-concept is forgiveness. It's the one self-concept that you can share with the Holy Spirit because it doesn't involve the ego.

It's still a self-concept. Imagine you reach a point and you just reach a state of mind that is so pristine and spectacular that you can say, with Jesus, *I have forgiven the world.* You can say with Jesus, *Satan is under foot, be of good cheer!* Imagine radiating that thought out to the whole universe: *Be of good cheer; I have forgiven the world!*

It's very simple to do that. And all spiritual pathways, all authentic spiritual pathways, always talk about emptying the mind. In Buddhism, they talk about going into the void. All the great teachers have said, *Lay aside the judgments and the thoughts of who you think you are and open your mind and your heart to the truth.*

29. Speak on the Deception of Seeking and Holding Idols

"Thou shalt have no other gods before me." (Exodus 20:3)

"Lay not up for yourselves treasures upon earth, where moth and rust doth corrupt, and where thieves break through and steal: But lay up for yourselves treasures in heaven, where neither moth nor rust doth corrupt, and where thieves do not break through nor steal." (Matthew 6:19-20)

"Let no man deceive himself. If any man among you seemeth to be wise in this world, let him become a fool, that he may be wise." (1 Corinthians 3:18)

"For thus saith the LORD of hosts, the God of Israel; Let not your prophets and your diviners, that *be* in the midst of you, deceive you, neither hearken to your dreams which ye cause to be dreamed." (Jeremiah 29:8)

"What profiteth the graven image that the maker thereof hath graven it; the molten image, and a teacher of lies, that the maker of his work trusteth therein, to make dumb idols?" (Habakkuk 2:18)

"Confounded be all they that serve graven images, that boast themselves of idols." (Psalms 97:7)

"A drought *is* upon her waters; and they shall be dried up: for it *is* the land of graven images, and they are mad upon *their* idols." (Jeremiah 50:38)

The Bible says to have no graven images before God (Exodus 20:4). This is because God knows no images, being pure Spirit. Forgive the images that never were, and experience indescribable happiness! The dreamer of a dream first realizes the dreaming. Nothing can hurt the dreamer once the Holy Spirit has revealed the dream as unreal. Without judgment, all dream figures are the same, for it was only the ego that made up the categories of victim and victimizer, abused and abuser, and enabled and enabler to perpetuate itself. Once the ego is released, perception has been healed, and nothing blocks the way to experiencing God's Divine Love. All glory to the living God!

~♥~

This world is like a childhood game called hide and seek. You hide your Christ identity, and then you seek out idols to distract yourself until you realize, *I don't like to play that game anymore. I would rather be authentic; I would rather acknowledge my feelings and face them.*

In this world we seem to have many desires and Jesus is saying: It's safe to take those desires off the altar of your heart and leave just one and let that be the desire for God. That is what a mystic is; the mystic is simply one who's devoted to God. And ultimately, we start to realize that desire is like our prayer. And if our desire is splintered and we want many different things from this world, we find we're not happy because we forgot who we are and we don't know ourselves with multiple desires.

~♥~

The Holy Spirit is the bridge back to eternity, the Holy Spirit knows the way. The Holy Spirit is the remembrance of that love in our mind. It's like that spark that could never be put out in the darkened mind. It's still there, and when we give ourselves over to it, we open up to becoming more and more consistently miracle-minded. Your happiness is not a matter of degree. But just for a moment, we'll say as if there are degrees: your happiness is proportional to the extent to which you're choosing the right mind.

The more habitually right-minded you are, the more habitually happy you are. And I'm not talking about being happy because you got a promotion, or because you met your soulmate, or happy because it's a sunny day, or happy because you like this specific form. We're talking about happy for no earthly reason. You're so happy you can't even think of a reason to be happy! That's another characteristic of the Holy Spirit's happiness. Because it is truly God-inspired, you are unable to identify the cause of your happiness. It's not inspired by anything in form. It's not inspired by any outcome. It's completely independent of outcomes. It wouldn't matter what was seeming to happen in form. You know you're happy for no good reason—for no reason at all in terms of the world—but you're happy because of your alignment with Source.

I was named after David in the Bible. One of the psalms you might have heard of is the 23rd Psalm, and the way it starts out is, "The Lord is my shepherd; I shall not want."; I shall not have multiple desires. Just the beginning of the 23rd Psalm has the key to awakening.

The difficulty with believing in the personality self and the ego is that the ego said, *There are plenty of things to want, and you can have them all; I'll give you the whole world, and you can have it all.* And it's a trick; it's been a big trick. The Bible said, "Hold no graven images before the Lord, thy God," and the problem with the human condition is that it's got these physical eyes that are growing big, and it wants a lot of idols; it wants to listen to a lot of idols, it wants to touch a lot of idols, and it wants to possess a lot of idols. The ego is the getting mechanism in the mind. And idols are not just golden calves or totem poles. Idols are any image that you value more than the light; anything, a twig, a toothpick. If you value a toothpick more than the light, that's enough to keep you asleep and dreaming. And when you value idols, you have unconscious guilt. And when you have unconscious guilt, you don't want to leave earth; you just want to reincarnate and come back, and then you get your exit. And you say, "When can I go back again and try to put some more idols on?" and then you exit, and then you come back again, and it just goes on and on until you finally go, *Oh, the Lord is my shepherd; oh my gosh, I shall not want!* Why? If I'm the Christ, why would I want anything from this world? Because this world was made as an attack on God and a place where God could not enter not. So, why would I go for idols when I could go for the Christ and wake up to my true reality?

The Holy Spirit needs happy learners. The only way we are going to get the final lesson is by becoming light, playful, and happy, and welcoming the happy lessons. And experiencing that, we can take the direct approach to happiness. And I think everything goes much quicker—that's how it went in my experience. Earlier on the lessons were harder, took a longer time to shift my mind, and the contrasts were even much more extreme. And then it got lighter and lighter, and lighter. And then it started to transfer exponentially, like lightning started to happen, where the contrast wasn't necessary anymore. Pain was optional. I was really getting, "Oh my gosh." And then I had years that started to go by where I didn't have a bad day. That was amazing after the track record I had before—that was miraculous! But that's when you can tell you are really coming into the happy dream, when you don't have a bad day. When you can't remember the last time you had a bad day, then that's where it just gets stronger and stronger. We learn best through attraction—we really are attracted to joy. Sooner or later, we give into that joy and we go yeah, that's actually the way I want it to go.

30. How Is Healing Accomplished?

> "But that ye may know that the Son of man hath power on earth to forgive sins, then saith he to the sick of the palsy, Arise, take up thy bed, and go unto thine house." (Matthew 9:6)

> "Jesus turned him about, and when he saw her, he said, Daughter, be of good comfort; thy faith hath made thee whole. And the woman was made whole from that hour." (Matthew 9:22)

Healing is accomplished just through the recognition that the mind decides and the body does not. People don't choose sickness, people don't choose health, people don't choose success or failure, because people don't choose! People are projections of the ego mind; the eight billion people in the world are all projections of one mind asleep.

The people aren't the problem because the Bible says, "God is no respecter of persons" (Acts 10:34), and God did not create the body; God did not create people. The ego invented the world, and we can start to realize: Wait a minute, I'm dreaming, and I don't have to give meaning to this world; I just need to forgive!

> "And Jesus went about all Galilee, teaching in their synagogues, and preaching the gospel of the

> kingdom, and healing all manner of sickness and all manner of disease among the people." (Matthew 4:23)

It gives me great joy to share the real alternative, the blameless perspective, the perspective of the dreamer. For in dreams, that is all that can be shared. How blessed we are in Christ! Glory to God in the highest for creating our Heavenly Kingdom in unchanging love.

Mind is singular, not separate or private. Joining is a state of mind, not an action. Correction is a perspective, not a process. Correction is unlearning or undoing concepts. Correction dissolves the questions associated with mistaken identity. This is, indeed, the point of focus. You will discover that there is no such thing as a *personal mind* or *levels* of reality. There is no Mind in matter, and this is why there are no "levels" of reality.

Spirit has never entered into the perceptual level of form. The Holy Spirit is the Thought that demonstrates the impossibility of Mind leaving its Source and entering matter. The *personal mind* is impossible because Mind cannot be divided and private, nor can Mind ever become physical, nor can the Infinite become finite, nor can the Eternal become time bound. This viewpoint is correct because it recognizes the impossibility of such an error. Wrong-mindedness is the belief in a personal mind that causation (Mind) can enter matter or time-space. God is the Author and the Cause. There can be no other Cause. You can't imagine the relief that comes from letting go of the belief in authorship. You cannot happily author a book, a newsletter, yourself, or the world. The only Author is God, and Christ is a joyful, perfect Effect. Everything else is meaningless. Such is the curriculum, and such is the unlearning of world belief.

The experience transcends words because words are symbols of symbols. There is no reciprocity in this perspective because there is no *other*. There is no *other* to write or read newsletters or books, and there is no *other* to buy or sell. There is no *other*. Forgiveness recognizes that the subject-object distinction is impossible. The cosmos is a tapestry that cannot be meaningfully divided into perceiver/perceived, observer/observed, a *me* and a *you*. Mind is one, and forgiveness reveals mortal mind (erroneous thinking) as one and corrected. Such is healing. Healing has nothing to do with specifics. Nothing can be separated from the whole. Healing is the liberation from part/whole thinking because Thought is whole and transcends the error of *parts*.

The joining is in the purpose or perspective. In awakening, the only *option* is purpose. This is the only joining. Joining is unrelated to words, thought forms, or bodies. It simply sees perception as a tapestry. Such is the beauty of simplicity.

The fictitious *personal mind* will never comprehend anything. It may appear to be in opposition to the experience of truth, but Spirit sees beyond the error, and truth remains forever in God's grace.

Fortunately, God is beyond any attempt at *definition*, and cannot be described or conceptualized. The peace of God is an experience that occurs when the belief in the *personal mind* is abandoned.

> "Not every one that saith unto me, Lord, Lord, shall enter into the kingdom of heaven; but he that doeth the will of my Father which is in heaven." (Matthew 7:21)

> "For the LORD giveth wisdom: out of his mouth *cometh* knowledge and understanding." (Proverbs 2:6)

> "For this cause we also, since the day we heard *it*, do not cease to pray for you, and to desire that ye might be filled with the knowledge of his will in all wisdom and spiritual understanding." (Colossians 1:9)

> "Happy *is* the man *that* findeth wisdom, and the man *that* getteth understanding." (Proverbs 3:13)

> "To know wisdom and instruction; to perceive the words of understanding; To receive the instruction of wisdom, justice, and judgment, and equity; To give subtlety to the simple, to the young man knowledge and discretion. A wise *man* will hear, and will increase learning; and a man of understanding shall attain unto wise counsels." (Proverbs 1:2-5)

"Behold, happy *is* the man whom God correcteth: therefore despise not thou the chastening of the Almighty." (Job 5:17)

Pain is always a misperception, for God has nothing to do with pain. There is no pain if God exists; there is no God if pain exists. The illusion of pain is always the result of wrong-minded thinking, and it is this that must be exposed and released in order to experience lasting peace and happiness.

Concern is another word for worry, and this emotion has nothing to do with true empathy or compassion. Concern is a painful emotion that arises from a desire to be correct about a specific person, situation, or event. One aspect of such anxiety is the belief that something untrue has already occurred. Another aspect is the belief that past events caused the fear and pain. This misunderstanding gives the past reality while rejecting the Holy Spirit's present solution. When you pray for a miracle, you are praying for a shift in your perception. This is true even when you appear to pray for "another." If you continue to be concerned about a brother after asking for a miracle, you are not allowing the miracle to be as it is. Miracles do not create or change anything; they simply observe the false and see that it has no consequence. Miracles offer only joy; once joy arrives, all pain is over.

Pain is correctly perceived as a call for Love, and the call to release the false perception of pain is always one's own. Because looking through a glass darkly never brings peace, happiness, love, or joy. Any apparent upset is a call to empty the mind of false concepts and thus clean the mirror. This is the mental preparation needed to accept the Atonement and remember God. Atonement is the realization that the separation never occurred. Until this correction is accepted, the world will appear to be real—and the ego's unreal emotions, which are one with the world, will appear to persist in awareness.

Allow the feelings to surface into your awareness. Then, with complete honesty and sincerity, surrender your thoughts, judgments, interpretations, and feelings to the Spirit. When darkness is raised to light, the darkness is gone. Do not protect the darkness, for the Spirit will not dissolve what has not been willingly offered for release. You have the Answer within but have been unwilling to let go of the ego's definition of the problem. The Holy Spirit must wait until you recognize that you have had a perception problem based on the ego's belief. Until this point is reached, the "problems" will seem to be projected onto the world and to brothers who appear to be apart from the mind. They are not. Apart from the mind, there are no problems. Healed perception will spring into awareness the instant the misperception is seen exactly as it is and not hidden or projected as "something else."

All illness is mental illness, and all pain is nothing more than a faulty interpretation of reality. Reality is Love, and Love is created eternally perfect. Love has no opposite.

Glory to God for creating Love as one forever and ever!

If you are identified with the ego, that is what hurts because that is denying your Christhood. If somebody seems to steal from you or harm you, the world would say you are just an innocent victim; you have nothing at all to do with that; you just happened to be in the wrong place at the wrong time. But I can choose to see peace and healing in every situation, or I can choose to see separation, defensiveness, etc.

A lot of new age systems will say you are responsible for things in form, but what happens when you take a mind-level principle like, *I am responsible for my state of mind*, and a worldly perception from the level of form, like cancer for example, and put these two together? You get: *I am responsible for my cancer*. Ah ha. The guilt comes in from taking something on the level of form and then taking a metaphysical principle of mind (I am responsible for my state of mind) and cross-pollinating or bringing those two together.

The question comes up straight away: Who in their right mind would choose sickness? And I always say that, of course, nobody in their right mind would choose sickness. You would have to be operating in the ego or the wrong mind to call forth such a witness in the world. And sickness is a very strong witness. The mind must believe that it is guilty to call forth a witness such as sickness. The good news is that once we learn to choose and be in our right mind consistently then we are free of the guilt and therefore we do not call forth the witnesses to reinforce that guilt. That is really the only escape from all pain and misery and suffering. If you are with Jesus and the Holy Spirit, you can discern between the purposes of the ego and the Holy Spirit; you understand that one is a fear-based thought system and one is a thought system of love. The ego is backwards; it believes that things out there in the world are taking away your peace of mind. But this is the flipside: the ego also tells us that things in the world can bring us peace of mind.

I know a particular island that I can picture and just be on. Or: There is a particular thought that is always peaceful to think about, but when my attention comes back to my job, I lose it. That is backward thinking, because as long as we think that there are things in the world that can give us peace or take it away, then we are literally co-dependent. Do not listen to that ego because it is telling you that there are things that you can get in this world that are going to bring you happiness and peace; and it is a scam, a big scam. Go within. That is where meditation comes in; go within your mind, sink down beneath these clouds of darkness of the ego, meditate, and go down beneath them to the Kingdom of Heaven.

And if you have trouble meditating, then relationships can really speed things up because they will bring up all the unconscious beliefs in your mind.

Jesus told us not to judge in the sermon on the mount. He gave us this information all along, saying: *You're an eternal being! Don't settle for less than the way God created you! Have fun, be spontaneous, and enjoy the present moment.* And this is what the Holy Spirit is doing through our healing relationships; they're reminding us to laugh. When you're getting into spontaneity, you're getting into the present moment.

He is saying: *Why don't you follow your heart's calling right now in the present moment?* And if you are sincere, loyal, and committed to the calling of your heart right now, your future will be a reflection of that commitment. Because remember, the ego is hatred. The world was made in hatred. That's what the past is: hatred, fear, and guilt, and if you succumb and say I can't do anything about it, then that hatred, guilt, and fear will be projected onto the future, and you'll feel hopeless. That's what death is. Death is a feeling of hopelessness.

My name is Hoffmeister, I'm the master of hope, I'm saying *join me!* Let's join in the present moment and have a different future! How about a happy future! If you believe in a future, have a happy future! That is what Jesus is teaching us.

31. Speak on Trying to Serve Two Masters

"No man can serve two masters: for either he will hate the one, and love the other; or else he will hold to the one, and despise the other." (Matthew 6:24)

Free will is another name for God's will, for it is eternally free, happy, peaceful, and joyful. This state of mind is perfection, reality, or truth. The will is free in perfect Oneness and union; this freedom is a characteristic of Spirit or eternal creation, which is the abstract light of unconditional Love. This light is total understanding and Love, or Oneness. God creates only light and Oneness.

~♥~

Duality is the illusion of the ego. Choice did not seem to arise until the "fall from grace," which reflects the belief that separation from God is possible. This belief in separation produces what appears to be a dualistic dream world of extremes and opposites: the time-space cosmos. These seeming "choices between specifics," which are the common "choices of the world," make it hard to see that the only meaningful choice left to the dreamer of the dream-world is the choice of purpose in his or her mind.

No one can serve two masters; the ego's voice and the inner voice of the Spirit are as different in purpose as night and day. Learn to discern between these two voices. Lay aside the ego. Align completely with the Voice for God. This is the goal of life, for God's will for us is perfect happiness. The

Voice for God leads to awakening from the dream-world of fear to the reality of eternal Love and Oneness.

> "For he that wavereth is like a wave of the sea driven with the wind and tossed. For let not that man think that he shall receive any thing of the Lord. A double minded man is unstable in all his ways." (James 1:6-8)

> "And Jesus knew their thoughts, and said unto them, Every kingdom divided against itself is brought to desolation; and every city or house divided against itself shall not stand." (Matthew 12:25)

Who are you attempting to follow to enlightenment—the ego or the Holy Spirit? Whom do you call master, remembering that you cannot serve two masters? If anger is your master, you will try to deny Christ and defend an illusion. If your master orders you to confront or fight someone who appears to be someone other than yourself, you are deceived in purpose and remain devoted to an unconscious death wish. Who can judge a brother and hope to awaken to a oneness that knows not of judgment? You can refuse to take a side, refuse to make a judgment, and refuse to align your mind with thoughts of the past or future, and in vigilance for this perspective, you will abide in the peace that passes the understanding of the world.

Anger is a false sense of control, attempting to tell reality what it must be. You must realize that the control issue or authority problem is not with something or someone outside of yourself. Clinging to the ego and a small self-concept is believing you can author yourself. You are as God created you. Accept the fact, and you are home in peace.

~♥~

Jesus says you cannot serve two masters. You can't serve two purposes; you can't live with a split mind. A split mind becomes intolerable after a while. So we are being guided to go deeper inside and say, *I don't have to live with a split mind.* I can forgive that which is not real and accept that which is real with the Holy Spirit's help—with help from inside, with help from above, so to speak.

~♥~

One aspect of the mind is blazing bright, and the other is very dark. As Jesus said in the Bible, "Ye cannot serve God and mammon [money]." (Matthew 6:24) He stated that you cannot serve two masters. In terms of the split mind, you can't serve both light and darkness at the same time, even though that's what schizophrenia is about. Trying to serve both light and darkness at the same time is pretty wild.

That split in the mind is so unnatural; God did not create the mind to be split. When the mind is split, the projection comes from a way to relieve the split by seeing it outside of oneself—out on the screen, similar to how the light passes through the film and then off onto the screen of images in a projector.

So, in order to relieve itself of the split, the mind projects out a world and then begins to interpret a dualistic world with right and wrong behaviors. Then it tries to return to the right behaviors and let go of the wrong ones, but it's an impossible situation. There are no perfect behaviors; rather, we must look beyond the screen, return to the holistic mind, and perceive the world through the eyes of the Holy Spirit. So that's why I say nobody's ever done anything wrong or right. If you still see wrong behavior and right behavior, you have not forgiven because God didn't create wrong behavior and right behavior; it's still attempting to take the split and apply it to behavior. That is why we forgive our brothers for what they have *not* done.

Confusion really comes from self-doubt. It's still coming from trying to listen to two teachers and serve two masters. And that's where all the confusion comes in, because the Holy Spirit and the ego don't teach the same lesson and don't have the same curriculum. And they don't offer the same guidance, so that's where the confusion is coming in.

Faith is the power of your mind, and your faith is always very strong because God created you with enormous faith. However, when you have a split mind, your faith is split between the right mind and the wrong mind. You're taking something that's extremely powerful, and you're dividing it—dividing your attention between the right mind and the wrong mind. This is ultimately what Jesus meant by, "No man can serve two masters." In terms of purpose, you cannot serve the Holy Spirit and the ego. You have to pick one or the other.

So, it's like in "Ghostbusters": *Who are you going to call?* Are you going to call on the Holy Spirit or are you going to call on the ego? Because faith and belief combined to make the cosmos. In other words, in Heaven there are no beliefs. The ego was the first belief. And when you have faith in the ego, it starts a big bang—a seemingly big bang of time and space—with such an emotion—a totally fictitious projection. It's totally fictitious, and nothing in the realm of belief is real; nothing in the realm of belief is true.

Forgiveness is the only belief that leads you out of all the rest; there's only one belief in the mind that is valuable, that leads you back to eternity. So, if you put your faith in forgiveness, which is the one belief that leads away from all the rest, then that faith in forgiveness, guided by the Holy Spirit, will lead you to eternity.

~♥~

In awakening, the split mind—or the mind that tries to serve two masters—comes up into awareness. This can give the impression of having a *split personality* of love and fear. Divine Love transcends the illusory aspects of the self-concept, or ego-image, which have been made to cover up and replace the real love deep within. The "good" aspects of the mask (or *persona*) are just as illusory as the "fearful" aspects, because illusions are all based on the mistaken belief that God's Love can have an *opposite*. God and Christ are unopposed. Love does not have an enemy or opposition.

Be grateful when the illusion of fear appears to rise into awareness, and don't try to battle, repress, or distract from the fear. See how the fear that had been denied from awareness, the fear that appeared to block the light of Love, is resurfacing in order to be forgiven forever. Look at the fear with the Holy Spirit and see its nothingness. Fear, when perceived correctly, is a call for love. And when this is acknowledged, you are answered in love. Love is knocking at the door of consciousness, asking that all self-imposed barriers to the remembrance of God be released.

Be happy that the awakening is occurring through your willingness and readiness, for nothing more is asked of you. Fear has run out of time and has nowhere to hide. Fear used time to conceal the wish to separate, yet under the Holy Spirit's direction, time is neutralized and used for miracles that collapse time and show its meaninglessness.

~♥~

In your mind, there are thoughts that come from God and thoughts that come from the ego, and all thoughts are endowed with equal power. The separation is giving those ego thoughts the same power that you give to God's thoughts. When you give the power of the ego thoughts as much power as those loving light thoughts of God, that is a split mind. No mind can serve two masters.

You cannot serve both God and mammon—God and money. However, money is just a symbol for the ego; it is not about the money but about the purpose. You cannot serve two purposes and be at peace. That is what "no man can serve two masters" means; you cannot endow all your thoughts with equal meaning when some of them are unreal and some of them are real. When you give equal meaning to all of these thoughts, you are saying, *Part of me is unreal, and part of me is real. Part of me was created by God and part of me was created by man, and I just give equal weight to both.* But that is not God's will. God's will is perfect happiness, so it is an error to attempt to give equal meaning to all apparent thoughts in the mind. It is this weaving, shifting pattern of dark and light that the sleeping mind has become accustomed to; the dark and light weaving is not natural at all.

32. What Does It Mean to Discern between Real and Unreal?

> "For I know the thoughts that I think toward you, saith the LORD, thoughts of peace, and not of evil, to give you an expected end." (Jeremiah 29:11)

The ego split off cause and effect, and then it turned it around so that the world seems to be doing something to you. The sleeping mind believes it's a victim of a world that's outside of itself, not understanding that all of this is made up to keep you from knowing who you really are.

Jesus was a great wayshower because he went through and passed linear time to realize that our reality is Heaven, our reality still is with God, and that right now in this instant there is a present cause that you can know, and that present cause is God. Jesus tells us that God is the only cause. The ego is not a real cause. If you believe in the ego, it will project and generate unreal effects because the ego is an unreal belief; it's a belief in separation. God has nothing to do with separation. But the ego is an unreal cause, and then you perceive a world of unreal effects, and you believe that they are real because in your mind you believe the cause is real. You see how it works? And what Jesus is telling us is that God is the only cause. Cause and effect go together; Christ can never leave the mind of God, and the creations of perfection can never leave their perfect creator.

~♥~

The question of discernment is your life's work, for all of us, to discern between those two voices: One is a death wish;

the other one wants us to remember who we truly are, healed and whole. Because of the ego, it seems like the voice of the Spirit is pushed out. The ego speaks first; the ego speaks louder. That's why we need a lot of discipline, a lot of mind training, a lot of discernment.

~♥~

The simplest, most direct way to discern between the two voices is what Jesus calls *the one right use of judgment*. We are used to thinking of judgment as an entirely negative thing. He says there is one right use of judgment, and that one right use of judgment is the question, "How do I feel?" So that's a good start. How do I feel?

The truth is within us; let's come together with the intention of becoming very clear in our discernment between the ego and the Holy Spirit. This requires looking closely at the mind and how it works. As we allow the Spirit to come among us, questions are asked, answers come, and experiences are shared.

We want to take practical examples from our lives and apply the ideas to them. All spiritual teachings are meant to be applied. We need to live the teachings. If there are parts of our lives that are not congruent with them, then it is helpful for all of us to be aware of those things, so the mind can shift and be a demonstration of the truth. As upsets come up in daily life, they can be traced back through the levels of mind, which are meant to be practical and useful. We must always come back to the awareness that it is our own perception that needs to be healed! Our minds make the decision to heal or not; there is never anything happening in the world of form that causes a change in mind.

A lot of us were trained not to pay attention to our feelings. We became so intellectual, so cognitive, and so into rational thinking of everything that we were divorced from our feelings. And that's the kind of biological family I projected. In all these years, no one in that family ever asked me how I was feeling. I was always told what to do, what not to do, what was right, what was wrong, what to eat, what's moral, what the bad things were, what the good things... A good inroad towards that discernment and intuition is to begin to get in touch with the feelings, and ask, *How am I really feeling about this?*

Now, having said that, I will say that the ego is sneaky, sneaky, sneaky. It is ingenious, and what it does is generate an entire range of emotions and sensations that feel good and are all part of its system. So, when you're asking the basic question, *How does it feel?* It's going to come in there with its best, feel-good disguise of how you authentically feel much deeper. This is because the mind is very deep, and the subconscious mind has these locked-away beliefs that generate a lot of emotions that are pseudo-good but aren't really good.

For example, pleasure and pain. In this world, it seems easy to tell the difference between pleasure and pain... If you knew that every time you seek pleasure, you're seeking pain in a disguised way, you would stop it.

It takes a while to start to raise these deep truths and principles—healing principles—in our mind to the point where we can voluntarily say, *The miracle offers me everything that I want!* Pleasure is fleeting; we all know that. It's temporary; it should tip us off right away because of its fleeting and temporary nature. And pain is temporary as well, although at times it can seem very common.

So that is part of this gradual work with discernment over the years, where if I see something that I desire to bring me pleasure, the Holy Spirit is saying, "Here, I need your attention over here. Remember, you are a miracle worker, and we have got some important miracles to do over here." And nothing is ripped away; I can't say that this has been a journey of sacrifice. I don't feel like, *Oh! I follow the Spirit and now it's just blah! I am totally neutral. I feel nothing.* No! I feel the joy and exuberance of the Spirit from all this following the miracle. But, also, there's been a lot of what I call "whims," lots of beautiful little things that came in along the way, which were just kind of like little signs and symbols, like, *Thank you for following me and thank you for devoting your mind to discernment.*

33. Do All My Distortions Arise from My Attack Thoughts?

> "And he saith unto them, Are ye so without understanding also? Do ye not perceive, that whatsoever thing from without entereth into the man, it cannot defile him; Because it entereth not into his heart, but into the belly, and goeth out into the draught, purging all meats? And he said, That which cometh out of the man, that defileth the man. For from within, out of the heart of men, proceed evil thoughts, adulteries, fornications, murders, Thefts, covetousness, wickedness, deceit, lasciviousness, an evil eye, blasphemy, pride, foolishness: All these evil things come from within, and defile the man." (Mark 7:18-23)

The mind denied all the attack thoughts and tried to push them out of awareness. Then another way the ego counsels is that the way to get rid of attack thoughts is to project them out onto the screen. If you consider what we would call a frightening situation, the form has become a concrete form of fear. There is something in my mind that I cannot accept, look at, or take responsibility for. It really is just a thought that I have or that I made up, and I do not want to look at that, so I keep it buried in the unconscious, and then I project it out, and therefore I see something objectionable in someone else or in some other situation or thing.

~♥~

In the Bible, it is written: "As you sow, so shall you reap." (Galatians 6:7) The way this world is set up, this translates into *whatever the mind thinks, feels, and believes about itself, the world will prove or bring witness to.* The ego-invested mind feels guilty, believing it separated from God, and therefore calls forth scripts and scenes from the world that bear witness to this guilt. Abuse, neglect, victimization, sickness, pain, and suffering are all, therefore, interpretations of the world that are based on the belief that one has separated from God.

A movie projector/theater analogy may be helpful here. In the projector room, inside the projector, is this glowing, brilliant, radiant light. That's a great metaphor for the Holy Spirit. That brilliant light seems to pass through the film, which is filled with a lot of dark images. We'll call those dark images "attack thoughts" or "ego thoughts." As these thoughts are projected, what seems to be produced on the screen are shadows. To the mind watching the movie, these shadows appear to have meaning. However, the only meaning the movie seems to have is given to it by the mind, which has forgotten that what it sees is just a movie. It has identified with figures on the screen and thought of itself as a person among other persons. The world perceived through the body's eyes and heard through the body's ears is also a screen of images. The world is just the shadowy reflection of the attack thoughts in the deceived mind. If one becomes aware of these attack thoughts and is willing to let them be replaced by clear, real thoughts, one is willing to clean the film up, so to speak, and let more light shine through. When this happens, the screen is going to light up more and more. The world will reflect the light in one's mind.

As the mind begins to let go of the ego belief system of separation, it opens up to the Holy Spirit's thought system, which is the memory of God in the deceived mind. This is a thought system that reflects love and offers a completely different interpretation of the world. As the mind embraces the Holy Spirit's thoughts, the world brings forth witnesses to that love. When one accepts the Holy Spirit, the world that was once seen as a place of *kill or be killed*, of violence, competition, and inequality, becomes full of miracles—witnesses of wholeness and completion. Only then is it possible to experience the peace and joy of forgiveness, what Jesus calls "the real world."

> Underneath this heavy, thick layer of attack thoughts, which are all thoughts of the past and the future, are these real thoughts. The Holy Spirit's job is to lead you into changing your mind about your mind—from believing in these attack thoughts to experiencing only thoughts that I think with God.
>
> Jesus says my mind holds only what I think with God. That's where it's all heading. It's swirling quickly down to that. Only the Holy Spirit can make that transition. How's the Holy Spirit going to go from a mind filled with attack thoughts to a mind that holds only thoughts that it thinks with God? It's called guidance. *Go here, go there. Call so and so.* All these thoughts are guidance thoughts, and they're from the Holy Spirit, and

they're loosening the mind from thinking that it knows anything about anything in this world. So, it's like you're unwinding from these attack thoughts, and you're going into these pure thoughts.

While you're asleep and dreaming, your brother and sister will always be a reflection of what's in your mind. Your brother and sister show you the contents of your consciousness. And that's important, because if you don't want to be a victim, you have to start seeing the judgment or attack thought in your own mind. If you don't want to feel at the mercy of a world that's external, you have to start to realize that everyone that you meet, or even think of, is simply a pictorial representation of what you believe you are. If you believe you're human, then you'll see everyone else as human as well. But that's subject to a lot of variation, and it's subject to a lot of judgment, positive-negative, good-bad. It's not true. It doesn't really show you the true essence, the true innocence, or the true joy of God's creation.

So we need reflections to help us be aware of what it is that we're holding on to in consciousness. In fact, Jesus says that you should always feel gratitude for your brother because of this mirroring that's going on. Without your brother and your sister in this world, the opportunity to realize the truth would be quite delayed. But if you allow the Holy Spirit to use relationships for forgiveness, you'll realize that there's only one of us; let's be honest here, we were created as one by God. But to the extent that we believe in the other, we need to forgive that perception. In the Bible, Jesus says, "Take the stranger in." (Psalm 146:9) He's saying take the stranger—the ego belief system—into the light of your heart, and it will disappear. Take the stranger in. It doesn't literally mean you should be inviting people off the street to live in your house. It's basically saying take the stranger, the belief in the ego in your mind, to the light inside of you where the Kingdom of Heaven is, and then the stranger will disappear, and you realize that there is only love. There is only love. There has always only been love. There's nothing but love.

34. What Do All the "Watch" Parables Mean?

"Then shall the kingdom of heaven be likened unto ten virgins, which took their lamps, and went forth to meet the bridegroom. And five of them were wise, and five *were* foolish. They that *were* foolish took their lamps, and took no oil with them: But the wise took oil in their vessels with their lamps. While the bridegroom tarried, they all slumbered and slept. And at midnight there was a cry made, Behold, the bridegroom cometh; go ye out to meet him. Then all those virgins arose, and trimmed their lamps. And the foolish said unto the wise, Give us of your oil; for our lamps are gone out. But the wise answered, saying, *Not* so; lest there be not enough for us and you: but go ye rather to them that sell, and buy for yourselves. And while they went to buy, the bridegroom came; and they that were ready went in with him to the marriage: and the door was shut. Afterward came also the other virgins, saying, Lord, Lord, open to us. But he answered and said, Verily I say unto you, I know you not. Watch therefore, for ye know neither the day nor the hour wherein the Son of man cometh." (Matthew 25:1-13)

"*For the Son of man is* as a man taking a far journey, who left his house, and gave authority to his servants, and to every man his work, and commanded the porter to watch. Watch ye therefore: for ye know not when the master of the

> house cometh, at even, or at midnight, or at the cockcrowing, or in the morning: Lest coming suddenly he find you sleeping. And what I say unto you I say unto all, Watch." (Mark 13:34-37)

> "Let your loins be girded about, and *your* lights burning; And ye yourselves like unto men that wait for their lord, when he will return from the wedding; that when he cometh and knocketh, they may open unto him immediately. Blessed *are* those servants, whom the lord when he cometh shall find watching: verily I say unto you, that he shall gird himself, and make them to sit down to meat, and will come forth and serve them. And if he shall come in the second watch, or come in the third watch, and find *them* so, blessed are those servants. And this know, that if the goodman of the house had known what hour the thief would come, he would have watched, and not have suffered his house to be broken through. Be ye therefore ready also: for the Son of man cometh at an hour when ye think not." (Luke 12:35-40)

> "Then shall ye return, and discern between the righteous and the wicked, between him that serveth God and him that serveth him not." (Malachi 3:18)

The awareness that leads to awakening is forgiveness of illusion. To forgive is simply to see the false as false, and there are no exceptions to this state of mind. It is impossible to achieve partial forgiveness. Forgiveness must be experienced completely to be experienced at all. Truth and illusion have no meeting point. Perfect Love casts out fear, and light abolishes darkness.

The awareness of dreaming is everything. This is absolutely everything. This is the perspective in which there are no problems; there have never been any problems. This is the state of mind that is still and silent. In this state of mind, everything, without exception, is in my own best interest, because this is the point. The point of my best interest is peace, joy, happiness, and love. And this was always the point. This ever shall be the point.

~♥~

The most beautiful thing is the experience of being able to watch the world with such calmness and stillness and a very deep, strong awareness that nothing in the world can be different than it is. There is a perspective in you that is so holy, and this is the Holy Spirit's perspective. That's why it's so important to be intuitive, because the more you practice being intuitive, the more you're merging your mind with this higher perspective, and you can see that there's only one way that you could see that all things are working together for good. Without judgment, all things are equally acceptable, so there's the key!

> Watch your mind as you go through the day, and you just start to notice that the sleeping mind, the egoic mind, wants to be right about something in form—right about how something should work out, right about what is good and

valuable and what's not valuable. The dreams that you think you like can hold you back as much as those in which the fear is present. It is this game of positive-negative, yin and yang. It's this game of trying to strike a balance to hopefully have more good outcomes than bad outcomes in your life. That is what the ego's whole game is; it's trying to separate out the good from the bad, so you can maximize the good and minimize the bad. Except, there are no good and bad things; only the ego's thinking makes it seem so. There aren't any good or bad outcomes. When you're happy and joyful, that's a good outcome. It's a state of mind outcome; it's not physical, it's spiritual. When you connect with the Holy Spirit, you find that the spiritual solution is always the only solution.

The Guide within first leads inward toward an experience, an adventure, and the discovery of the awareness of dreaming. In this state of awareness, it is always apparent that nothing real is happening in the world. The forms seem to shift and change, the dream figures seem to come and go, but the dreamer can no longer be fooled by the fact that appearances have no real meaning. From the point of view that comes from thinking with God, the matrix of the illusion of control has no appeal or charm. Dream softly of a sinless world devoid of judgment. God does not judge, for there is literally nothing to judge between. Forgiveness might be called the acceptance of a wholeness that knows no parts.

Often, spiritual awakening is associated with giving something up. This false association springs from the belief in lack, which was the impossible attempt to deny wholeness. What God creates is forever whole and knows not of lack. There is no need to give up something that never existed. When the desire to be separate has been let go of, it is clear that dreams are not real. Instantaneously, it is evident that wholeness never went anywhere, for it is always so. The willingness to awaken also includes the release of the desire to get out of here, for in the discovery of wholeness, there is neither here nor there. You can't go after something or try to get away from it without "seeming" to prove that something other than wholeness exists. Wholeness transcends all apparent appearances.

If Christ is real, the world is not. Spirit comes not into time or space. Awakening is the recognition that Spirit is real and identity in God is changeless. The body has no meaning because the mind is one and Spirit is one, and there is no gap in what is forever one. The withdrawal of faith from the illusion of meaning projected onto time/body/world, and the awareness of present meaning are apparent as All. I am Spirit. Rejoice in this fact! Thank you, God, for creating all as one in Spirit!

Following the thinking of the Holy Spirit is easy, as there is no desire for something else. Awakening is natural and only seems difficult if appearances are given value. Value no appearances, and the truth instantly leaps into awareness. How simple and obvious is the truth.

35. Distinguish between Our Father's Law of Love and the Make-Believe Laws of the Ego

> "Think not that I am come to destroy the law, or the prophets: I am not come to destroy, but to fulfill." (Matthew 5:17)

We are dealing with double oblivion. When people say, *I don't like society; I don't like all the laws and rules of this world; and I don't like how I have to do certain things all the time; I don't like having to conform,* those are all projections. There's only one law, and that's the law of Love; that's what we were created as: is Love. We're dealing really with one law from God which is the law of Love—that's what we were created in.

And now all these other laws are make-believe laws of time and space that the ego has made up—laws of medicine, laws of economics, laws of disease, laws of hierarchy and striving for ranking; it's a world of competition. It's a world God did not create because there's only the law of Love, which is the light, and it's pushed out of awareness, and it's covered over by this unconscious darkness.

The ego is a false belief, and not only is the whole cosmos that is perceived generated from the ego, but all laws of competition, reciprocity, and economics—that's ego. God didn't create economics, nutrition, exercise, thermodynamics, or all the laws of Newtonian physics. All the laws of this world are part of this mesmerism, and so the mind has fallen asleep and forgotten its reality. And now it believes a bunch of make-believe laws and sees a world that reflects those make-believe laws. So, this is why I am pointing out that all attempts to improve the world, to improve your body, to improve your personal situation, to better your life as a person, all the attempts to make a better self, a more happy self, a more vibrant self, a more loving self, are all still within the realm of the ego. Even attempts to improve yourself as a person or attempts to "make a better illusion," it won't help you escape from this world, because even attempts at personal self-help, and personal betterment are all still egoic attempts.

~♥~

The goal of the curriculum, regardless of the form you choose is, "Know thyself!" There is nothing else. Know thyself as the Christ. That is coming to the truth—coming to the Oneness! So, it's a perceptual problem. The very idea of perceiving through the body's eyes and perceiving a fragmented world is the problem. The problems aren't relationship problems, economic problems, disease, or environmental problems. The problems are not of an interpersonal or personal nature; the problems are not even of a personal psychic nature. The problems are perceptual problems of believing in a world that has no reality or existence, and then having an investment in anything of that cosmic projection. If you believe that you want something from the world, the world will seem to want something from you. When people say, *Well, I have trouble with society and the rules of society. I'm having trouble with my own rules in my own home. I have trouble with the laws and the rituals and the rules of this world*—well, they came from the ego, and as long as you believe in any aspect of the cosmos, you are saying that you want those limitations. These are all limiting laws that have nothing to do with heaven or the laws of love—they are all limitations.

~♥~

Jesus had to come and correct the Scribes and the Pharisees, because they got so much into the letter of the law—*what you can do on the Sabbath and what you can't do.* All these rituals start to take over. And Jesus came to show the spirit of the law, not get caught up in the letter of the law. And basically, the ego thought Jesus was breaking the law, doing things that he shouldn't be doing on Sabbath, and he wasn't keeping all these little rules. Jesus was there to demonstrate the spirit of the law, to fulfill the promise, and to fulfill the commandments. And he was the fulfillment, the living experience, of all these things. The ego was nitpicking and even trying to trap him with laws.

Miracles are always only for the mind of the perceiver or dreamer (the mind is one), and what seems to occur in form is merely symbolic. Miracles are for the mind that has the ears to hear, so to speak, or the willingness and readiness to behold. Seeming changes in form reflect the shift in mind of the miracle-minded, and though some of these changes seem to transcend "known physical laws," in reality there are no "known physical laws." The law of Love (Spirit) is the only reality. Feeding the multitudes and raising the dead were symbols of the divine law of Love which has no limit or lack. It is truly the beatitudes, or state of mind, that demonstrates the miracle has come. It is this state of mind in which consistency is possible, and this is a characteristic of awakening. "Consistent form" is a contradiction in terms, although behavior can seem to become more "stable" for the miracle-minded. The easy way to remember that miracles are not intended to be used as spectacles to induce belief is to remember that miracles are the means of awakening for a mind that already "believes" yet is also willing to go beyond belief and to be still and remember God.

> “Let every soul be subject unto the higher powers. For there is no power but of God: the powers that be are ordained of God.” (Romans 13:1)

Heaven is Love. There is no other love than God's Love; there are no different types of love. There is only one love, and that is God's Love, and when you begin to pull your devotion, efforts, and pursuits away from ego goals, you will be giving your mind's energy to the Holy Spirit, and you will devote yourself to God, to peace, joy, and happiness. As you withdraw the ego's false pursuits, the ego begins to fade away; it needs something to hide behind—a world of false pursuits to hide behind. As you begin to devote yourself to God, the mask of the ego, which is a death wish, begins to peel away.

Suffering comes from being devoted to a death wish. That's what reason would tell you: follow a death wish and suffer, or follow the present moment, the Holy Spirit, and Jesus and awaken to eternal life. Those are basically the only two options, and really only one is a real option; the other one is a facade of an option.

Today is the golden opportunity to choose to be God dependent—to choose to listen to the Holy Spirit and be guided—not in some things, but in all things without exception. This is where we make the shift from vigilance to peace, where we shift from perceiving two worlds—from believing in two thought systems, one of love and one of fear. We take a stand in the mind. We devote ourselves so wholly and completely to right-mindedness and following the Holy Spirit, that we experience a state of complete invulnerability and complete wholeness. The peaceful perception of the entire cosmos in this instant; everything from this instant, without exception.

And our mind shifts into a natural state of rest without the need to be vigilant against the ego and for God. We rest in the certainty of a single unified purpose, one clear intent that guides us, that sustains us. This is a very practical application of experiencing the Love of God.

We do not attempt to manage the world. We do not attempt to understand linear time or figure out the laws of the world. We are sustained by the Love of God. Every breath is a symbol used by the Holy Spirit, as is every piece of food eaten by a body and every place where the body can lay itself down at night. Every form of help that seems to come from many different directions in this world—all can be summed up in the very simple idea: "I am sustained by the Love of God." This idea frees the mind of concerns about work, about debt, about survival. The acceptance of this idea, wholly and truly, frees the mind in an instant. It is handing over all the symbols of the world to the Holy Spirit.

Money does not mean anything. Food does not mean anything. Travel does not mean anything. Nothing in form means anything in and of itself. It is all a beautiful backdrop for witnessing perfect safety, perfect security, perfect love, perfect certainty. That is the only purpose that the symbols serve. There is no dependency on the symbols. The symbols only represent the purpose in the mind when the purpose is to forgive and open to divine Love. Divine Providence is the law of God, the law of Love. Everything is provided easily and naturally, without exception.

The Holy Spirit will provide everything you need and will renew it as long as you have need of it, but the Holy Spirit will not have you linger in time. That is not God's will for you; that is not your holy will. The Holy Son of God is not meant to linger in time but to reside in eternity. I Amness, truth, holiness, and perfect innocence; today we remember this and give thanks.

36. Speak on the Topics of Money and Possessions

"And he spake a parable unto them, saying, The ground of a certain rich man brought forth plentifully: And he thought within himself, saying, What shall I do, because I have no room where to bestow my fruits? And he said, This will I do: I will pull down my barns, and build greater; and there will I bestow all my fruits and my goods. And I will say to my soul, Soul, thou hast much goods laid up for many years; take thine ease, eat, drink, *and* be merry. But God said unto him, Thou fool, this night thy soul shall be required of thee: then whose shall those things be, which thou hast provided? So *is* he that layeth up treasure for himself, and is not rich toward God." (Luke 12:16-21)

"For the sun is no sooner risen with a burning heat, but it withereth the grass, and the flower thereof falleth, and the grace of the fashion of it perisheth: so also shall the rich man fade away in his ways." (James 1:11)

"Jesus said unto him, If thou wilt be perfect, go *and* sell that thou hast, and give to the poor, and thou shalt have treasure in heaven: and come *and* follow me. But when the young man heard that saying, he went away sorrowful: for he had great possessions. Then said Jesus unto his disciples, Verily I say unto you, That a rich man shall hardly enter into the kingdom of heaven. And again I say

> unto you, It is easier for a camel to go through the eye of a needle, than for a rich man to enter into the kingdom of God." (Matthew 19:21-24)

The thing about wealth in the Bible is where it says, "It is easier for a camel to go through a needle's eye than for a rich man to enter into the kingdom of God." (Luke 18:25) It was saying there is nothing wrong with money. It's not to judge the money or the accumulation of money; it's the identification. It's all about possession. Love does not possess. It is the possession part—the belief in the parts and the belief in the possession of the parts—that block the awareness of Love's presence.

~♥~

In truth, what you have is what you are, because what you are comes from Source. You have a Source, and anything in this world that is used to deny that Source is self-deception. It is playing little; it is playing small. It is identifying with personality instead of the vastness of beingness.

~♥~

The state of mind, or how one feels, is the outcome of which thought system one is aligned with: God or ego. Money is nothing, though if a mind believes in ego (belief in lack of or reciprocity), money is endowed with false value. The belief in lack or reciprocity is the belief in substitution, for the ego is the chosen substitute for the Source, for God. The reason money seems valuable is because it seems to be highly exchangeable for many "things" that meet illusory needs, whether they seem emotional, physical, or spiritual. Like medicine, money is like a magic spell in the world that seems to make illusory problems disappear for a while. Yet until the ego has been released entirely, the mind perceives needs and uses external means (false sources) to meet the perceived needs.

The construct is a construct of lack. To deny your selfhood as the Christ, and instead accept a false self that has been made up, is to accept the belief in lack.

It all comes down to this: one must accept one´s self as changeless Divine Mind. The only step to this is realizing that the world cannot change, for it is an unreal effect of an unreal cause. The world *cannot* change. Asking for things to be different than they are, is an impossible request. Money, like all effects (images of the ego), is never a source. The meaningful request is a request to see the world differently—as an unreal effect of an unreal cause—and to thus accept the fact that there is only one Source. God is the *only* Source.

> "Lay not up for yourselves treasures upon earth, where moth and rust doth corrupt, and where thieves break through and steal: But lay up for yourselves treasures in heaven, where neither moth nor rust doth corrupt, and where thieves do not break through nor steal: For where your treasure is, there will your heart be also." (Matthew 6:19-21)

> "Again, the kingdom of heaven is like unto treasure hid in a field; the which when a man hath found, he hideth, and for joy thereof goeth and selleth all that he hath, and buyeth that field. Again, the kingdom of heaven is like unto a

merchant man, seeking goodly pearls: Who, when he had found one pearl of great price, went and sold all that he had, and bought it." (Matthew 13:44-46)

"For the love of money is the root of all evil." (1 Timothy 6:10)

There is one construct that is valuable, and that is forgiveness. Forgiveness is the construct of stepping back, back, back to the point where you can see it all as a construct, until you have stepped back so far that you only have the purpose of healing and wholeness in the mind. All of the judgment and valuing, all of the ordering of the thought-forms are gone; there is no hierarchy among them. There is no meaning read into them, and no associations are made. In one metaphor, there is a blanket that covers all thought-forms; the cosmos is seen as a single fabric with no particular threads singled out as more or less valuable. Forgiveness is a meaning in the mind that is given to everything in form. It is still a construct in the sense that it is perceptual. Forgiveness is the one helpful construct—the one all-inclusive construct—where there is no ordering among the thought-forms.

I would read about the saints and the mystics, poverty, chastity, and obedience. I would say, "What does poverty really mean?" Jesus said, "Poverty is ego thinking." It has nothing to do with the forms. Don't try to define your abundance and deprivation in terms of form. Just know that ego thinking is poverty. When you take a vow of poverty, you are taking a vow of dis-identification with attachments and possessions.

When our life is about commerce—buying and selling, saving money, investing money—we have gone way off the track, because there are none of these things in Heaven. And our stress levels get higher if we get worried and concerned about things that mean nothing to God.

We think about someone like St. Francis, who lived in Europe around the twelfth century. Why do people relate to St. Francis? Why are they so drawn to St. Francis? Because he had the same temptations that all of us have, but he lived a very simple and devoted life. He came from a very wealthy family, just like Siddhartha came from a very wealthy family. Siddhartha lived in a palace, and St. Francis lived in a big, beautiful house in Assisi, Italy. But neither St. Francis nor Siddhartha were fulfilled in their lives in the world. Siddhartha did not really want to be the king. Many people in this world would want to be the king or queen. But I think he knew there was much more than that. And St. Francis' father was a trader; he bought and sold many items, including clothing, fine silks, and fine fabrics. And his father was willing to give him the whole business, but St. Francis did not want it. He would rather go out with the flowers, bees, and butterflies. He would rather loaf with his life and just be—stay out with the birds and the butterflies. And really, in our hearts, we want to feel peaceful.

I used to believe that poverty was tied to material conditions. Jesus taught me that poverty was the same as ego thinking. There are many people who have great material wealth but truly live in poverty because of a sense of lack and ego thinking. To the ego, there is never enough. This helped me realize that poverty was a state of mind. In trusting in the Holy Spirit, everything I seem to need to share the message is provided effortlessly. Going to Argentina is a good example of this. Frequent-flier miles were donated for the plane tickets so we could go. We use donated money for taxi fares and for food. It is the Holy Spirit's money and resources. It is the Holy Spirit's plan. We do not consider which countries are rich and which are poor. In the Holy Spirit's plan, we listen and follow, and it is always a gift to ourselves.

Jesus started to break down the Protestant work ethic I'd been taught and helped me become more open to Divine Providence. You must be very humble to accept sustenance from God. That was my biggest difficulty in my early travels: letting go of pride and the belief that I was personally responsible for my survival on this planet. At first, this was hard to believe; all my training had taught me the opposite. I had lived a life of competition, competing in sports, competing for grades, competing for jobs. Jesus said to me that the messenger is worthy of his keep. "If you will let me speak words through you and bring hope and cheer to your brothers and sisters, I will take care of all the details of your life." He has kept his word. Everything I seem to need is provided for me, with no effort on my part.

37. What Thought Need I Give to My Earthly Needs?

> "Therefore I say unto you, Take no thought for your life, what ye shall eat, or what ye shall drink; nor yet for your body, what ye shall put on. Is not the life more than meat, and the body than raiment? Behold the fowls of the air: for they sow not, neither do they reap, nor gather into barns; yet your heavenly Father feedeth them. Are ye not much better than they? Which of you by taking thought can add one cubit unto his stature? And why take ye thought for raiment? Consider the lilies of the field, how they grow; they toil not, neither do they spin: And yet I say unto you, That even Solomon in all his glory was not arrayed like one of these. Wherefore, if God so clothe the grass of the field, which to day is, and to morrow is cast into the oven, *shall he* not much more *clothe* you, O ye of little faith? Therefore take no thought, saying, What shall we eat? or, What shall we drink? or, Wherewithal shall we be clothed?" (Matthew 6:25-31)

> "But seek ye first the kingdom of God, and his righteousness; and all these things shall be added unto you." (Matthew 6:33)

Let's bring it back to the practical. When we think about the world and when we think of ourselves as persons in the world, it seems that we have needs on different levels. We can talk about the mental level; we can talk about the emotional level. Maslow's hierarchy of needs talks about the basic levels of needs—food, clothing, warmth, sex, etc. He also talked about self-actualization needs and reaching your full potential. To be more specific, what if we talked about things that we were really interested in and believed in? Some people might talk about environmental issues; others might talk about eradicating AIDS. Other people may have interpersonal problems in their minds, problems with their husband or daughter, or it may be financial needs, chronic conditions, sickness, or disease. There are so many different topics.

It seems like saving the dolphins, fighting cancer, and having an interpersonal relationship with your mother are different things. This is the illusion of levels of need. It seems like every day you have to deal with problems, interpersonal problems, survival, and so on and so forth. But you only have one problem, and there is only one solution to that problem. Isn't it nice to think it's so simple? If there is such a thing as truth, it will be simple—one problem and one solution. If I perceive the problem to be in the world, it cannot be solved. Because the Holy Spirit is the one answer to that one problem, and the Holy Spirit is in the mind. God did not place the answer where the problem was not. He did not place the answer on the screen. He did not place the answer in the world; he placed the answer in the mind of the sleeping Son. And that is where the Holy Spirit is.

~♥~

Do not look to anything in the world to sustain your life, for all needs are met only by following the Holy Spirit. The structures of the world that seem to offer support will fade, grow dim, and disappear from awareness as light dawns in the mind.

~♥~

There's nothing, there's no person, place, or thing that can interrupt your connection with the one inside that's there to awaken you. So that's why Jesus said, "Be not concerned with the things of this world; be not concerned with what you shall wear or what you shall eat; take no thought for tomorrow. Seek first the Kingdom of Heaven and all else will be added unto you," because it's a direct connection.

> Jesus began with practical instructions 2,000 years ago. His teachings were greeted with much resistance, as if they were impractical. He said things like, *Take no thought for what you should wear and what you should eat.* In terms of vocation, he simply said, "Follow me." (Matthew 9:9) It did not matter if they were tax collectors or fishermen. It did not matter if they were single or married. He just looked into their eyes and said two words: "Follow me." For a young, wealthy businessman, he said: "Sell all that thou hast, and distribute unto the poor, and thou shalt have treasure in heaven; and come, follow me." (Luke 18:22) When a man protested that his father had just died, Jesus said, "Let the dead bury the dead." (Matthew 8:22) There was not even an allowance for a period of grieving because Jesus was the "way, the truth, and the life", and had

nothing but good news to share, nothing to grieve about.

After I left the university, I realized that if I opened up and became dependent on the Spirit, that would be the answer to all my problems, and that spiritual dependency would be a good form of financial dependency. Jesus is always teaching, "Consider the lilies of the field, how they grow; they toil not, nor do they spin," (Matthew 6:28) and "Take no thought for what you should wear and eat." "Seek ye first the Kingdom of Heaven and all things else will be added unto you." The lilies certainly did not fight or compete, and Jesus said, "Look how our heavenly Father has clothed them." The message of Jesus has not changed, not in 2,000 years, and it never will.

For myself, I had to realize that in order to serve God completely, I would have to learn how to trust. There is no way I could even attempt to live his message without taking a leap of trust.

With my spiritual journey, I've found that everything I need to fulfill my function comes very effortlessly and very easily. I've never been into vision-boarding or trying to visualize goals for the future. It's been more like, *Okay, tell me what You want of me, where You want me to do Your work, and I'll gladly do it.* Things have come very easily.

38. Are There Plans I Need Make to Follow You?

> "Take therefore no thought for the morrow: for the morrow shall take thought for the things of itself." (Matthew 6:34)

> "And as ye go, preach, saying, The kingdom of heaven is at hand. Heal the sick, cleanse the lepers, raise the dead, cast out devils: freely ye have received, freely give. Provide neither gold, nor silver, nor brass in your purses, Nor scrip for *your* journey, neither two coats, neither shoes, nor yet staves: for the workman is worthy of his meat. And into whatsoever city or town ye shall enter, inquire who in it is worthy; and there abide till ye go thence." (Matthew 10:7-11)

Jesus was telling us to let go of the past, take no thought for tomorrow, and trust me right now. He will provide all the guidance you need now. Let's look at it from a different angle: Suppose you've got this powerful voice and force in your mind—we'll call it a commitment—you have the power to commit. And Jesus is saying to take that entire power of your mind and put it all on forgiveness. When anybody says, *What about this and this?* Remember forgiveness, salvation, resurrection, light, love, and joy. This is it! Focus all your mind's energy, like a laser beam, on this.

~♥~

The sole purpose of this world is to let the Holy Spirit use the symbols to wake you up from this dream. The Holy Spirit sees the world as a learning device to bring you home.

~♥~

Jesus Christ is the master teacher. Ultimately, he's the master professor because he is demonstrating what he's teaching; he is in the state of mind that he is pointing towards. Just radiating a state of mind and giving you practical guidance too.

Jesus is calling us to strengthen the ideas by giving them away. There is no loss involved in sharing true ideas, and that is why everyone's given a teaching function—to share true ideas—and really, it's not you who do it. You could just speak from your heart. That's the beginning stage of learning to clear away the darkness and let those true ideas pour through you and be strengthened in your awareness. Now, that is generosity! If Jesus tells me that the only function the body has is to let the voice of God speak through it, I'm going to take that very sincerely.

It gives you an opportunity to just let the love flow through you in an involuntary way. Jesus will go before you and tell you which miracles to perform.

> "Humble yourselves therefore under the mighty hand of God, that he may exalt you in due time: Casting all your care upon him; for he careth for you." (1 Peter 5:6-7)

> "Behold, I send you forth as sheep in the midst of wolves: be ye therefore wise as serpents, and harmless as doves." (Matthew 10:16)

You are being called. Everyone is called. The ego's voice and goals can seem to crowd out the Holy Spirit's voice in this world. And while everyone is called, few seem to listen and answer. To answer is simply to be happy, for God's Will is for perfect happiness. The time-space cosmos was made as a mechanism to avoid the perfect happiness of the Kingdom of Heaven. But there can only be happiness in answering the call.

Trust in the Holy Spirit is the key to awakening. You will become increasingly aware of your lack of problems as you learn to trust the Holy Spirit. A simple life of listening, trusting, and following will extend the forgiveness lesson throughout your entire perception. Trust would settle every problem right now. A simple life of trust will yield immediate results in terms of peace of mind.

Salvation is not for sale. Enlightenment is not for sale. Those who truly give freely offer what they have received from the Holy Spirit. Rituals fade as the mind surrenders to divine spontaneity. True giving dissolves the desire to get. Travel can be a symbol of the willingness to share and flow, to accept and not expect. What shows up is perfect, in that it is orchestrated and provided by One who knows your best interests in every seeming situation.

In healed perception, everything is for the best. Surrendering means giving up one's personal perspective in favor of the flow of Spirit—Oneness. Do not try to activate the past, organize the present, or plan the future if you want to trust. If there are plans to be made, your inner wisdom will inform you of them, and they will be for the benefit of all. In one gentle perspective, the miracle meets every perceived need and leaves a blessing for all. We walk together every step of the way. We cannot fail in a plan destined to awaken all in Oneness and Love. Take my hand and we shall skip along singing and rejoicing as we go; for we but seem to travel in happy dreams of forgiveness, all the while safe at home in God.

Jesus has said to take no thought for tomorrow. And I said, *Wait a minute, and this is the master speaking!* I'm willing to let go of 18 years of education if the master—the one who's awakened from time and space—is telling me something. I'll listen to the master, even though of course my parents, friends, and family have all said, *You are nuts. David, that worked for Jesus, but it's not going to work for you.* That was a rare experience; he got away with it 2,000 years ago.

I can talk for months and years about letting present trust lead the way. It's only by opening to the present trust that we are able to really tune in and hear and follow what the guidance is. Remember, the guidance is to unwind you from the belief in linear time. That is what Jesus means by *the Kingdom of Heaven is at hand*; it takes you to an experience of the present moment, and it's very convincing when things start to happen and things start to show up in an involuntary way. Your prayer is just saying, I want to allow myself the permission to be shown that I can live a very happy, fulfilled life, moment by moment, without planning for the future.

Goals and ambitions seem useful in the real world, but if they are about the future and what will happen there, I can tell you that they are ego motivations. Present peace is a "goal" worth desiring, for it is more than possible; it is inevitable. The experience of present peace results from listening only to the Spirit within, and to the Spirit, there is no tomorrow. The Holy Spirit uses time to teach that there is no time. This is the purpose that inspires, blesses, and even seems to motivate action until the realization dawns that nothing is really happening. The happy dream is like a lucid dream, in which the dreamer is aware of dreaming. Dreams are not taken to be reality, and sleep is not taken to be wakefulness.

If you feel like you are driven to "do things," ask yourself if there is a fear of consequences. If you believe that not "do things" will result in fearful consequences, then it is wise to examine what is believed. As long as fearful beliefs are held to be true, thoughts and actions will be fear-driven. Forgiveness is a miracle, and it releases the mind from fear of consequences. Let the Holy Spirit be the purpose that gently guides, and you will never feel "driven" again! Value not one belief the ego sponsors and enjoy the experience of divine ease. Not one seeming difficulty but will melt away before you reach it.

39. How Will I Know What Words to Speak?

> "Take no thought how or what ye shall speak: for it shall be given you in that same hour what ye shall speak. For it is not ye that speak, but the Spirit of your Father which speaketh in you." (Matthew 10:19-20)

I find that the Spirit and the presence of God are what give you the strength and the guidance to do the most helpful and appropriate thing in any given instance. It's not trying to figure out what's appropriate. It's a lot of work to figure out what's appropriate in form. Looking back at the past and all past learning and trying to judge what's appropriate, what to say, and what to do takes a lot of work.

When you put the purpose out front to forgive, it is like you're handing over all attention, concern, and worry about outcomes in the world to the Spirit and the presence of God.

~♥~

Holy Communion is being in alignment and letting the Spirit guide, and that means giving over the concern for the form and saying, *if there's a word I need to speak, you give it to me; if there's somebody I need to meet, I'm happy, you tell me how to meet them or you bring them to me. If I'm supposed to travel somewhere, then let's do it; you be you in charge.*

~♥~

Jesus was able to come and speak the Word because he had transcended the ego system. There was nothing threatening to him—not the Pharisees or any of the different groups that would come to claim blasphemy. *How dare you forgive people's sins? No one but the Father can do that.* Jesus was able to remain above the battlefield because of his certainty of who he was. If you remove all falsity and false beliefs, you will have that certainty too.

> "They are of those that rebel against the light; they know not the ways thereof, nor abide in the paths thereof." (Job 24:13)

> "Show me thy ways, O LORD; teach me thy paths." (Psalms 25:4)

> "Trust in the LORD with all thine heart; and lean not unto thine own understanding. In all thy ways acknowledge him, and he shall direct thy paths." (Proverbs 3:5-6)

The point of our forgiveness journey is to feel the connection and feel the love—to not try to separate, to not get into tit for tat over beliefs or theology. If Jesus says that there's only one belief that takes us back to heaven and that belief is forgiveness, I'm interested in joining in the experience of that belief. And, the way that I do that is I pray before my encounters and Jesus just gives me the words to use. But it's all unintentional. I just have a heartfelt desire to join with everyone; I have no enemies. I'm here to connect with everyone—everyone I meet and everyone I think about in my mind. I'm here to connect. The only reason I think about people is to connect with them in a true, deep equality and love. We are here to put into practice what has been given to us. By really giving our hearts over in a very devoted way, we go into an experience of that direct connection with God.

You're a perfect, holy, innocent child of God, and the only place you're happy is in your natural environment, which is Spirit, which is eternity! If you want to find eternal happiness, happiness that lasts, you must go to the environment where happiness exists. Christ is our Identity in the Kingdom of Heaven, and the Kingdom of Heaven is within us. Christ has not left Heaven's Kingdom. Jesus is saying that what you perceive as your daily life is an illusion made up of beliefs and thoughts in your mind, and that you must bring those beliefs and thoughts to the light within for them to vanish. However, do not attempt to bring light into the projection. This is a world of projection, and Jesus tells us that projection is the attempt to get rid of something you do not want. You finally get to the point where you say, *I don't want the ego*—and then you don't project the ego; you forgive it and reel in the projections. Of course, you'll be tempted to get upset with others. You'll be tempted to be upset by temperatures, noises, sounds, animals, and pets. You'll be tempted many times to be upset by something on the world's screen. You'll be tempted to be upset by the images. The ego is always saying, *Something is wrong with this picture;* it's always pointing to the picture.

When you realize Jesus is showing you that *you are never upset for the reason you think*, and that you *can be hurt by nothing but your own thoughts*, you will begin to bring your attention back to your mind, which is exactly where it needs to be. Not on the people, the situations, the things, or the political issues. *No,* Jesus is telling you that *you need to withdraw the projections and bring them back to the mind.* He says that in order to forgive, you must first recognize that these are all thoughts and beliefs in your mind; you will not be able to let them go as long as you see them as something outside of you. As long as you see yourself as a person with all these things going wrong inside of the body and outside of the body, you're at the mercy of the ego; you've bought the ego's belief system hook line and sinker, and you're sinking. You're captive to the ego if you believe in the projection, but to the extent that you can withdraw the projection and just pay attention to your thoughts, feelings, and beliefs, you're bringing it back to your mind.

~♥~

We are so accustomed to perceiving a world in which all of the characters, places, and faces appear to be witnessing that the dream is real. Jesus is saying that, *The mind that is dreaming has forgotten that it is dreaming*. And now it's playing a character, and it's perceiving everything around it in a problematic way. It sees political and economic problems, racial and gender issues, and all types of diseases and threats. It sees everything as if it were a real problem, but it refuses to acknowledge that it is a perceptual problem. And Jesus and the Holy Spirit will wait until you do.

As soon as you're willing to admit that you have a perceptual problem, your life is going to get very interesting. You're going to have the most amazing adventure with the Holy Spirit. Once you get out of the driver's seat and admit that you have a perceptual problem, then you're going to let the Holy Spirit and Jesus show you the correction. But if you want to be correct about all of these relationship, economic, and political issues; all of these things that are a part of earthly life require you to simply say, *Oh my gosh, I have a perceptual problem.* That is the issue. *And, if I want it, the solution is within my mind*. I can see with the Holy Spirit and Jesus and put an end to the war for good. Jesus says, *The war against yourself is almost over.*" Isn't that beautiful? The battle with yourself is nearly over. You are the Christ. But you forgot who you are, and now you appear to be at odds with yourself. However, you are not at war, because your reality is reflected in your right mind, which is where the Holy Spirit is. And the wrong mind is not and was never you. You've never been the ego. You may have thought it was you, but it wasn't.

God's mind does not change. You are, without a doubt, the Christ. God created everything. That is not going to change. So now I have the option of changing my mind and accepting my divinity. The belief in abandonment and rejection is a major ego defense against the truth. It's one thing to talk about it, but when it comes down to actually taking the steps in your life that are guided and inspired that will liberate your mind from ego tyranny; that's when the real celebration begins. Not because you memorized some passages from a book, or because you became a theologian or a philosopher, but because you have said to yourself, *Oh my gosh, I've been mistaken about so much, and I'm willing to change my mind.* That's how you let go of the fear of abandonment and rejection.

So it's all about the living experience. Words on a page are just a starting point, but the experiences we have prove the words are true. The only way we know the words come from the Holy Spirit is that when we practice the principles, we become happy. Then, once you're overjoyed that your time with the book is up, your attitude becomes the teacher. You don't even have to worry about saying the right words, because miracles are involuntary and the Spirit will speak them through you.

It's wonderful not to have to worry about words. Despite the fact that I've been speaking a lot of words for many years, I was recently invited to a silent retreat where they told me, "You don't have to say anything, just show up." They said, "At the end of your name, we will put nothing, no contact information, no biography, no description." And I thought, *Oh, I like that.* So this is where the Holy Spirit is leading me, and before long we become anonymous before God as the little me fades away. You may reach a point where they call you by name and you do not respond; you may forget your name. This happens occasionally, but you simply feel this love in your heart. There is no need to maintain anything, and there is no point in attempting to keep anything up to date when the present moment is always up to date and very simple.

> There is nothing, not even words, in that pure beingness. All I wanted to do was say to Jesus, "You guide my words, you guide my interactions, you guide everything; it's all yours," and that's why I am not advocating a particular form. I could not advocate for form when the parable of David has been filled with so many different forms.

Jesus said pray, ask your question. If that's my prayer—to be shown, to be guided, to be led—it's going to come from everywhere, and so for me, that's the purpose. And the purpose is consistent with the prayer of the heart. I'm more interested in all of us praying together, and not just praying together with words but being on the same channel. Being all tuned in to the same purpose makes it like a dance; that's what communion is.

If you start to trust and you start to flow and let the Spirit orchestrate things, then you start to realize that everything in this world is a backdrop. All one has to have is the willingness, and the Holy Spirit will undo the false self-concepts and replace them with forgiveness. Start with this prayer: "Abide with me, Holy Spirit. Guide me in what to say and do and where to go." If you welcome and trust Him, you will experience immediate results.

40. Speak on Trust

"What time I am afraid, I will trust in thee. In God I will praise his word, in God I have put my trust; I will not fear what flesh can do unto me." (Psalms 56:3-4)

"The God of my rock; in him will I trust: *he is* my shield, and the horn of my salvation, my high tower, and my refuge, my saviour; thou savest me from violence." (2 Samuel 22:3)

"And they that know thy name will put their trust in thee: for thou, LORD, hast not forsaken them that seek thee." (Psalms 9:10)

"How excellent *is* thy lovingkindness, O God! therefore the children of men put their trust under the shadow of thy wings." (Psalms 36:7)

"Blessed *is* that man that maketh the LORD his trust, and respecteth not the proud, nor such as turn aside to lies." (Psalms 40:4)

"Trust in him at all times; ye people, pour out your heart before him: God *is* a refuge for us."

"But *it is* good for me to draw near to God: I have put my trust in the Lord GOD, that I may declare all thy works." (Psalms 73:28)

"And such trust have we through Christ to God-ward." (2 Corinthians 3:4)

Trust in the Holy Spirit is the key to awakening. To the extent you are able to trust the Holy Spirit, you will be increasingly aware that you have no problems. A simple life of listening, trusting, and following will transfer the lesson of forgiveness to your entire perception.

A simple life of trust will yield immediate results in terms of peace of mind. If you would trust, do not attempt to bring up the past or plan and organize the present or the future. If there are plans to be made, you will be told of them by your inner wisdom, and they will be for the benefit of everyone. The miracle meets every perceived need in one gentle way and leaves a blessing for all.

~♥~

You can trust the Spirit within. The ego has no sense of trust in anything, and it is the ego that doubts and judges and strives to stay alive and well as a "body." You are not the ego. The Spirit within is always alive and doesn't need anything to keep it that way. Relax and be still, and allow your awareness to sink below the fear of illness and restrictions of any kind. There is a state within that offers peace and rest.

Trust in the Holy Spirit will continue to grow. No one can accept forgiveness without trust. Trust is the basis on which miracles are founded. Trust is the way to open the mind and release false concepts and idols. Future planning can be laid aside, for present trust directs the way. Confidence and surety come with trust, and this is how you become aware that you are truly a miracle worker. Time is in your hands, so to speak, as you trust the Holy Spirit. Aligned with the Holy Spirit, you no longer have an enemy to "overcome." For the light has come!

Trusting the Holy Spirit is not determined by the situation in which a mind believes itself. Whatever the apparent situation, Help is available and accessible. The willingness to open up to the guidance of the Holy Spirit is not limited by circumstances. If there appear to be earthly responsibilities and commitments that have been made, they will be handled with the compassion and love of the Holy Spirit's plan of forgiveness. This cannot be understood from a personal perspective, but be assured that all things work together for good. There are no exceptions, for under the Holy Spirit's teaching, everyone must gain. There can be no loss.

A general rule of guidance can be stated this way: pray, listen to, and follow the Holy Spirit. Do just what you are given to do and be open to the solution of the stillness within. Question and bring to the light all beliefs and thoughts that obscure the light from awareness. Bring the illusion to the truth. Be willing to change your mind and accept yourself as having a changeless mind. And do not be concerned with the form in which the lesson of forgiveness appears to come.

Trust is the key. Don't try to "figure out" what cannot be understood, such as ego dynamics, as the ego enjoys studying itself. Simply desire the experience of God, let the Holy Spirit be the "how," show up moment by moment with nothing but willingness, and watch the "accelerated" undoing of what never was. Old ways of thinking will keep coming up until the belief at the core of the system is changed. Be aware, keep an eye on your mind by noticing your thoughts as objectively as possible, and be willing to question the programming that lies just below the surface of your consciousness. The choice of interpretation or judgment is best consciously given over to the Holy Spirit. The Holy Spirit will guide you specifically if you are willing. You need not use ego judgments of the past to tell you what kind of "listener" you are. Present trust will light your path now.

41. What If I Cannot Do What You Ask?

> "Then came the disciples to Jesus apart, and said, Why could not we cast him out? And Jesus said unto them, Because of your unbelief: for verily I say unto you, If ye have faith as a grain of mustard seed, ye shall say unto this mountain, Remove hence to yonder place; and it shall remove; and nothing shall be impossible unto you." (Matthew 17:19-20)

It doesn't matter the form of things, but this calling to wake up to God is there and will not go away. That is the mustard seed that Jesus refers to, and the Holy Spirit places it on our hearts. It's a very tiny seed, but it can grow and grow, far beyond its tiny size. That's like a little mustard seed of faith, that we would find our way back home to Eternity. Faith that we would come to know our creator, faith that we would come to know ourselves spiritually as we really are. It's the faith of self-realization.

When you hear an inner calling and you feel called to follow the Spirit, it is important in the sense that you're accepting a correction for everyone, not just for your little personality-self. There aren't any personal saviors. You simply have to go into your mind and see if there is any splinter or fragment of doubt, guilt, or fear there, and simply say, *I'm worth more than this. I'm worth everything. My peace of mind and everyone else's peace of mind are worth more than this scrap, this tiny little scrap, this little seed of guilt.*

~♥~

Your mind is not at the mercy of the world. It is limited only by ego thoughts. As you release the ego thoughts, your mind is free and limitless. Jesus demonstrated this 2,000 years ago—calming the seas and saying things like, *If you have faith like a grain of mustard seed, you can move mountains.* Nothing is by accident. Nothing is random. The mind calls forth witnesses to what it believes. We are questioning the beliefs to be free. It is very empowering; you are no longer at the mercy of the world. You see that you are not a small human being in a vast world. You see that the world is in your mind. It is a reflection of your thoughts. As you change your mind, the world you see changes as well. As within, so without. And enlightenment shows there is no within or without; there's only one mind! One mind cannot be split, even into the inner and outer. In God's Love, all are one.

~♥~

Jesus was a follower of the Holy Spirit; he was a devoted follower, and that is what allowed him to accept the atonement for himself. And then, when he accepted the Atonement, Jesus became the leader of the plan of Atonement. He is the first one to accept his part perfectly, and therefore, he is in charge of it; that's the wording, in charge of. And any kind of embarrassment or a little resistance to Jesus is quite common, but he is the one in charge. He is the one, you might say, who orchestrates time and space. He says I will go before you, and if you will be a miracle worker for me, I will arrange time and space for you. That is quite amazing; it means that you don't have to hold on to these personal ideas of "I have to do this." So, if you have already given your consent and Jesus is saying you are ready now, He is the one in charge.

"Hast thou faith? have it to thyself before God. Happy is he that condemneth not himself in that thing which he alloweth." (Romans 14:22)

By opening the heart and being willing to trust, we learn to let go of the past and release the *source* of all hurt, anger, and blame. Forgiveness equals guiltlessness. We finally open our eyes and ears to hear the soft Voice of Love. The Holy Spirit tells us again and again, *It's not your fault. What you think you did wrong never happened.* Error has no basis and can't be true, since only the truth is true.

This very moment is a sparkling, clean, clear, and fresh rebirth, reminding us of our eternal innocence. The descent into fear that seemed to occur was just a dream, a belief in the impossible. Only the ego, which is an unconscious false belief, sought to put a limit on the beautiful, magnificent inner being that wants to shine brighter and brighter. When the mind is ready and willing, it can see the inner beauty of the divine Mind. This is because being aware of love has nothing to do with time. When all the idols are taken off the altar of the mind and desire becomes singular, all that is left is Love extending Love.

~♥~

The Holy Spirit is here to help us completely forget about problems. The plan of salvation is for us to get to a place in our minds where we are so close to divine innocence, divine connection, and divine love that we no longer see problems. If the Holy Spirit looks at everything and everyone and sees Himself, then what is seen can only be love. That must mean that everything and everyone should be seen through the lens of forgiveness; until in the end, we recognize ourselves as the one Christ, an idea in God's Mind. This is very different from how we usually solve problems, where we are asked to identify the problem so we can find the solution.

~♥~

Jesus says that the ego made people. *The ego peopled the world.* People is a verb for him, not a noun. So, what he's saying is, *You need to come back with me and line up with me in the truth of your mind's light.* Then you'll realize that the world was just a mistake. It wasn't linear at all. It wasn't separated at all. The Holy Spirit corrected it. And once you had the correction, that was it. Game over. You're not going to fight against something or resist it. You're not even going to find fault in a brother by saying, *You know, well, this is what you're doing wrong. And here's what you should do instead.* No, because now, the mind is so filled with light that it can't see the mistake at all. That's where the mind is going—to be so pure that you can't see the mistake. You don't first see the mistake and then try to pray and figure out how to fix it. Instead, you become so purified and so merged with the light that you don't even notice the mistake. This is what the Holy Spirit does. And you can only find the Holy Spirit right *now*, not in the past or the future. As you go deeper, you start to let go of all your thoughts and plans for the future, as well as all your regrets and anger from the past. You were wrong about everything you ever thought. Jesus is saying, *Choose again*! Do you really want to hang onto the belief in wrongness? Talk about a downer. Don't bring the party down by focusing on an error. Join the party of innocence, joy, laughter, and love instead!

~♥~

The Holy Spirit can watch what the ego seems to think, say, or do without concern because He knows they aren't true. So, the contrast is that, if you're watching your own ego, you're just analyzing, criticizing, or judging it. Something is wrong with that mode. It's like watching a fight from inside the ring, instead of as a spectator a safe distance away. If there's a sense of believing that the ego is real, there will just be a sense of thoughts watching thoughts, but there won't be any peace, happiness, or joy. Because to forgive is to *look past.*

The Holy Spirit always looks at things with perfect innocence and doesn't care about mistakes. The Holy Spirit sees the world as a whole, so it is impossible for mistakes to be seen. Instead, the Holy Spirit always looks past them. This is a good reminder: When you see a mistake and think or say, "That's wrong"—that's the ego talking. This is why Jesus said, "Turn the other cheek" (Matthew 5:39) over 2,000 years ago. He knew there was an innocence beyond all wrongdoing. Even the story of Judas betraying Jesus was based on the ego's perception because the actions of Judas were part of a script that would be used later as a teaching aid. Jesus knew exactly what Judas would do and told him, "That thou doest, do quickly." (John 13:27)

> "Jesus beheld them, and said unto them, With men this is impossible; but with God all things are possible." (Matthew 19:26)

So, it always amazes me how the Spirit just goes ahead of us and provides whatever we seem to need. Whatever credentials, documents, transportation, residency, or anything else that would help you shine, share, and spread your love and joy from your heart, will come to you easily when you decide to let God use you. And that is so different from how we've been taught to think in a world where you have to go through a series of steps to get things done." But when you give your heart to God, anything is possible, and when your goal is just to shine and share, all you have to do is open up and let things happen naturally.

We can look at Mother Teresa as an example because she lived in our century, while St. Francis and some other saints lived hundreds of years ago. Mother Teresa lived during the era when passenger airlines first became available, and I know there were times when she and her nuns were determined to get on a plane and travel to another country. When they went to the airline desk, they were asked, "Do you have a reservation?" And they said, "*No.*" "Have you bought your ticket yet?" "No, but we need to get somewhere else." Imagine going to an airline desk and being asked, "Do you have the reservation you made? Show us something..." and then having a holy encounter and being put on a plane! That's how God works, and it still happens today.

I hear so many stories of doors opening. When one of my friends in Africa tried to cross the border from one country to another, he was stopped at passport control and told that he didn't have the papers he needed to go to the next country so he couldn't cross the border. I asked him what he did then and he said, "Well, I just went to the corner of the office and started singing praises to God. I just kept singing and singing and singing." I think he sang for hours, just in a corner of the passport control office, until they told him, "Get in there, go on." I like hearing these stories. He was so dedicated. He just went to a corner of the office and kept singing praises to God! People might say that's not practical, but it worked.

We need to remember that the Bible says, "With God, all things are possible." I translate that verse to mean that if you're living a life devoted to God, everything you need in this world will show up for you. Our minds are very powerful, and I can't even tell you all the miracles I've seen in the last thirty-five years as I've traveled all over the world and the United States, where doors just kept opening and opening and opening. That's how you'll know you're following the Spirit: when doors keep opening in front of you. You don't have to struggle or try to figure things out because everything will unfold before you effortlessly. It doesn't even sound human, and it isn't. It comes from God and happens naturally when our hearts are devoted to Him and committed to doing His Will.

> "A Psalm of David. The LORD is my shepherd; I shall not want. He maketh me to lie down in green pastures: he leadeth me beside the still waters. He restoreth my soul: he leadeth me in the paths of righteousness for his name's sake. Yea, though I walk through the valley of the shadow of death, I will fear no evil: for thou art with me; thy rod and thy staff they comfort me. Thou preparest a table before me in the presence of mine enemies: thou anointest my head with oil; my cup runneth over. Surely goodness and mercy shall follow me all the

days of my life: and I will dwell in the house of the LORD for ever." (Psalms 23:1-6)

Jesus shows that *forgiveness is the key to eternal life*. Forgive your brother. That means seeing a brother without the past. That's not a small request. That's huge.

We're praying for God to save us—for the dead to rise again. We're praying for divine innocence, which means to see the perfect innocence in everyone and in ourselves. So that's a really big prayer. This is a very big prayer, and we're going to say it today. Today, we're going to escape from fear. We're going to turn away from guilt. And to do this, you have to realize that every time you look at a person—whether it's the person you think you are or a partner or someone else—you're looking at a reflection of yourself. Every time you look at a person or a body, you have more than one way to see it.

The Holy Spirit shows us another way to look at the body and the world. And that's amazing. It's a real miracle. And this is a time when you can see the world without making any decisions about it. Without putting anyone down. Without thinking about what is good, bad, right, wrong, advanced, beginning, rich, poor, pretty, or ugly. Beyond all the judgments of the world is a pristine interpretation that leaves you with a smile on your face, because you behold the world as the Holy Spirit sees it. You behold the happy dream. You behold the forgiven world. You see the whole world sparkling. And the main characteristic of this interpretation is that you still have a self-concept but the self-concept is forgiveness. It's still a self-concept but it's the one self concept that you share with the Holy Spirit, because it doesn't involve the ego.

Imagine that you reach a point where your mind is so clear and beautiful that, like Jesus, you can say, *I have forgiven the world.* You can say that Satan is underfoot, just like Jesus. Have a good attitude. Imagine sending the thought, *Don't worry, I've forgiven the world*, out into the whole universe. Now in order to do that, it's very simple. All real spiritual paths talk about clearing the mind. In Buddhism, they say, "Go into the void." All of the great teachers have said to *put your judgments and thoughts about who you think you are aside and open your mind and heart to the truth*. What you're really seeing is the nothingness of what you thought was you, your former self-concept. So this can sometimes seem like a blind spot. The unconscious mind is the blind spot. When you think you're happy, flying along, gliding down the highway and then something shocks you and pulls you out of a peaceful state of mind, that's a self-concept belief from your unconscious mind saying, "Here I am!"

> "He saith unto them, It is I; be not afraid." (John 6:20)

The deceived mind is untrained and unwilling to pay attention to the present because it is afraid of it. All of the mental chatter, drama, busy distractions and outlets are defenses against the present moment, where the still Voice for God reminds the mind of its home in Heaven.

The deceived mind is afraid of the Holy Spirit. The reason for this may not be obvious. The deceived mind believes the ego (and thus separation from God) is real and is attached to a tiny, imposter concept of self that God did not create. In the stillness, the Holy Spirit speaks for God and appears to be a threat because He reveals the truth of the mind's origin and being. All goals and purposes of the self-concept are of the ego and were created to obscure the Holy Spirit's single purpose. The fear, then, stems from the mind's attachment to the fictitious, make-believe self-concept. When the ego is questioned and investment in it is withdrawn, peace and joy follow.

Detachment is frequently mentioned as a possible solution. And there is often a sense that detachment would truly bring peace if it were possible. But attempting to be detached is met with resistance because the mind is unsure what to detach from, unsure about form (appearances) and content (purpose). We come together willing to have our errors of thought and misperceptions healed or corrected from the ground up.

In other words, we do not begin with the abstract (God's Love, Knowledge, Heaven) as a solution to perceived problems. The apparent process could be described as a very open dialogue in which no questions, concerns, or topics are off limits; a kind of spiritual psychotherapy in which everyday perceived problems are traced back to false beliefs and resulting misperceptions in the mind. However, this is merely an interpretation. Perceptions of what occurs vary. One thing is certain: feelings of peace and joy are indicators of choosing to hold the Holy Spirit's single purpose.

Cultivating a sincere intention to discern the nature of ego thought, or raising it to awareness, leads to a greater willingness to choose peace over fear. Why would anyone choose fear unless it appeared to offer something of value?

A permanent solution is more than possible; it is inevitable. However, it must first be understood that it is a perceptual correction, not a change in worldly conditions. In other words, before the *one Correction* can be accepted, the problems must be redefined from form problems to thinking problems, or from problems in the world to problems in the mind. If we are willing to consider the possibility that we have been mistaken about everything we have believed, a radical shift in consciousness is possible.

~♥~

This entire world has been an attempt to flee from light into darkness, fragmentation, and duality. No one wants to ask an honest question because he is afraid of the answer. What we are discovering is that the Holy Spirit is the answer. God sent a spark of light, the Holy Spirit, into this darkened mind that believes it is separated from God. That light will grow and grow until it literally illuminates the entire mind. However, the mind is terrified of it.

~♥~

At one point in my life, maybe my mid to late twenties, I was contemplating things and I started to realize that it didn't really matter so much what I would do with my life or how I would behave. I started to take myself off the hook a bit and not be so concerned with what I've done or what I haven't done—what I did or didn't do that I thought was wrong and mistaken. There is a lot of guilt from all those things. I started to take a look at the way the script had played out and

I thought, *Wow I have been living a very fearful life.* I was very shy. I had a life of hiding and protecting and there was a lot of fear with it. It dawned on me that I had been living my life out of fear of consequences, making these timid decisions and avoiding things, avoiding people. I thought, *Hmmm that's certainly not going to get me anywhere.* I started to ponder it a little bit more and I started to see, *Hmm, it's the motive underneath that's been the problem; it's not what I seem to do or not do.* So at one point I just started to ponder what my life would be or could be if I changed the motive and I allowed myself to follow my heart, live from inspiration, live from peace and joy and happiness. How would it go if I just started to follow a different drummer—go in a completely different direction— living for things that were inspiring to me, even if I had to search a bit to find that inspiration, I thought, *Well if I do find that inspiration, I'm just going to start making decisions based on that.*

~♥~

I was having lunch with a friend who is a magnificent teacher, and she was telling me about how she went out the other day and was in a store. She approached the checkout line and abruptly turned to her friends, saying, "Um, I think I need to leave the store for a moment. I'm about to puke." And she walked out. She walked over to the first garbage can and threw up in it, then went back to the store and on her way. What was cool about how she told the story was that she didn't feel any shame or embarrassment about it. If she was embarrassed, she wouldn't be telling me. She wasn't trying to hide it. That, you see, is the key. When something appears to happen in the world and we read meaning into it or interpret it in such a way that we feel even a tad embarrassed, Jesus tells us that this is still fear. Intense rage, a slight bit of irritation, annoyance, or even a slight bit of embarrassment is all fear, and the Holy Spirit is teaching us not to hide it. Don't hide it from the Holy Spirit because the Holy Spirit isn't embarrassed. The Holy Spirit is saying, *Bring it to me. Bring it to me and I'll take it from you.*

> "Be strong and of a good courage, fear not, nor be afraid of them: for the LORD thy God, he it is that doth go with thee; he will not fail thee, nor forsake thee." (Deuteronomy 31:6)

The ego is very good at frightening the mind. It's the master of fear, no doubt. But Jesus is telling us that Love is stronger than fear. He says "Fear not. I am with you." (Isaiah 41:10) Your identity is secure and it will always be so. Nothing can oppose God's will. Nothing can change God's Will. What God creates is forever. So don't be concerned about a blip that's here one moment and gone the next. Don't be concerned about the hallucination. Jesus says, *Seek not to change the world, rather, seek to change your mind about the world.* Give it a new function. Instead of hating it, forgive it. Change your mind about the world. But don't be concerned about fixing the world. Don't be concerned about making the world a better place. Don't think you'll have to destroy the entire world. The ego is destruction, and when you forgive the ego, you are free of it. You are forever free of destruction.

> "For thou wilt not leave my soul in hell; neither wilt thou suffer thine Holy One to see corruption. Thou wilt show me the path of life: in thy presence

is fullness of joy; at thy right hand there are pleasures for evermore." (Psalms 16:10-11)

When you have peace as your goal, everything that is contrary to that inner peace will rise to awareness, allowing you to look it in the eye with the help of the Spirit and simply see the false as false, and thus the Spirit heals the mind. False perceptions are thus expelled, dissolved, and washed away. It may take some rinsing at times, but Spirit is inevitable. What is, is inevitable. So now is the time to honestly ask yourself, *Am I willing to trust, listen, and be open to the possibility of a fast track to Heaven*? It's a straight shot, the straight and narrow that Jesus mentioned in the Bible.

~♥~

Time is a learning device that the Holy Spirit can use to teach you that there is no time. So, if that sounds like a contradiction, it isn't. To those who believe in time, it is simply a paradox. And the more content you are with the present moment, the less of a paradox you have. You're happy now, and that's the end of the story. Heaven has no paradoxes. There is no contradiction with the Holy Spirit. And the Holy Spirit will simply keep repeating this simple forgiveness lesson for the sleeping mind until the time it is accepted, which is inevitable. Jesus and the Holy Spirit rejoice at the inevitable. The ego fears the inevitable because it associates it with loss and destruction. It's frightening to tell the ego that your existence is fading. But what is Spirit will never vanish. What is Spirit is Eternal.

The body is now just a tool for learning forgiveness. That's all. It serves only one purpose. And the simpler that is for you, the better, because the more you realize that the body has only one purpose, the more you start to relax and think, Okay, I got this. I'm being led home by the Holy Spirit. And I am capable of doing so.

~♥~

The Holy Spirit intends for you to live a joyful life before ascending back to the Creator. Keep this in mind when you are worried about your job or your family, worried about your success in the world, or even worried about your survival. Just keep telling yourself, *There's a much bigger plan than this. I am here to experience joy before returning to my Creator.* That plan is too much for the ego. That is unrealistic, according to the ego. Actually, that is the most realistic.

~♥~

Jesus, the Holy Spirit, inspires miracles in and through us, and joy will sweep you away like nothing else. When you begin to experience intrinsic bubbling joy, it is undeniably real. There is so much inspiration and help that it just becomes your life. You think to yourself, *I'm not sure what I was doing before but I was lost; now I'm found, and now the joy is bubbling.* That is inspiring. That literally transports you. Because if you had joy, do you think pain and pleasure would be as important to you? If you were filled with joy from your Source, you would not hesitate, and it would not be a sacrifice to you...Who can be sad when nothing is sacrificed?

~♥~

It is really just a call, as you keep practicing and watching your mind; opening to miracles and being used in miracles; becoming more joyful, and even more consistently joyful. You cannot change or fix anyone, but you can present an attitude, a demonstration of a changed mind—of a mind that is aligned with the Source. And in doing so, you have accepted full responsibility. There is nothing more responsible you can do; your attitude is entirely your responsibility. It's very glorious because you realize how relaxed you are if you're not responsible for other people's actions.

In fact, you could go a step further and say that you are not directly in control of even your own body, because it is part of a predetermined script and you have no control over the world you created, so you cannot actively control the body. What you do is a result of what you think, and while you can choose your thoughts, you have no direct control over the puppet. The purpose you choose to align with in your own mind—the Holy Spirit or the ego—will move the puppet. It is difficult to comprehend because we are so accustomed to judging. It is your fault if you are overweight, and you must stop putting food in your mouth. You can see how the world always looks at it from a behavioral perspective: If you smoke, stop smoking! If you drink, put it down! Quit drinking! People who have been through Alcoholics Anonymous or alcoholism will say, *Yeah, yeah, stop drinking...okay, yeah, I tell myself that, stop drinking*. You see, you have to go much deeper than that; you have to go really, really, really deep into the mind.

We really have to give up this sneaky idea of personal responsibility. Many of us were taught the concept of personal responsibility as children: You are personally responsible for earning a living; you are personally responsible for everything, including everything you do and do not do. Now, if you *were* responsible for the behavior, that is where some guilt can arise, because the puppet is prone to a variety of misbehavior. And if you are directly responsible for the behavior, you believe you have to prove your innocence. You'll have to find innocence where you're accountable for your actions. Consider Charlie Manson or Adolf Hitler, are they responsible for their actions?... Guilt arises from associating the behavior with some kind of standard, and you will be guilty if you continue to do so.

What if you were held accountable for what you think rather than what you do? Because what you do is simply a result of what you think. Wouldn't it be better to concentrate all of your efforts on shifting your thoughts from ego to Holy Spirit and letting go of concern about the behavior and all of the judgments that go with it, as well as all of the judgments that go with the body? Consider how much guilt is involved in judging the body as *too* this, *too* that, good at this, good at that. You can see how the ego has quite a system in place. But Jesus says that you are responsible for what you think, not what you do.

It is at this level—the level of thoughts—that we must work. So, this was really helpful for me because I had to be convinced of it. My entire life, the whole parable of David, was concerned with the body, personality traits... *I am shy, it is a curse...how will I meet girls, how will I meet women, how will I be in a relationship if I am...with the curse of shyness, the curse that follows me*. You can see that you're going nowhere with that; you're just stuck. You might think, *oh, personality traits don't change much*, but in my case, there was quite a transformation. But those are just symbols; it was really a change in my thinking that caused everything else to follow suit.

I was flying back from Brazil, and I had my iPhone on shuffle, and this song came on, and I just started to feel the love welling up in this song, called "High," and then it got to a certain part of the lyrics, and the tears just started to flow down my cheeks when I heard, "Even the impossible is easy when we are together."

Now that line, "Even the impossible," got to me because you could say that the Atonement or innocence from the worldly perspective seems to be impossible in a world of sin, in a world that is generated out of error, where every nuance, every fabric of this dream is projected error.

That is why it is so depressing. That is why it seems like such a closed system. That is why it seems like there is no escape. That is why there is no awareness in the mainstream of it being a dream of escape. So that is why there is so much focus on scraps of pleasure and scraps of good feelings because it is so dark that the scraps are even emphasized, but even the impossible is easy when we are together.

It reminds me of that saying, "With God all things are possible," and that song with the lyrics, "There ain't no mountain high enough," and all those songs that just talk about how inevitable awakening is through this Love and this innocence. But without this Love and innocence, it just seems bleak. It seems bleak and meaningless, I mean in a dark sense, dark and meaningless and empty in a very dark sense, not like when the Buddhists talk about an empty mind.

Really, we are just sinking back into that experience and feeling the gratitude of that. We are not trying to accomplish anything. It is not going for an accomplishment. We are not fishing for a reason, or something that makes sense in the world. We are so willing to let go of whatever things mean, just for that Love, just to have a good taste of that true Love. Your worth was established by God; it is so far beyond the things that we have associated with worth. And we are worthy.

~♥~

Let's go on a journey inward together. I'm thinking of the Macy's Day Parade, where there are big floats filled with helium and cables that keep the floats from flying away. Let's look closely together to see if we can find and let go of some of those tethers, since that's what we're doing. We are letting go of the ropes. We know intuitively that our birthright, our inheritance is the Kingdom of Heaven; it is Nirvana; it is perfect joy and happiness. We know that in our hearts. We know that it's there and nothing can take that away. All Jesus asks us to do is remove the obstacles to the awareness of love's presence. This is the only reason we are here. We don't want to *get* anything. We're not here to get anything done. We're not here to get more stuff. We're not here to come up with new ideas. We're not even here to make something happen.

I go around the whole world talking about the impossibility of manifesting. Those talks are not always popular but if you want to enter the Kingdom of Heaven you have to see that manifesting is also an illusion. It has some value for a while, as it helps you start to gain the power of your mind, but you do not want to get stuck in it. Because if you get stuck into trying to manifest the things that you want, you are still stuck in wanting.

I will guarantee you that fulfillment is better than wanting. I will guarantee you that contentment is better than wanting. I will guarantee you—I will promise you—that peace of mind, present peace, reverent presence is better than wanting and there is nothing that wanting will ever bring you except illusions.

In the Bible, there was a King called David who wrote songs. He wrote one called the *23rd Psalm*, which is well-known to Christians. He starts the song by saying, "The Lord is my shepherd; I shall not want." He was singing to God, telling him, *I won't want anything.* But, in the mind, the point of prayer/desire is the point of power. So, in a way, saying, "I shall not want" means, *I don't want to know how powerful my mind is.* This is because you think that power is often abused. So, when you really pray, you join the Spirit in His power and also in His ability to help you forget the things you think you need. We should trust the Holy Spirit to take care of everything. Jesus says that the key to real prayer is to forget about the things you think you need. This song is also about being thankful. It's like singing to God, *Thanks for giving me everything I need*, but not really thinking about what you need.

So, in a way, this is what you've been praying for and what you've been wanting, but the Holy Spirit also knows that you can't skip over any beliefs. Say you want a soulmate; this can be a way of asking the Spirit, *What would help me wake up?* In this way, the Spirit turns special relationships into holy relationships by giving them a new purpose without trying to change what you still believe. So the ego is a filter in the mind, and for the Holy Spirit to get to where the mind thinks it is, it has to go through the filter.

In monasteries and convents, monks are often asked to swear to be poor, chaste, and obedient. If their mind is ready for the vow, it can be helpful. If the mind is not ready, it goes into repression and denial. Part of the mind wants to get rid of the desire, while the other part of the mind wants to keep the desire. This means that there is resistance and conflict in the mind. Because of this, the prayer needs to be useful.

The Holy Spirit knows how to free the mind from guilt, but it doesn't come from wanting or trying to stop certain things from happening. In the movie, *The Matrix,* the Oracle is talking to Neo, and she is telling him that no one can understand an answer from a level they are not ready to understand. When Morpheus took Neo to see the Oracle, he asked her if she thinks he's "the One". First, she tells him to show her his hand, and then she gives him more time. The Oracle then tells him, "Open your mouth." She gives him more time by looking at his teeth and mouth. Then she looks into his eyes and says, "But you already know what I'm going to tell you." *No one can tell you that you are the One; you have to find out for yourself*. But he is still looking at her, waiting for her to tell him the answer. So, he's not ready to find out that he's *the One*, and she tells him that. In fact, he is the one who says, "I'm not the One." She says, "Sorry, kid. You got the gift, but it looks like you're waiting for something."

The same is true of prayer. We can't pray for things we aren't prepared to get. This is why getting in touch with your inner voice feels good, asking your inner Self what things or steps would be best for you to do next. That will make you feel happy because the Spirit is responding to you. If you want to be forgiven and wake up, the Spirit will go through your beliefs and give you what you need next. It will also keep helping you let go of all the beliefs you need to let go of. So it really shows a lot of love.

42. Speak on Your Appearance on the Road to Emmaus

"Lo, he goeth by me, and I see *him* not: he passeth on also, but I perceive him not." (Job 9:11)

"And, behold, two of them went that same day to a village called Emmaus, which was from Jerusalem *about* threescore furlongs. And they talked together of all these things which had happened. And it came to pass, that, while they communed *together* and reasoned, Jesus himself drew near, and went with them. But their eyes were holden that they should not know him.

And he said unto them, What manner of communications *are* these that ye have one to another, as ye walk, and are sad? And the one of them, whose name was Cleopas, answering said unto him, Art thou only a stranger in Jerusalem, and hast not known the things which are come to pass there in these days?

And he said unto them, What things? And they said unto him, Concerning Jesus of Nazareth, which was a prophet mighty in deed and word before God and all the people: And how the chief priests and our rulers delivered him to be condemned to death, and have crucified him. But we trusted that it had been he which should have redeemed Israel: and beside all this, to day is the third day since these things were done. Yea, and certain women also of our company made us astonished, which were early at the sepulchre; And when they found not his body, they came, saying, that they had also seen a vision of angels, which said that he was alive. And certain of them which were with us went to the sepulchre, and found *it* even so as the women had said: but him they saw not.

Then he said unto them, O fools, and slow of heart to believe all that the prophets have spoken: Ought not Christ to have suffered these things, and to enter into his glory? And beginning at Moses and all the prophets, he expounded unto them in all the scriptures the things concerning himself.

And they drew nigh unto the village, whither they went: and he made as though he would have gone further. But they constrained him, saying, Abide with us: for it is toward evening, and the day is far spent. And he went in to tarry with them. And it came to pass, as he sat at meat with them, he took bread, and blessed *it*, and brake, and gave to them. And their eyes were opened, and they knew him; and he vanished out of their sight." (Luke 24:13-31)

And they drew nigh unto the village, whither they went: and he made as though he would have gone further. But they constrained him, saying, Abide with us: for it is toward evening, and the day is far spent. And he went in to tarry with them. And it came to pass, as he sat at meat with them, he took

> bread, and blessed it, and brake, and gave to them. And their eyes were opened, and they knew him; and he vanished out of their sight." (Luke 24:13-31)

Jesus was very gentle, uncompromising, and certain, even though the examples were kind of extreme—the crucifixion and the resurrection. It was just a wonderful opportunity to teach defenselessness and to teach that communication between the Father and the son is unbroken. And, in the end, to teach that there is no death, using the symbols of bodies. The body seemed to be crucified and resurrected, but the real teaching is that the mind that lets go of judgment—that lets go of the ego—is resurrected and remembers itself as the Christ.

When Jesus came, it wasn't just a public ministry where he just said the two words "God is" and then just sat there in silence. He seemed to move about. He seemed to be on many walks, moving around quite a lot around Galilee and in many places. And he did a lot of his teaching as he was sitting down and eating dinner with people or as he was walking along the road to Emmaus, and he did not try to beat anyone over the head with the Kingdom of Heaven. He was a demonstration. His beatitudes—his manners of living—were so loving and gentle that everyone was invited.

Do you think that Jesus Christ just tried to live a normal life on earth? No. He was so interested in waking up and knowing his Heavenly Father that he realized that thoughts were very important to get in touch with, and beliefs were very important to get in touch with. And he knew that he had some kind of great destiny, and if he followed this inner guidance, transformed his consciousness, and released all attack thoughts and false beliefs, he would rise up in awareness just like the Phoenix rising. He would rise into a state of mind that we call the Christ mind, he would transcend the world, and he would say things like, "Before Abraham was, I am." (John 8:58)

He would identify with the 'I Am' Presence. He wasn't saying, *Lead a normal life.* I don't think raising the dead, healing the sick, or walking on water are very normal. And I don't think rising after you've been crucified and stuck in a sepulcher and then coming out, rising, and going around to teach are normal. How many people before Jesus were walking around after they were dead? Jesus was walking around talking after he had spikes in his arms and legs, and he came out and had risen and was teaching. Do you think that you will lead a normal life if you follow the Holy Spirit completely like Jesus and hear only one voice—the Holy Spirit? It's just not an ordinary thing to raise the dead and heal the sick. Those are great expressions of a miracle, of the power of the mind—of mind over matter.

~♥~

Your willingness will carry you farther along than you can imagine. It cannot be difficult to do all that Christ has appointed for you, for it is Christ who will do it through you until the realization dawns that you are the one. Jesus says that if you knew who walks beside you along the way, fear would be impossible.

I am always with you, and you can always call on the "I Am" Presence to join you in whatever circumstance you seem to be facing. My heart goes out to you, beloved one, for you are my Self. Our joining carries the power of all of Heaven! Trust in that, and watch the fears of the ego melt away and disappear forever.

> "Jesus saith unto her, Touch me not; for I am not yet ascended to my Father: but go to my brethren, and say unto them, I ascend unto my Father, and your Father; and *to* my God, and your God." (John 20:17)

> "Jesus saith unto him, Thomas, because thou hast seen me, thou hast believed: blessed *are* they that have not seen, and *yet* have believed." (John 20:29)

I must emphasize that the guidance of the Holy Spirit, which is the inner guidance of your intuition, is extremely practical. You will never be given advice that you cannot follow. The guidance will only give you what you *can* follow. That makes sense to me because if the guidance gave me something that was far beyond what I could expect myself to do, I would question whether it was coming from the Holy Spirit and would begin to doubt the voice. But, since the late 1980s, every time Jesus and the Holy Spirit guided me, everything has turned out beautifully. My heart kept opening, and I started traveling even though I didn't like to travel.

I began speaking about God, even though my parents had told me, "Don't talk about God or politics in public." Jesus apparently thought it was okay to talk about God in public, but that's not something I would have done. *Do you have to put me out there?* I would have said. Is it *really* necessary for me to go? *I could get fried!* Remember what happened to the prophets in the Bible? And what about what happened to Joan of Arc? *You really want to speak through this David character? Maybe there is another character you could use instead.*

The guidance is all for you, so what can you do? You can't really go against guidance when you hear it. I tried that too at the beginning. I tried to ignore the guidance and I made myself sick. I was in the school psychology program back around 1984-85, and the guidance I received was to leave the program, but I resisted the guidance, and then I got sick. I got sicker and sicker and sicker, seemingly, until I finally did what the guidance told me to do, and then I felt relief. Wow, what a pleasant surprise! Take the advice, be happy, and find relief. Or, don't follow the advice and feel guilt, struggle, pain, or suffering. It's very straightforward and obvious.

~♥~

The world will reflect your own doubt until you completely withdraw your mind from the ego. So, if you believe you have friends and relatives who are trying to slow down your spiritual journey, it is because they are acting out the ego beliefs; there is still doubt in your mind about your identity. Nobody on the planet is slowing anyone down. Nothing exists in the world. There is nothing in the world that can slow you down.

If you think you have an angry boss, it is simply that you are still invested in the ego's anger. If you have angry parents or children, or if you have problems with authority figures—lawyers, police officers, or government officials—it is all the authority problem of thinking you can make up an identity other than God's. And that is what is happening in the world. It is never related to what seems to be happening around us. The issue of authority is still attempting to believe in a thought system that God did not create. And that is where all the specialness comes in—you've heard all the conditioning: *You're special, you're very special*—comes in. Instead of simply being one, the ego asserts that you can do better than Oneness by being unique. You can be your own unique, individual, special person, and that is what the ego is attempting to convince you of—*you've got something valuable now, it's your own individuality*—but it is still part of a lie. Sorry for dampening your sense of individuality. Instead of being an individual, you are *indivisible*. That word sounds more restful.

> "And I will pray the Father, and he shall give you another Comforter, that he may abide with you for ever; *Even* the Spirit of truth; whom the world cannot receive, because it seeth him not, neither knoweth him: but ye know him; for he dwelleth with you, and shall be in you." (John 14:16-17)

You are being led back toward God's Will by the Holy Spirit, which acts as a bridge to connect the gap between you and God. When the Holy Spirit is present, you cannot fulfill your will. The Holy Spirit often shows up in the form of an inner voice because the mind seems lost in a foreign land and has forgotten Oneness, so it requires a Guide to lead it back to truth. And so, to accept that God wants only perfect happiness for me is to remember my identity. God's will is for me to live in the Kingdom of Heaven. Yet in this world, there is still one slight reverberation of will remaining in the universe, and it is known as choice, which is the belief in duality. In Oneness, there is no choice because there is nothing to choose between. There are no options available. So, you can see why choice is not the true will. Without duality, you cannot have choice! You decide between one and one. It is absurd to associate Heaven with free will because there is only absolute Oneness in Heaven. However, there is a choice in the tiniest ripples of God's Will or of Oneness in this universe—since there is no option in Oneness, it is not really a choice; it's rather a matter of following the Holy Spirit or listening to the ego. That decision is significant in the split mind context, but it is not significant in the sense of Allness.

~♥~

Two thousand years ago, Jesus said, *Judge not*. He said, "The Kingdom of God is within you." (Luke 17:21) Not on another planet or in another galaxy, but within you. It's a spiritual kingdom. But we can't know it if we judge, so we are being taught to let go of all judgments. The Christ is unaware of any judgments. So how do you let go of your judgments when that's all you've ever known? All you have to do is pray and say, *Holy Spirit, Jesus, decide for God for me*. What does that mean? It means letting go of what you think you know and listening to your intuition, that small, still voice inside your head that knows how to get away from the world. It will show you where to go, what to do, and what to say, with everything that arises in your life. It's extremely useful. You can call it whatever you want, the words don't matter, it's all about listening to the guidance and following your heart. Those daily nudges and prompts are there to assist you in learning how to be truly helpful. Help your brother, help your sister, because everyone you help with the Holy Spirit's guidance is assisting your mind in escaping the ego, which is the path to true freedom. This is the path that will lead you to true happiness.

The ego's world is all about stuff, and everything in the ego's world is for sale. But, according to the Bible, Jesus asked, "What shall it profit a man if he shall gain the whole world and lose his own soul?" We lose touch with everything important when we lose touch with the Spirit. The ego says forget about it; you can be content with time and space: you can buy a lot of things if you have a lot of money; you can have a lot of nice things; you can own the body and other people's bodies. But Love does not own. We are here to teach that we can follow guidance, that we can hear the Voice that will lead us to the truth. We are more than a body, more than something that must die, more than separation; we are truly more than One Self, and that we do not need to be duped. I want to share the good news, the joy. I don't want to be ruled by fear and guilt; it is *possible* to live a life inspired by Love, and that is what we are here to discover.

~♥~

When you read the words of Jesus, the red letters, in the Bible, you can feel the ease and comfort that come through them. That is what we would expect God's Voice to say, but when we are learning to tune in and listen, God's Voice sounds more like, *Turn left; call so and so; you can let that go now; you need to call so and so now.* It's very soft, gentle, and loving, but also very precise.

"Who only hath immortality, dwelling in the light which no man can approach unto; whom no man hath seen, nor can see: to whom *be* honor and power everlasting. Amen." (1 Timothy 6:16)

"I will instruct thee and teach thee in the way which thou shalt go: I will guide thee with mine eye." (Psalms 32:8)

When Jesus walked the earth 2,000 years ago, he taught the importance of, "*Let thine eye be single.*" (Matthew 6:22) He was not referring to a perceptual eye, but rather the "singular eye" of the Spirit—the spiritual observer. He was speaking about the vision of Christ that comes by way of the Holy Spirit. That's the direction we're heading. We're heading into the vision of Christ. Glory to God! Hallelujah!

~♥~

Jesus is inviting us to embrace our Christ vision, our spiritual eye, and our higher way of seeing the world. He wants you to know that the angels are with you, and he wants you to let your mind be lifted up so you can laugh at this world. The only way to laugh at it is to not judge it, because once you judge it, you try to make a part of it real. You try to have only a sliver of vision. When you judge, you put on blinders. And when you don't judge it, it's actually quite a lovely world. It's not beautiful in the way your parents taught you, but beautiful in the way the present moment shows you, seeing the world through new eyes.

~♥~

When we say, "I am as God created me," we are essentially acknowledging a spiritual fact: that God, the *Cause*, and

Christ, the Spirit, the *Effect*—the Creator and creation—are *one*. In Spirit, cause and effect are one. That is a proven fact and this *is* Heaven. So basically, all you have to do is recognize that cause and effect are one and the same, and that God and Christ are joined and inseparable. It is impossible for an effect of God to leave God and enter a world of make-believe, go down the rabbit hole, enter the matrix, enter time and space, and create a different identity—a time identity. That is not possible. And Jesus discovered that this is impossible. You cannot abandon God. You can't abandon your Creator. It's a fantastical fantasy. It's a work of fiction. It's a fantasy to think you can exist apart from your divine Creator. And, to his delight, Jesus realized, "I and *my* Father are one." We share the same spirit.

~♥~

There may be situations where you have had to seemingly counsel or comfort someone, such as a mother who appears to have lost her child, a family whose home has been washed away in a flood, or someone who has just been diagnosed with terminal cancer. Someone calls you in deep grief over something that has happened. What is it that unites all of these things? What is the link between everything I just mentioned? The link is the belief in attack and when that belief is shared you cannot comfort someone. Only the mind believes in attack and is desperately seeking the spiritual eye, the Lord's eye. It's just the mind pleading for the Lord's eye, for the healing balm. The attack is incredible; it has not occurred. You are, after all, trusting in something that God did not create. You've got a Source—a genuine Source from which you came, and that genuine Source does not generate attack. All of the situations I mentioned are exactly the same. And the Holy Spirit is asking, *Are you ready now to help me save the world?* It's not about saving the outside world. It's about rescuing the mind that believes in attack. The mind that believes in attack is in need of salvation. That is what requires redemption. That is what needs to be resurrected.

> "*Let your* conversation *be* without covetousness; *and be* content with such things as ye have: for he hath said, I will never leave thee, nor forsake thee." (Hebrews 13:5)

It has nothing to do with correcting our brothers and sisters. They are not the issue. Our thoughts are the issue. Accepting the correction means accepting Christ within us, within our minds. It is the acceptance of the love within. It isn't about trying to change the world. I had a woman write to me on YouTube after watching my video and ask, "Does this mean I have to accept mandates—vaccine mandates?" That's exactly what she wrote. I replied back to her and said, "Well, render to Caesar what is Caesar's, and to God what is God's." Because God created you, your holy state of mind is what you render to God. You will be happy if you surrender your state of mind to the Holy Spirit—to Jesus.

Government mandates or societal mandates cannot take away your peace of mind unless you believe there is an outside world that has the power to make you a victim. It's really quite simple: you either believe in separation and an external world, or you believe in unity with the world. I believe the world is in good spirits. I truly believe in a happy world. But I also see that it's my mind at work, so I take full responsibility for my happiness, and I see a happy world. Do you understand how that works? I perceive it if I accept it. I see a happy dream if I accept that the world has been forgiven.

~♥~

The Bible gives us a good look at principle through the Golden Rule, "Do to others as you would have them do to you." (Luke 6:31) Then in the Gospels we see examples of principle in action. It is helpful to have some kind of example or demonstration when we believe we are human beings. Otherwise, it's, *Mmm hmm, nice word—love, but can you be a little more helpful and practical than just saying love, love, love all the time?*

Out of the Ten Commandments, I believe the first two were the most glorious and lovely, and those are the ones that Jesus emphasized. *Love the Lord thy God with all thy heart, and with all thy soul, and with all thy mind, and with all thy strength; Love thy neighbor as thyself.* Why do you need three through ten if you can get the first two? Who is coveting when you're loving? Who is stealing or committing adultery? If you're operating in love, you don't even have to think about the remaining Commandments.

~♥~

Once I was in a Pizza Hut and I saw a poster that said, *A bite of heaven is just a moment away.* It is beautiful, you can even get the principles on the wall of Pizza Hut. We really need to learn the *how*, we need to practice with the principles. Because when we ignore the principles or forget the principles or have it out of mind—it does not do us any good—we get distracted into minutia, into things of the world, all these specifics of the world. But the Holy Spirit is calling out to us, saying, *I am here, I am here to save the day.*

You want a happy day? I am here. And we are just not aware of it because we are focused on the gap instead of the bridge that leads us over the gap.

We get away from practice and more into the letter of the law when we start analyzing and breaking things down and trying to feel like we even have to conform to these things, like the scribes and Pharisees of old. "Love one another and love God," was all Jesus was just saying. He was ringing the bell of those first two commandments and saying, *Do not be so worried about what you should not be doing, here is what you can really focus on*. These two guidelines simply remind us to return to openness, transparency, directness, and to not hold back, because it takes so much energy to hold back thoughts, push down feelings, and suppress our emotions. Now we have the Gospels, which are examples of principle in action. And if you want to see how it goes, watch how defenseless, how meek, how strong and loving, and yet so gentle the principle is when it appears to be dancing on earth for a few years—Jesus was such a demonstration of the simplicity of salvation.

~♥~

Because his mind was so clear, Jesus was extremely telepathic. He had cleared the mirror in his mind, and he could pick up on the thoughts of the scribes, the Pharisees, and the Sadducees. A woman who was considered as sinful, came in and poured expensive perfume on Jesus´ feet in front of a Pharisee who had invited him to his house. The Pharisee thought to himself that Jesus couldn't be the Messiah because he was allowing a sinful woman to touch him. Jesus answered his thoughts by sharing a parable about forgiveness. Jesus then turned to the woman and forgave her sins. The Pharisee didn't have to say it out loud; Jesus knew what he was thinking.

He knew what the Apostles were going through, and he knew all their doubt thoughts. However, he was aware that there was only one mind. So he knew there was no issue. Because Jesus knew it was impossible, sickness could not exist near him. Sickness is the belief in privacy, secrets, and fragmentation. Jesus understood that fragmentation does not exist. It's just the wrong mind, which he forgives. He pardoned the wrong mind. He was not obligated to forgive specific people, such as Herod or Julius Caesar or the Roman empire. He didn't have to forgive anyone who was trying to trap or kill him because he knew that the wrong mind was impossible. That is why he did not die on the cross.

~♥~

This is what the inward journey to healing is all about: learning to trust your intuition and letting go of your belief in external rules and regulations. Jesus is not telling us to simply disregard the ego's rules. He was a good role model. During his time on earth the Jews had a rule that you couldn't go into the temple to pray unless you paid the temple tax first. So, when Jesus and the apostles went to the temple, they paid the temple tax. They paid the tax, which is significant. Because Jesus said, "Render unto Caesar the things which are Caesar's; and unto God the things that are God's." (Matthew 22:21) Jesus is returning us to the one law, the law of love. But he's not telling us to openly defy and overthrow the laws of the land. He is showing us how to transcend the entire world through love. He is teaching us that if we identify with who we truly are, we are subject to none other than God's laws. He is teaching us that if we follow our intuition and the Holy Spirit, everything will work out perfectly. Without rebelling against the ego or the world; rather by following inner guidance, you can transcend this world and come to expand your perception from a limited ego perception to the Holy Spirit's holistic perception of the world. That is the essence of spiritual awakening. It's about allowing the Holy Spirit to broaden your vision.

~♥~

The psychiatric diagnosis of multiple personality disorder is about split personalities seemingly within one body. There are two movies—*Sybil* and *Split,* which both feature split personality disorders. The thing about split personalities is that they are so distinct; the voice seems to change, the facial expression changes, they dress differently. One may have cancer, while the other may not. If you like to do research, these cases of multiple personalities should be the first evidence of the power of the mind: One personality character may have diabetes and require insulin and injections, while another does not. Or, one may have active cancer cells, while the other does not. This shows how powerful the mind is, and how it generates everything about the body, including all the symptoms, and can even shift to another personality and cause symptoms to disappear instantly. When the mind is simply shifted to a different personality, the diabetes and cancer vanish in an instant.

Let's take that a step further: what if we're all one sleeping mind of Christ, and the seven billion bodies, seven billion different personalities on this planet are just one big case of multiple personality disorder? You're concerned about your physical symptoms, but your friend doesn't have them. You tell your friend, *Well, I'm glad you're healthy, but I'm sick.* But wait a minute, this is all a projection. It's the ego that tells some bodies they are healthy and others that they are sick. That's just the judgment. This multiple personality disorder involves seven billion personalities and the disorder is in the mind. Just like in the movies *Sybil* and *Split*. What effect does this have on your perception of symptoms? Can it be that some of our brothers and sisters are sick or dying while others are healthy and alive? That doesn't seem fair; to have some sick people and some healthy people, and then the healthy people are the doctors; they get paid a lot of money. Doctors, nurses, and practitioners make a lot of money because they help people get rid of symptoms, but what if it's all psychological? What if all illness is psychological in nature?

Jesus wants us to know that all illness is mental illness, but not in our own *private* minds. *People* do not suffer from mental illness. *The sleeping mind* is insane. The sleeping mind is creating an unreal world. There is only one problem and one solution, and all you need to do is admit for just an instant that you made it all up. I mean all of it, all of history; you have to admit that you made it all up. And then you'll be ready for the correction, for the happy dream that gives you a new perspective on everything. It is not on a linear timeline, but it will show you everything at the same time. Scientists talk about parallel lifetimes, but everything is parallel, everything is happening at the same time, and only the ego strings it out over past, present, and future. So when you begin to feel pain, it is being raised up into awareness for one reason only: not to punish you, because God is unaware of punishment, but, rather to demonstrate the need for a shift. You are in need of a shift when you are in pain.

> "Lord, now lettest thou thy servant depart in peace, according to thy word." (Luke 2:29)

Inner peace is always the goal; it should always be at the forefront, and there is really nothing else we need to focus on except that inner peace.

Peace of mind is not a small gift, and we *are* deserving of it. We were created in peace, and we are deserving of that peace.

> "Peace I leave with you, my peace I give unto you: not as the world giveth, give I unto you. Let not your heart be troubled, neither let it be afraid." (John 14:27)

True forgiveness is taught and learned by being aware that one is never upset by anything other than erroneous thoughts, and that those erroneous thoughts can be released. True forgiveness is the release of all hurts, grievances, and grudges that obstruct awareness of God's Divine Love, which exists in everyone and everything. True forgiveness is the release of all anger, hatred, guilt, and fear by recognizing that they stem from an error, a mistaken belief, in forgetting God's Love. Living and extending inner peace is the natural result of true forgiveness, because peace reigns when error is set aside and a healing Correction is accepted in its place. To spread peace, one must first be peaceful. To teach peace, one must first learn it. No one can give a gift that they do not already have. Similarly, peace of mind cannot be found outside of one's own mind because it is not dependent on the world. Peace is a natural extension of God and comes from Him. As a result, prayer and meditation are promoted as methods of achieving inner peace and harmony. Religion is the experience of inner peace and *true* education, which is the unlearning of falsity, is but a means of coming to the experience of inner peace.

~♥~

The ego is like the Big Bang that scientists talk about that seems to be in the cosmos. It's the same as believing a false idea with a powerful mind. How else could a Big Bang occur? It is said in the Bible that if you had the faith of a grain of mustard seed—a tiny little seed—you could move mountains. What if you had the ability to do more than just move mountains? What if your mind was the driving force behind the Big Bang—a powerful Christ mind that was given over to an insane idea. And it appeared to cause an explosion; not a nuclear explosion, but a cosmic, galactic explosion of time and space. And what if the Big Bang had already been healed, and you had the ability to accept that healing on behalf of everyone?

That's how significant this is. That is why, when you hear an inner calling and feel compelled to follow the Spirit, it is significant because you are accepting a correction for everyone—Not just for your tiny personality. Personal saviors do not exist. You don't have to stand on a soapbox in downtown Stockholm and say, *Repent, repent, turn from your ways! The Kingdom of Heaven is at hand!* You don't have to do that. You simply have to go into your mind; if there is any splinter or fragment or mustard seed of doubt or guilt or fear in there, simply say, *I'm worth more than this. I'm worth everything.* My peace of mind and everyone's peace of mind is worth more than this scrap, this tiny little scrap, this little seed of guilt.

~♥~

Put the purpose of peace out in front with all your encounters. When you have peace out in front, I mean completely out in front, you will perceive the situation as a whole. What does that mean? That everyone is playing their part perfectly—isn't that lovely? Imagine having peace out in front and having all these encounters and interactions and instead of trying to break the situation apart thinking, *Oh, I like this, I didn't like that. Well they said this and I like that, but I didn't like that.* Instead of breaking things apart and seeing a fragmented world of likes and dislikes, good and bad, imagine if peace of mind was so important for you—so absolutely important— that you put it out in front. You trust that everyone is was playing their part perfectly and you have a unified perception of everything. And you can extend the blessing of peace to everything and everyone because of your devotion to peace.

~♥~

A lot of us were raised in Christianity and the word "salvation" had different meanings. Perhaps they weren't the most positive meanings; perhaps we were not overjoyed by the idea of salvation or it wasn't something we were looking forward to. But it is important because what is being saved or salvaged is our peace of mind. That is so important. If "saved" means *peaceful*, then I'm ready; being saved is peaceful, so I'm all for "saved." It's not personal *salvation*. But it's very important.

~♥~

Do I truly desire peace above all else? When I truly open my mind to that, I just start to watch and see if there is anything else coming in there. Is peace on my altar? Is peace on my heart's altar, or are there other things on my altar that are attempting to coexist? We are accustomed to wanting things and having ambitions, desires in the world for things and desires for specific outcomes, concepts, and so on. That, I believe, is where it all begins. It all begins with our desire; not to judge or evaluate it. It's about starting to come to a sense of honesty with ourselves around it. There is a trust involved with that too, where if I start to just feel I really want peace of mind—and I'm really sincere about wanting that—but I don't know the way. I don't know how to get there, but I'm willing to be shown. I'm willing to ask and give over my personal ideas of how I think I can get peace of mind.

Then that starts a dismantling process. We have a desire for peace and there is a dismantling that begins to occur, and we can just welcome it and say, *Okay, I don't know the way, but there is one inside of me that does. I'm willing to just tune in and really listen to that.* That speeds up the whole process. It takes a lot of faith. Do not rely on previous knowledge. *This I know, that I know. I learned this in school. I learned this from my parents. I learned this from whatever.* That previous knowledge has never completely freed us. But, that intuitive voice or that intuitive feeling inside of us, that will guide us along, that does know the way.

~♥~

I was raised in Christianity but had never felt a strong connection. But as I went through this process, I began to sense Jesus' presence guiding and leading me. I was in a state of surrender, complete surrender to that presence. So a guide was essential for me in order to come to a very strong intuitive feeling. It is important to honor those intuitive feelings because they may differ from society, and they may differ from family voices and influences. Taking this journey towards truth, divinity, or love necessitates a lot of stepping outside of the box—letting go of thinking in very structured ways and coming to nurture ourselves, giving ourselves full permission to have an actual experience. This leads to being drawn towards others who are also dedicated to being intuitive.

Guilt, regardless of country or culture, is very suffocating, and any theology, teaching, or religion that still incorporates guilt—that you should feel guilty for this or that— just misses the mark. We're not condemning or praising specific behaviors and actions; we're saying look at consciousness or the psyche to find a way to innocence, a way to peace, harmony, and connection. Don't let theological beliefs get in the way. For example, India is no different from other parts of the world where there have been religious wars, riots between Muslims and Hindus. Where is the love, where is the harmony if we cling to religious beliefs as an identity and begin to judge and point the finger at others who have different religious beliefs?

> "Finally, brethren, whatsoever things are true, whatsoever things *are* honest, whatsoever things *are* just, whatsoever things *are* pure, whatsoever

things *are* lovely, whatsoever things *are* of good report; if *there be* any virtue, and if *there be* any praise, think on these things." (Philippians 4:8)

"Create in me a clean heart, O God; and renew a right spirit within me." (Psalms 51:10)

"These words spake Jesus, and lifted up his eyes to heaven, and said, Father, the hour is come; glorify thy Son, that thy Son also may glorify thee: As thou hast given him power over all flesh, that he should give eternal life to as many as thou hast given him. And this is life eternal, that they might know thee the only true God, and Jesus Christ, whom thou hast sent. I have glorified thee on the earth: I have finished the work which thou gavest me to do.

And now, O Father, glorify thou me with thine own self with the glory which I had with thee before the world was. I have manifested thy name unto the men which thou gavest me out of the world: thine they were, and thou gavest them me; and they have kept thy word. Now they have known that all things whatsoever thou hast given me are of thee. For I have given unto them the words which thou gavest me; and they have received *them*, and have known surely that I came out from thee, and they have believed that thou didst send me.

I pray for them: I pray not for the world, but for them which thou hast given me, for they are thine. And all mine are thine, and thine are mine; and I am glorified in them. And now I am no more in the world, but these are in the world, and I come to thee. Holy Father, keep through thine own name those whom thou hast given me, that they may be one, as we *are*." (John 17:1-11)

"These things have I spoken unto you, that my joy might remain in you, and *that* your joy might be full." (John 15:11)

"And, lo, I am with you always, *even* unto the end of the world. Amen." (Matthew 28:20)

When the Holy Spirit's guidance is followed, the result is joy. When you become aligned with the Spirit, you lose all future ambitions and experience profound contentment because it is about being truly happy, and that happiness comes from our source, God. Even in our relationships, we are learning to let go of possessions, to be very intuitive, and to have a sense of inner guidance that directs and guides us in all aspects of life. You have the impression that nothing is being taken away from you; instead, you are filled with gratitude and appreciation for everything.

~♥~

The Holy Spirit is the link between what God cannot comprehend and what God knows to be true. In other words, God does not understand error or sin because God did not create them. God does not understand suffering or struggle; the Holy Spirit is the bridge that knows the mind believes in these things but knows they are not true. That is why the Holy Spirit is the comforter, offering comfort, wisdom, and instruction.

Guidance should be your number-one priority in your interactions with the world. Guidance is the Holy Spirit using the words and symbols that the ego made to unwind your mind and bring you back to the light. Using what the ego made—words, bodies, planets, stars, flowers, and mountains—to take you in another direction and transcend it all; to first recognize that you are the dreamer and then to awaken from this dream to eternal life, the Kingdom of Heaven. It's really straightforward and simple; guidance is the key to mind training. Guidance is the fastest way to awaken from duality and enter the Kingdom of Heaven. Let's go over that advice again. If guidance is that important and the ego doesn't want you to listen to it, it's because if you do, the ego is basically out of business: "Perfect Love casts out fear." (John 4:18) When you know yourself as Light, then the darkness is no more. There isn't even a battle going on; darkness can't fight light, just like when you go into a dark room at night and turn on the light. There isn't a fight to see who will win. We don't have to wonder, *Will there be light or not?*

The real does not struggle with the unreal. It is only when you believe in the unreal that the struggles come in. To look at this in a more practical way—in terms of daily experience, let's relate guidance to decision making. Consider that you're really making decisions continually all through the day and all through the night. Some of them are unconscious—you're not aware of some of the decisions that you are making—but you are consciously aware of some decisions that you make every day. Are you making them with the Holy Spirit, or are you making them with the ego? How can you tell? You can tell by how you feel. If you are consistently joyful, peaceful, loving, happy; if you're just gliding along without any turmoil and drama in your life and your mind, then you're making all your decisions with the Holy Spirit, by default. If you're happy, you don't even have to ask, "Is that okay?" You're happy. The Holy Spirit is happy that you are happy.

~♥~

I recently did a teaching session called "Do Only That." This is a beautiful way to live your life, but you must be very clear in your mind. People usually live by a mantra of *Don't do this, don't do that*. We have a whole society of rules and laws that result in punishment. And if you live your life by saying, *Don't do this, don't do that*, or *Here are the consequences and punishment*, then consequence and punishment is what you will seem to experience. Imagine how your life would be if you were always tuned in to guidance and inspiration. You would simply speak and act on guidance and be joyful and happy. And in that sense, you are no longer in an interactive world—you are only being guided—but the ego wants you to believe that there is a world outside your mind with which you must constantly interact.

~♥~

When you follow guidance, you don't have to think about potential outcomes; you just have to think about how you feel right now. *What feels like a happy, peaceful choice?* You don't have to go through all the options in the world; you can let the Holy Spirit guide you to the final decision, which

Jesus refers to as the Atonement, or correction. It's beautiful; the more direct we are, the more time we save.

> Jesus demonstrated his teachings through his attitude. When you live in the Christ mind, you're in fearlessness, and in this state, you take the stranger in. In my experience, I could be driving along and picking up a hitchhiker or meeting a stranger in a laundromat or grocery store. You're always meeting yourself, and we teach most by demonstration.
>
> What you do is go inward to the Christ mind, and you're in such joy that you don't take the symbols and images of the world so seriously. You're into the inner listening and the inner joy, which is what it's all about. Therefore, you're not into trying to correct brothers and sisters; you're simply into living with the Correction in your own mind, which is staying in the one-mindedness. And then what occurs is just a gentle outflow of that one mind, a reflection of the beauty in that one mind.
>
> Shine your light to all your brothers and sisters! You will shine your light on the sorrowful. You have to teach what you would learn to strengthen it in your awareness.
>
> In the mind, you have a calling. Jesus is calling

us out of the past because, in the past, you felt guilty. When you have a new experience of the real you, then you are innocent.

~♥~

Because Thomas was renowned for having doubts, Jesus responded to him, "Because you have seen Me, you have believed: blessed *are* those who have not seen and *yet* have believed." (John 20:29) The Spirit will use the elements of perception and individually design them in a way that will work for you. Throughout my travels, I have met people who have had extrasensory perception, out-of-body experiences, manifestations and other people who appear to them, much like what happened to the little boy in the film *Sixth Sense* when he said, "I see dead people." So, there are individuals who perceive apparitions, and then there are others who would be so terrified even if Mother Mary showed up at the foot of their bed that they would immediately jump out of it.

The Holy Spirit will employ things that will work with you according to a very specific curriculum based on what you are willing to tolerate and accept in your mind. Some experience what are referred to as "near-death encounters." I like to refer to them as near-*life* encounters because they go to the light. People will experience this sometimes more than once, and that is often how they first become spiritual. It seems like the body's heart and brain waves cease for a while.

However, if you see these issues more from a holographic or quantum perspective, you will never be given more than you can handle. It's the comparison that introduces strain and tension. This happens when you start doubting yourself, you begin comparing your experiences to those of others, or you try explaining them to friends and family members who respond by asking, "What are you talking about?" However, Jesus says that love is all-inclusive and is therefore incapable of comparing. You have to come to the place where you are comfortable with the pathway—the signs and symbols that are being presented to you, and this requires a lot of practice.

It can be very helpful to pray straightforward prayers like, *Please show me signs and symbols that I am not alone, that I am loved and I am being watched over.* Those kinds of symbols can show up frequently, whether *wordly* or *heavenly* in nature. I have given so many talks and have discussed a wide range of topics where people have told me, *Oh, I am glad you talked about that because I did not want to share it with anyone else for fear of looking strange or being rejected.* When attending a conference for those who have had a Near Death Experience (NDE), some people shared their relief in being able to talk to a whole conference of others who have had an NDE: *I cannot share it with my family, or, I cannot share it with my husband [wife]—but now I can talk to these people.*

When those needing help attend 12-step meetings and are all working the steps and going through these experiences, there is a synergy that occurs. They start to realize that their issue is not specifically their own. All of a sudden, the notion that, *I am the black sheep and nobody else can relate to me* begins to fade as a result of the Holy Spirit at work in the group. When they hear the same words coming from all these various bodies, they think, *Wow, I am not alone at all, I feel great.* The things that the Spirit can utilize to take you to a gathering of people or to meet someone are signs that, *I am not alone in this.* Staying on track and moving forward when you have the feeling that you are completely alone is definitely the toughest thing to do.

~♥~

I was once guided to watch *The Oprah Winfrey Show* and Oprah's topic for the week was religion. Oprah brought in a panel of experts and as soon as the show began, they all started talking about Jesus. Look out! When you discuss Jesus in a public forum on *The Oprah Winfrey Show*, strong feelings about him will emerge. Everyone in the audience began standing up and shouting and the energy started to escalate. Then one woman in the crowd came forward and said, "Jesus Christ is our Savior and the only way to God!" The camera started shaking—and there was so much energy and reaction. Even Oprah began to respond to that remark, saying, *Jesus is a wonderful guide, but there are many pathways to God.* She was coming in hard, the camera was shaking, it got really wild and everything started spinning out of control into chaos. And then Oprah looked up into the camera and said, *Jesus, if you're there, help us.* And they cut to a commercial break.

The show returned to Oprah and the panel of experts, which consisted of maybe five people sitting in chairs on the stage. And the experts, as they always do, got into it. One was yelling, and another was pointing fingers… I sat and watched because, out of those five people, one man who was sitting in the middle of the panel was smiling and completely calm. While one expert would scream and shout from one end, the man sitting in the center didn't say a word. And he stood out like a radiant, shining star of non-judgment. As he watched the debate among his colleagues, he remained totally peaceful. No words were needed; the smile on his face said it all.

The only way we can be at peace without judgment is to practice putting peace first. Perception is selective; we only see what we want to see in the world. We have preferences, which we choose to see, and they are exaggerated in our world. You buy a brand new car in a specific color and model, you drive it down the highway, and as you look around you see this same car everywhere. Your mind is so powerful that it's focused on a specific model and color; out of all the cars you could see, here they come, disproportionately showing up at every turn.

But what if you put your mind at ease first—before anything else—before any other ego preferences? What you give your mind over to, you perceive. And if you give it over to peace, you're training your mind to experience that peace in every person and every situation because you've made that your purpose. That's exactly how it works; you have to put peace first. Whether we're talking with family or meeting new people, regardless of the context, peace is at the forefront, and that will be your perception.

A peaceful purpose that is focused on, elevated above anything else, and held out in front results in a peaceful perception of the world.

Jesus is teaching a practical gospel of love because it involves guidance. Pray, listen and follow. He will provide the guidance you need.

Bibliography

The Bible, King James Version

Resources

Books by David Hoffmeister

This Moment Is Your Miracle

The Mystical Teachings of Jesus

Awakening through A Course in Miracles

The Movie Watcher's Guide to Enlightenment

Quantum Forgiveness: Physics, Meet Jesus

Unwind Your Mind Back to God: Experiencing A Course in Miracles

Available at store.livingmiraclescenter.org *in print, eBook, and audiobook formats. Select materials available in thirteen languages.*

Online Resources

the-christ.net
Practice and Living the Mystical Teachings of Jesus

davidhoffmeister.com
A website about David Hoffmeister and His Teachings

tribe-of-christ
Practice and Live the Mystical Teachings of Jesus

youtube.com/user/DavidHoffmeister
Teachings by David on his YouTube Channel

spreaker.com/show/the_david_hoffmeister_show
The latest audio talks by David

livingmiracles.org
Learn more about the Living Miracles Community, personal silent retreats, to browse our online store

store.livingmiraclescenter.org
David Hoffmeister Books and Resources

mwge.org
Online Portal to Movies for Awakening

acim.me
Searchable Audios by David

levelsofmind.com
The Levels of Mind Instrument and the Fast Track to Peace

Made in the USA
Columbia, SC
23 March 2024